e-commerce
vs
e-commons

Communications in the Public Interest

Edited by
Marita Moll
Leslie Regan Shade

A collection of essays on public interest issues
in a new communications environment

Canadian Cataloguing in Publication Data

E-commerce vs e-commons : communications in the public interest

Includes bibliographical references.
ISBN 0-88627-242-4

1. Information superhighway--Social aspects--Canada.
2. Communication policy--Canada. I. Moll, Marita II. Shade, Leslie Regan, 1957- III. Canadian Centre for Policy Alternatives.

HM1017.E23 2001   302-23   C00-901637-6

Printed and bound in Canada

Published by The Canadian Centre for Policy Alternatives
410-75 Albert Street, Ottawa ON K1P 5E7
Tel 613-563-1341   Fax 613-233-1458
www.policyalternatives.ca   ccpa@policyalternatives.ca

FINANCIAL ASSISTANCE FROM THE UNIVERSITY OF TORONTO,
FACULTY OF INFORMATION STUDIES, INFORMATION POLICY RESEARCH PROJECT (IPRP)
IS GRATEFULLY ACKNOWLEDGED.

Contents

About the Contributors

Marc Bélanger worked for the Canadian Union of Public Employees for 25 years, the last 15 years as the union's Technology Co-ordinator. He now works at the training centre of an international labour organization in Turin, Italy, where he teaches computer technology to unionists from developing countries.

Andrew Clement is a Professor in the Faculty of Information Studies at the University of Toronto. His involvement with public access to information began in 1974 when he served as programmer and project leader of an early community networking experiment. More recently, as coordinator of the Information Policy Research Program (IPRP), he co-organized a series of Universal Access workshops which led to the development of *Key Elements of a National Access Strategy* discussed in this volume. Besides information policy, his research and teaching interests include: participatory design; computer supported cooperative work; workplace privacy; and the "information society" more generally. <http://www.fis.utoronto.ca/faculty/clement>

Ursula Franklin, C.C. FRSC, holds a PhD in experimental Physics and a number of honourary degrees and civic awards. She has been a member of the Science Council of Canada and served on the Boards of NRC and NSERC. In addition to her teaching and research in the field of Metallurgy and Materials Science, Dr. Franklin has been active in the areas of peace and justice, the social responsibility of science and scientists, and issues affecting women. During the past decade she has written extensively on the impact of modern technology on various facets of life including education. A new and enlarged edition of her book *The Real World of Technology* was published in 1999. Dr. Franklin is now University Professor Emerita and a Senior Fellow of Massey College.

Penny Goldsmith is a long-time community worker in Vancouver, B.C., and has for many years been involved in creating public legal education materials in clear language for anti-poverty advocates. She is past-president of the Vancouver Community Network and is currently the co-ordinator of PovNet, an online resource for anti-poverty information. She is also the owner of Lazara Press, which publishes progressive pamphlets, books and broadsides.

Garth Graham is currently in Hanoi, Vietnam, working as Project Director for the CIDA-funded Vietnam-Canada Information Technology Project. VCIT supports the Government of Vietnam's capacity to design and implement policies that enable the uses of information and communications technologies for development. As one of the co-creators of Telecommunities Canada, he says, "I had a front-row seat on what happens as ordinary citizens plug the Internet into dynamic social processes at the grassroots level. I learned how governments had come to believe that citizens were consumers of services, and that governments could abandon almost all of the defense of the public interest, if only they could price those services correctly. It has always struck me that, in a democracy, the separation of the body politic into governors who supply services and their clients who receive them is the most dangerous of false assumptions. In a digital world, where the edges disappear, the assumption of such a separation becomes intensely difficult to sustain."

Jesse Hirsh is a writer and public speaker based in Toronto. For the last five years he has helped build the tao.ca networks into a unique facility for social change activists to use and learn about the Internet. His most recent project is to build a public interest research organization called OpenFlows.org which seeks to offer facilities for the development and maintenance of Open Source Intelligence concerning all aspects of our emerging Network Society. As a dynamic speaker, he loves to give presentations and workshops to all sorts of groups and students, regarding all aspects of the political economy of culture and technology, and is thus often available and eager to share his ideas in person. Helping to build a co-operative worker-owned Internet, Jesse is also unionized with IU560 Local 42 of the IWW. <jesse@tao.ca>

Marita Moll is a Research Associate of the Canadian Centre for Policy Alternatives and a researcher and technology policy analyst with the Canadian Teachers'

Federation (CTF). Her interest in communications issues led her to form an early Internet-based lobby group to encourage broader participation in forums receiving input on communications issues, such as the Canadian Radio-television and Telecommunications Commission (CRTC) and the Information Highway Advisory Council (IHAC). She later helped found a broad-based alliance of public interest groups concerned about the evolving communications landscape—accessibility, affordability, public participation in communications policy development, and the impact of new communications technologies on jobs. She was an early member of the National Capital Freenet and a director of Telecommunities Canada—the national coalition of community networks.

Heather Menzies is a writer, mother, gardener, peace activist, and an Adjunct Professor at Carleton University where she teaches a Canadian Studies course called "Canada in the Global Village." She is the author or six books, including the 1996 best-seller *Whose Brave New World? The Information Highway and the New Economy.*

Vincent Mosco is Professor of Communication, Sociology and Political Economy at Carleton University, Ottawa. He received his Ph.D. in Sociology from Harvard University and is a research affiliate with the Harvard Program on Information Resources Policy. Professor Mosco is the author of four books and editor or co-editor of seven books on telecommunication policy, mass media, computers, and information technology. His most recent book is *The Political Economy of Communication: Rethinking and Renewal* (London: Sage; also Spanish, Korean and two Chinese editions). Professor Mosco has held research positions in the U.S. government with the White House Office of Telecommunication Policy, the National Research Council, and the U.S. Congress Office of Technology Assessment, and in Canada with the Federal Department of Communication. He has also served as a consultant to governments, universities, corporations, and trade unions in Canada, the United States, Malaysia, and South Africa.

Leslie Regan Shade is an Assistant Professor at the Department of Communication, University of Ottawa. She has been researching the social and policy issues surrounding ICTs for many years now, and has published in many venues, including *Computers & Society, The Information Society, Ethics and Information Technology,* and the *Canadian Journal of Communication.*

Sandra Smeltzer is a SSHRC doctoral candidate in communications at Carleton University. Her academic interests include international communications, specifically in the developing world, the political economy of new information and communication technologies, and the privatization of public space. Her academic background is in both Anthropology and Communications. Sandy has conducted research on the privatization of television in East Africa and is currently carrying out research on the Malaysian government's information technology policy at the University Science Malaysia. In addition to other travels, she spent a few years at the Department of Canadian Heritage working on the social and cultural ramifications of new information and communication technologies and the future of the 'knowledge based economy and society' in Canada. Previously, she has lectured at the University of Ottawa and has published in the area of Canadian cultural policy and the economic benefits of cultural expositions.

Valerie Steeves is an Adjunct Professor in the Department of Law at Carleton University. Her main area of research is the impact of new technologies on human rights issues. Professor Steeves has spoken and written extensively on privacy, and is the author of a number of interactive, Web-based educational games designed to teach children about protecting their human rights in cyberspace. Her game *Sense and NonSense*, produced by the Media Awareness Network, won the Race Relations Foundation's 1999 Award of Excellence in Race Relations Education. In 1997, she served as a Special Advisor to the House of Commons Standing Committee on Human Rights and the Status of Persons with Disabilities, where she organized and facilitated a series of national public consultations on privacy rights and new technologies. She continues to be an active participant in the policy-making process, and appeared before the Standing Committee on Industry and the Senate Committee on Social Affairs in regard to Bill C-6.

Gregory J. Walters is Professor of Ethics at Saint Paul University, Ottawa. He is the author of "Information Technology, Human Rights and Community/ Technologie de l'information, des droits de la personne et de la communauté." *Human Rights Research and Eduction Centre Bulletin/Droits de la personne Bulletin d'information sur la recherche et l'enseignement,* Number 36 (1998):1-11; "A New Way of War in the Information Age." *The Ottawa Citizen,* (March 14, 1998):B7;

"Canadian Information Highway Policy, the Right of Access to Information, and the Conditions of Human Action," *Science et esprit*, XLIX/2 (1997):193-229; "Information Technology, Work and Human Development: A Human Rights Perspective," *Canadian Journal of Development Studies*, XX/No.2 (1999):225-254; and "Deterrence and Information Warfare," in Frank P. Harvey and Ann L. Griffiths, eds., *Foreign and Security Policy in the Information Age*, pp.115-143 (Halifax, Nova Scotia: Dalhousie University, The Centre for Foreign Policy Studies, 1999). He is currently working on a book entitled *Ethics and Canadian Information Highway Policy: A Philosophical Analysis*]

PREFACE
The Usual Suspects

WELL BEFORE THE DAYS OF THE WORLD WIDE WEB AND MP3, THERE WAS AN UNUsual surge of spontaneous public activity challenging the powerful market model of what was then referred to as the "Information Highway." Canadian media activists lined up against big government, telephone and cable interests in a battle to preserve some Canadian perspective in the rapidly changing communications environment.

These people were not paid professional lobbyists. Most of them stretched their own financial and personal resources, writing, speaking and participating in various activities such as CRTC hearings, public forums, and policy development workshops.

Did these efforts have any impact on public policy? Is there a Canadian perspective in the global roll-out of new communications strategies? *e-commerce vs. e-commons: Communications in the Public Interest* presents a reality check of what has been lost and what has been gained under the global imperative of harmonization of communications policies through deregulation of the communications industry.

Much of the activity centred around Ottawa and Toronto, although activists were busy in Montreal and Vancouver, Guelph and Chebucto. For many of us, when we appeared at a CRTC hearing, an IHAC press conference, or a government, industry, academic, or community conference, we joked that we were once again meeting the "usual suspects." Some of us "usual suspects" had a vision of producing a document of these public interest activities, in order to preserve the energy and commitment of this activism. Years passed, and the rhetoric of the "information highway" changed to that of jumping on the "e-commerce" bandwagon. For many Canadians, the Internet was becoming a domestic item, and the media was suffused with breathless exposes of dot.com millionaires and teenage "netrepreneurs."

Last year, we decided that a book documenting the vitality of Canadian activism and highlighting the importance of public interest perspectives for the Canadian communications environment was both overdue and timely. Many luncheon meetings later, rushed e-mails, late-night phone calls, bleated entreaties and coercions to the contributors, thanks to the patience of authors and the CCPA, we are pleased to bring you this collection.

We hope that this book will be useful to students and academics, and especially be suited for courses on the policy and social uses of new media. We also hope that the book will also be of use to policy-makers, pundits, and media practitioners, as well as activists and agitators alike.

We would like to thank the Canadian Centre for Policy Alternatives, particularly Bruce Campbell, Ed and Kerri-Ann Finn, and Diane Touchette for their support and the many contributors to this collection for their perseverance and patience in the making of this book. Because of time and space considerations, there were also many worthy interventions which deserve a higher profile than they have received here. For this we apologize. We do harbour thoughts of producing another volume, but we are mindful of John Lennon's warning: "Life is what happens to you while you are busy making other plans."

Andrew Clement and the Information Policy Research Project at the University of Toronto deserve thanks for their contribution to this project, which has enabled us to put together an accompanying website of resources related to the themes of this book. Here you may find some of the original policy documents from the CRTC and IHAC, as well as a selection of submissions made to the CRTC, and other links to public interest groups and assorted policy platforms. The website is accessible through CCPA's website *www.policyalternatives.ca/ICTpolicy/*.

We hope that this book will record the diligent work of Canadian activists in sustaining a public space for Canadians in the communications environment. We hope that it will arouse your critical sensibility and energize you to keep up the momentum that these activists have forged. It is now more important than ever, as media mergers continue unabated, and as the allure of dot.com-everything reaches its fevered pace, that we remember to protect and extend the public interest.

Marita Moll
Leslie Regan Shade

September 25, 2000
Ottawa

INTRODUCTION
Myth-ing Links: Power and Community on the Information Highway [1]

Vincent Mosco

THE NEWS MEDIA, POPULAR CULTURE, AND GOVERNMENT POLICY DEBATES ARE INCREAS-ingly filled with some variation on the theme that society and culture are in the process of a great transformation brought about by the introduction of computers and communication technology. Supporters of this view typically maintain that we are going through a period that rivals in significance the development of agriculture, which, about 10,000 years ago, took us out of a nomadic hunting and gathering way of life, and the development of industry, which, starting 300 years ago, made manufacturing products more central than farming for modern economic and social life.

This view maintains that today computer communication is bringing about an Information Revolution which links people and places around the world in instantaneous communication and makes the production of information and entertainment a central economic and political force. Yes, it is agreed that not all societies are at the same level of informational development—the revolution is well-entrenched in the richest and only beginning in the poorest. But, insist supporters, no society can resist the powerful impact of the computer, particularly when linked to advanced telecommunications and video systems. In fact, information technology is widely perceived to be a key to economic and social development. Indeed, the computer, the telephone, television, radio, and associated devices like the facsimile, photocopier, printer and video camera are making information and entertainment defining characteristics of life at the dawn of the millennium.

This paper argues that one cannot understand the place of computer communication technology without taking account of some of the central myths about the rise of global computer communication systems, particularly those identified with the Internet, cyberspace, or the so-called information highway. It maintains that myths are important both for what they reveal, in this case a genuine desire for community and democracy, and for what they conceal, here the growing concentration of communication power in a handful of transnational media businesses.

A simple, but also quite limited way to understand a myth is to see it as a falsehood, a promise not fulfilled or simply unfulfillable. I like the way my mentor Daniel Bell put this view, in characteristic curmudgeonly fashion: "One hears that new adventures in technology—mixed media, computer-generated images, radical juxtapositions of materials, virtual reality—will open up new horizons. It reminds one of the radical agitator who proclaimed that Communism was on the horizon, until he was told that the horizon is an imaginary line that recedes as you approach it.[2] Could the promised land that Bill Gates trumpets in his book *The Road Ahead* turn out to be a mirage?

Much has been written about the history of technology from this conception of mythology. We look with amusement, if also with some condescension (what the historian Edward Thompson called the "massive condescension of posterity"), at 19th century predictions that the railroad would bring peace to Europe, that steam power would eliminate the need for manual labour, and that electricity would bounce messages off the clouds (though turn of the century references to "celestial advertising" contain a modern ring). But we certainly have contemporary variations on this theme. After all, in the 1950s supporters of nuclear power boasted that the "Mighty Atom" would soon bring us heat and electricity "too cheap to meter" and, when applied to treating the oceans, would deliver a near limitless supply of drinking water to the world.[3]

These are all myths in the sense of seductive but false tales containing promises unfulfilled or unfulfillable. As myths, they promote what historian David Nye has called a vision of the "technological sublime," a literal eruption of feeling that briefly overwhelms reason only to be recontained by it. Or, better still, as his mentor Leo Marx put it, "the rhetoric of the technological sublime" involves hymns to progress that rise "like froth on a tide of exuberant self-regard sweeping over all misgivings, problems, and contradictions."[4]

Such a vision may have succeeded in winning popular support for the railroad, steam, electricity, and nuclear power. And, particularly in the case of the first three, many would say that on balance they generated more good than harm. Nevertheless, society has also paid an enormous price for their false promises—in lives and resources sacrificed to realize impossible dreams.

Some would argue that we are giving in to similar false promises about the new computer communication technologies. Guarantees of instantaneous communication throughout the world, of a genuine global village, are, in essence, pledges of a new sense of community and of widespread popular empowerment. They offer a world in which people meet directly across borders without the intervening filters and censors set by watchful governments and profit-conscious businesses.

But, critics contend, these promises are no less mythological than boundless cheap energy or water.[5] Yes, they concede, many people are making use of relatively inexpensive computers to trade messages with people around the world. But the number doing so is relatively small in a world most of whose people have yet to use a telephone. In fact, a parallel can be drawn between the people who regularly travel down the information highway and the early users of radio.

In the 1920s, amateur enthusiasts and educators pioneered in the new wireless technology, communicating over vast distances without political or economic controls. Emboldened by their new invention, many of these people also felt the allure of virtual community and popular power. How could any material force get in the way of invisible messages travelling through the ether? But, the critics remind us, a lot got in the way of their dreams of democratic community. Once businesses figured out that they could make money by selling the ether or, more specifically, by selling radio audiences to advertisers (giving new meaning to T. S. Elliot's "patient etherized upon a table"), they pressured governments to open radio to commerce. These same governments quickly recognized the power of the new technology and either took complete control or shared it with business, leaving the amateurs, educators and other pioneers with little. By the 1930s in North America and Europe, radio was no longer the stuff of democratic visions.[6]

Today, governments worried about the loss of control and businesses eyeing cyberspace as a new marketplace—as a source of new commodities and a means to repackage old ones —lead critics to conclude that history is in the process of repeating itself. Part of the process of preventing another lost opportunity is to unmask the myth that today's information highway is inevitably leading us to a new sense of community and to democratic communication.

Notwithstanding its value, debunking these myths reflects a limited view, one restricted to the idea that myth simply falsifies reality. But myths are more than fabrications of the truth. As the anthropologist Claude Levi-Strauss tells us, myths are stories that help people deal with contradictions in social life that can never be fully resolved.[7] They are one response to the inevitable failure of our minds to overcome their own cognitive or categorical limits to understanding the world. One such contradiction is the desire to retain our individuality and yet participate fully in a collective community. Another is the wish to control our circumstances, even as we also desire to give up some control to bring about democracy. The inability to figure out how to "have our cake and eat it too" leads people to embrace myths that help them to deal with the irreconcilable.

In this respect, as the philosopher Alisdair MacIntyre concludes, myths are neither true nor false, but living or dead.[8] A myth is alive if it continues to give meaning to human life, if it continues to represent some important part of the collective mentality of a given age, and if it continues to render socially and intellectually tolerable what would otherwise be experienced as incoherence. To understand a myth involves more than proving it to be false. It means figuring out why the myth exists, why it is so important to people, what it means, and what it tells us about people's hopes and dreams. Put simply, myth is congealed common sense, with common sense understood as being what Antonio Gramsci meant when he said "Every philosophical current leaves behind a sedimentation of common sense: that is the document of its historical effectiveness. Common sense is not something rigid and immobile, but is continually transforming itself, enriching itself with scientific ideas and with philosophical opinions which have entered ordinary life. Common sense creates the folklore of the future, that is, a relatively rigid phase of popular knowledge at a given place and time."[9]

This conception of myth as living, meaningful story is particularly powerful because it suggests why people embrace it even in the face of otherwise compelling contrary evidence. Myth does not just embody a truth; it shelters truth by giving it a natural, taken-for-granted quality. According to the literary critic Roland Barthes, myths naturally conjure up a desired end, rather than suggest how to deflect or critique it. In this respect, myths transform the messy complexities of history into the pristine gloss of nature. As he puts it in his *Mythologies*, "Myth does not deny things; on the contrary, its function is to talk

about them; simply, it purifies them, it makes them innocent, i
natural and eternal justification, it gives them a clarity which is not that of an
explanation but that of a statement of fact."[10]

Myth provides a "euphoric clarity" by eliminating complexities and contradictions. In essence, myth is depoliticized speech—with "political" understood broadly to mean the totality of social relations in their concrete activities
and in their power to make the world. More positively, following Thomas
Hine, myths are "an attempt to invest our lives with a meaning and a drama
that transcend the inevitable decay and death of the individual. We want our
stories to lead us somewhere and come to a satisfying conclusion, even though
not all do so." [11]

The information highway is a powerful myth because it goes a long way
to satisfying these characteristics. It is a story about how ever smaller, faster,
cheaper, and better computer and communication technologies help to realize,
with little effort, those seemingly impossible dreams of democracy and community, with practically no pressure on the natural environment. According to
this view, the information highway empowers people largely by realizing the
perennial dream of philosophers and librarians: to make possible instant access to the world's store of information without requiring the time, energy and
money to physically go where the information is stored.

Moreover, the story continues, computer networks like the Internet provide relatively inexpensive access, making possible a primary feature of democracy—that the tools necessary for empowerment are equally available to
all. Furthermore, this vision of the information highway fosters community
because it enables people to communicate with one another in any part of the
world. As a result, existing communities of people are strengthened and whole
new "virtual" communities arise from the creation of networks of people who
share interests, commitments, and values.

All of this is accomplished safely, because violent crime does not invade
virtual communities, and with generally sound environmental consequences.
Energy use is more than counterbalanced by savings in travel. In essence, by
transcending time, space and resource constraints, (approximating what Marx
called in the *Grundrisse*, "the annihilation of space with time"), the information
highway provides the literal and figurative missing links that bring genuine,
sustainable democracy and community to a world in desperate need of both.

Versions of the myth come in various shapes and sizes. It is increasingly common to have it presented with what Barthes called in his *Mythologies* "inoculation." This is the admission of a little evil into the mythic universe in order to protect against a more substantial attack. Yes, these more sophisticated versions admit, there are potholes in the information highway. Not everyone has access to the network, nor does every virtual community feel like a neighbourhood. Not all information is available, and some of it is too expensive for many people. Breeches of privacy take place and some people log on to the net with mischief on the mind. Such admissions serve to protect the myth by granting that there are flaws in cyberspace. But the flaws, it is concluded, are well outweighed by the unique potential to overcome time and space with communication.

Inoculation is particularly strong when combined with another protective covering that Barthes found in most major mythologies: the tendency for myth to transcend history. Here the myth says ignore history because the information highway is genuinely something new, indeed, the product of a rupture in history: the Information Age. Until now, information was scarce; it is now abundant. Until now, communication technology was limited; it is now universally available at prices that are rapidly declining. Until now, people had to work primarily with their hands making things; they now work primarily with their heads, creating knowledge and providing services. Until now, your choice of community was limited mainly by accident of birth; today it is entirely open to choice and subject to constant renewal and change. There is no need nor genuine value in placing the Information Age in historical context, because everything that came before is pre-history, of little value save to account for the extent of the contemporary rupture. Like the division between Old and New Testaments in the Christian Bible, the Information Age and what came before are fundamentally different worlds.

Nicholas Negroponte, the director of M.I.T.'s world-renowned Media Lab, provides one of the more extreme versions of this radical break-with-history viewpoint. In *Being Digital*, Negroponte argues for the benefits of digits (what computer communication produces and distributes) over atoms (us and the material world), and contends that the new digital technologies are creating a fundamentally new world that we must accommodate. In matter-of-fact prose, he offers a modern-day prophet's call to say good-bye to the world of atoms, with its coarse, confining materiality, and welcome the digital world, with its infinitely malleable electrons able to transcend spatial, temporal and material constraints. The world of atoms is ending; we must learn to be digital. [12]

In the world of mythology, Negroponte would be considered a bricoleur, someone who, following Levi-Strauss's usage, pulls together the bits and pieces of technology's narratives, to fashion a mobilizing story for our time—what Nerone has called the heroic narrative with didactic effect. [13] Negroponte and others like him (Bill Gates in *The Road Ahead* does likewise) are fashionable rag and bones men, in the sense that William Butler Yeats gave the expression when he said that myths are forged "in the foul rag and bones shop of the heart."

The denial of history is central to understanding myth as depoliticized speech, because to deny history is to remove from discussion active human agency, the constraints of social structure, and the real world of politics. According to myth, the Information Age transcends politics because it makes power available to everyone and in great abundance. The defining characteristic of politics, the struggle over the scarce resource of power, is eliminated. History has a new beginning with the end of traditional politics.

This compelling vision is increasingly the subject of critical accounts that debunk the mythology. According to these, the information highway is increasingly in the hands of corporate giants whose base in television, telephony, Hollywood, publishing, computer hardware and software, gives them the resources to control pricing and product on the highway.[14] Yes, information and power are intimately connected, but only insofar as computers deepen and extend the power of Time-Warner, Rupert Murdoch's News Corp., Hachette, Disney, Silvio Berlusconi's Fininvest, Microsoft, Matsushita, and other information conglomerates.

Yes, amateurs, educators, and computer hackers, the contemporary version of the mythological trickster, continue to ride the highway at little or no cost, creating furrowed brows in the executive suites. But it is just a matter of time, critics contend, before a handful of transnational companies take near-complete control of the highway and its product. The early warning signs, such as Internet advertising, shopping, banking, access fees, tightening security controls, and the explosion of "firewall-protected" intranets point to the inevitable victory of the market over democratic communication.

Inoculated against this powerful criticism, myth-makers and their believers hold onto the faith. But, the critics insist, if they were to look closely at the powerful forces mobilizing to make the information highway just another profit centre, they would have to admit that, far from a rupture with history, computer communication is little more than business as usual. A world of information haves and have-nots is far more likely than a global village or a world of virtual communities. Furthermore, the computer enthusiast, alone in front of the screen, is less the new model of human participation in community and more its sad caricature. Community, they insist, requires social interaction, a genuine coming together of people in physical contact to exchange ideas and feelings, to debate and plan, to make use of all of the senses with all of their nuances.

At best, community in cyberspace is one small tool, one extension of the senses to build social networks.[15] Critics maintain that the energy invested in mastering the technology and in simply dealing with its demands would be better spent in building direct connections with people. For people skeptical of virtual community, computer communication reflects little more than the extent of human alienation. The claim that the technology provides the literal missing link between power and community is little more than myth.

Another approach to critical reflection on computer communication requires a slight shift in the meaning of mythology. If myths are viewed not so much as true or false but as living or dead, then we need to do more than determine how well the myth stacks up against reality and address what the myths mean for the people who profess them. What do they tell us about what matters to people today? Why such a strong response to the promise of power and community? Why do the myths work in spite of the evidence suggesting that cyberspace is seriously flawed?

The myths of cyberspace work in part because people genuinely want power and community. They provide strong evidence that people desperately want to control their lives and also want to be part of a larger social totality that provides emotional and intellectual support. And they are potent evidence of just how difficult it is for people to accomplish this today. The rise of transnational businesses whose power rivals that of national governments and the decline of public institutions which, however flawed, once offered a buffer to organized power, makes it difficult to envision how people can regain control over their lives and create viable communities. Critics conclude that it will take a substantial force to overturn what appears to be the inexorable concentration of power in the hands of corporate giants and the decline of community and neighbourhood.

At this point, a detour in this narrative is tempting. For is not the yearning for community and neighbourhood itself the response to a myth of a golden age when neighbours mattered and communities were distinctive places where people chose to build a public life? As the University of Toronto's Barry Wellman has recently shown, following a long tradition of community research in sociology, the neighbourhood was also a place of exclusion—not particularly golden for racial minorities or gays, nor for many women who experienced place as where they were kept. There were good reasons why the song "We've gotta get out of this place" resonated with a generation!

And yet, we need to be cautious about overreacting, about falling prey to the tendency to see all communities as, in the title of Benedict Anderson's delightful but overcooked book, *Imagined Communities*.[16] It is important to resist the tendency to adopt a variant of E. P. Thompson's "massive condescension of posterity" which, while rejecting the inevitablity of progress, nevertheless refuses to see decline or to admit to the possibility that the past may have offered a superior social form, such as the sense of physical, social, and spiritual place embodied in historic communities.

Nevertheless, whether the longing is for a real or imagined community, the longing is real, and for many people computer communication—and specifically the information highway—offer a near magical means to overcome it. Faced with the enormous challenge, and understandably discouraged that the traditional ways of organizing people to bring about social change can possibly work, people turn to technology for the answers. The technology offers a seductive deal. In return for learning how to navigate the information highway, you can increase your power and your sense of community without having to leave your home or office. The promise of overcoming age-old constraints on mobilizing people for social transformation is at hand. Everything from the banality of dealing with people one face at a time, to the resources it takes to get from place to place and to maintain solidarity, are solvable from the keyboard.

The magic wand of computer communication is undeniably seductive. It is also undeniable that much of the allure is manufactured by the very companies that stand to benefit from the sale of computer technology, software, and access to the information highway. Indeed, we are in the midst of a worldwide effort, organized by many different companies and governments in many different ways, to make computer communication a transcendent spectacle, the latest iteration in Nye's "technological sublime."[17] Everything from advertising to trade shows, from demonstration projects to conferences, speaks of a campaign to market the magic, to surround computer communication with power, speed, and the promise of freedom.

There is nothing new here. Students of the history of technology will recall similar attempts to make electricity a spectacle by lighting up streets and buildings in the downtowns of many cities and towns, turning them into miniature versions of New York's Great White Way. Moreover, one can argue that such spectacles as the Internet's Electronic World's Fair, a cyberspace version of the great exhibitions that touted earlier technologies, are valuable in overcoming people's natural reluctance to try something new. But in doing so they make it easier for people to turn to the technology for solutions to problems better addressed through the admittedly old, admittedly banal, forms of social mobilization. However one feels about their politics, last year's Million Man March in the United States and the recent mass protest in Toronto demonstrated that traditional forms of social mobilization and opposition can still speak louder than messages transmitted in electronic space.

When we begin to understand computer communication as a mythology that speaks to genuine unmet needs and aspirations, we can understood its seductive power, why it is that people are so taken (and taken in) by it. We can also begin to comprehend why a critical minority dismisses making use of the technology as just another form of co-optation.[18] Again, there is nothing entirely new here. In the 1920s and '30s, trade unionists debated the value of using commercial radio to get out labour's message.[19] The key to a useful response to computer communication, as it was for radio, is to recognize that it is less than its enthusiasts make it out to be and more than rejectionists maintain.

Computer communication is not a transcendent, magical force that marks a break with history, let alone a shift from a world dominated by atoms to one controlled by digits. Computer communication by itself does not bring about social change and is no less banal than any other technology. Nevertheless, like other technologies, including newspapers, radio and television, computer communication can be used effectively as one among a wide range of instruments to mobilize people, foster communication, produce, process and use information. This must be done carefully because the terms of access and use are increasingly set by corporate giants who have little sympathy for movements that might challenge their own hegemony. Nevertheless, the development of networks to connect peace, environmental, feminist and labour organizations provide models of alternative use. So too do the admittedly embattled community computing networks or freenets that serve as a resource for cities and towns.

It is important to nurture these networks, not to complete Marx's annihilation of space with time but to enrich space, particularly those neighbourhood spaces that include our homes, schools, playgrounds and shops. The test of sustainable computing is not how fast it moves or how far it travels, but how well it deepens ties in our neighbourhoods and cities, and how meaningful are its messages. Computer communication does not signal a digital Utopia, but can, along with other equally banal organizing tools, serve as an instrument for democratic social change.

NOTES

1   Annual Davidson Dunton Lecture, Carleton University. November 1996

2   Bell, Daniel. (1992). "Into the 21st Century, Bleakly," *The New York Times*. Sunday, July 26. p. E 17

3   Nye, David. (1990). *Electrifying America: Social Meanings of a New Technology, 1880-1940*. Cambridge, Mass.: MIT Press, 1990; Nye, David. (1994). *American Technological Sublime*. Cambridge, Mass.: MIT Press.

4   Marx, Leo. (1965). *The Machine in the Garden: Technology and the Pastoral Ideal in America*. New York: Oxford University Press.

5   Stoll, Clifford. (1995). *Silicon Snake Oil: Second Thoughts on the Information Highway*. New York: Doubleday.

6   Barnouw, Erik. (1990). *Tube of Plenty: The Evolution of American Television (2nd rev. ed.)*. New York: Oxford University Press.; McChesney, Robert, W. (1993). *Telecommunications, Mass Media, and Democracy: The Battle for Control of U.S. Broadcasting*. New York: Oxford University Press, 1993.

7   Levi-Strauss, Claude. (1978). *Myth and Meaning: Cracking the Code of Culture*. Toronto, Ont.: University of Toronto Press; Levi-Strauss, Claude. (1987). *Anthropology and Myth: Lectures, 1951-1982*. Oxford: Blackwell.

8   MacIntyre, Alisdair. (1970). *Sociological Theory and Philosophical Analysis*. New York: Macmillan.

9   Gramsci, Antonio. (1971). *Selections from the Prison Notebooks* (Geoffrey Nowell Smith, Trans.). London: Lawrence and Wishart.

10   Barthes, Roland. (1972 (orig. 1957). *Mythologies* (Trans. by Annette Lavers). New York: The Noonday Press. p.143

11   Hine, Thomas. (1991). *Facing Tomorrow: What the Future Has Been, What the Future Can Be*. New York: Alfred A. Knopf.

12   Negroponte, Nicholas. (1995). *Being Digital*. New York: Knopf.

13   Nerone, John. (1987). "The mythology of the penny press." *Critical Studies in Mass Communication* 4. p. 376-404.

14   Schiller, Herbert. (1996). *Information Inequality: The Deepening Social Crisis in America*. New York: Routledge; Mosco, Vincent. (1996). *The Political Economy of Communication: Rethinking and Renewal*. London: Sage.

15   Stoll. (1995).

16   Anderson, Benedict. (1991). *Imagined Communities: Reflections on the Origin and Spread of Nationalism* (Rev. 2nd ed.) London, Verso.

17   Nye. (1994).

18   Postman, Neil. (1996). *The End of Education*. New York: Knopf.

19   McChesney. (1993).

Designing Policy: Whither the Public Interest?

MANY PEOPLE EITHER GROAN AT THE THOUGHT OF POLICY, OR ARE CONSUMMATE POLICY junkies. Policy is often presented as something cut and dry, or as something that "experts" do. This is a pity, since so much policy affects us—as ordinary citizens—in our everyday lives. This is especially the case with communications policy.

The public interest spirit that has guided the communications sphere has historically included the mandate towards universal service to telephone services, and the creation of non-commercial public affairs, arts, and cultural programming services in the radio and television broadcasting spheres.

With the advent and proliferation of new communications technologies, these public interest media attributes in the "information age" have become more elusive and complex. The era of telecommunications deregulation has brought about an ambiguous relationship between public and private interests: privatized and commercial interests vs. governmental regulation and control. As well, networked technologies are constantly evolving and being deployed in new social arenas which transcend constrained geographic boundaries.

The current realities and prognostications of the information and communications infrastructure highlight the need to reconceptualize public interest perspectives, and re-evaluate the role of these technologies in participatory democracy. At a minimum, these policies should:

- ensure that a heterogeneous public is represented in policy discussions, so that the perspectives of those groups in society that may be affected by the introduction and deployment of new technologies are consulted;
- research the needs of diverse user communities to ascertain what essential services are needed for social service and community development delivery;

- research access issues as related to user interface;
- research vital policy issues related to privacy, copyright, and intellectual property;
- guarantee that the public has facilitated access to the existing public information services while the transition to the electronic medium is underway; and
- ensure that public education and information related to electronic networks is provided for the public at large.

What's the killer app for Internet policy? This section offers several perspectives on emerging and salient policy issues that affect citizens. The first article by Andrew Clement, Marita Moll, and Leslie Shade looks at attempts by public interest groups to forge a national access strategy for Canadians in light of recommendations made by the federal Information Highway Advisory Council (IHAC). Although access advocates had some influence on the wording of official policy recommendations, there has been, so far, little discernible effect on actual policies or practices.

Valerie Steeves describes ideological debates over the nature of privacy. Is privacy an inherent human right, or is it merely an accessory to calm fears of consumer reticence in shopping online? Steeves looks at Bill C-6, the *Personal Information Protection and Electronic Documents Act*, designed to promote electronic commerce by ensuring that Canada remains competitive in the global marketplace. The civil rights issue for the 21st century could, indeed, be privacy: those who are active and informed about their privacy rights vs. those that are not—the privacy have-nots.

Jesse Hirsh offers a compelling, yet chilling, look at the terrain of digital information amid the manic mergers and convergence of media behemoths. What these patriarchs still control is intellectual property. Hirsh argues that, despite the dominance of AOL/Time Warner, "the kids are alright": youth are creating innovative and awesome products that are the antithesis of those of "wunderkids" Steve Case (AOL) and Jeff Bezos (amazon.com).

Two competing moral visions of the Internet—that of e-commerce versus e-commons—are explored by Gregory Walters, with specific reference to work and workers in the digital economy. Walters examines the debates on whether information technology is a job creator or a job killer, situating it within an ethical framework. The increasing gap between the information haves and have-nots, and the obscene pay-gap between wage earners and CEOs, offer sober reflection on where our societal values are headed.

Debating Universal Access in the Canadian Context: The Role of Public Interest Organizations[1]

Andrew Clement, Marita Moll, and
Leslie Regan Shade

THIS ARTICLE DISCUSSES KEY EVENTS IN THE POLICY DEBATES SURROUNDING THE EMERG-ing information and communications (IC) infrastructure[2] from 1992 through the end of 1997, and presents a public interest perspective on those events. Although there is no single "public interest perspective," here the concept "public interest" is used:

> to refer not only to long-standing shared aspirations and visions of citizens of a nation-state, but also to the interests and objectives that remain to be discovered as new concerns and policy problems arise over time. The government, public interest advocates would argue, should seek to serve the broad interests of all members of the political public, and not just the interests of a more narrow sectoral group that happens to have the ear of the government of the day.[3]

Issues of public interest relevant here include privacy, employment, governance and, most importantly for the purposes of this article, universal access. The focus on universal access, one of the most prominent public interest issues, illustrates some of the strengths and weaknesses of the public interest group role.

Current IC infrastructure debates must be situated historically within the Canadian context of the state's mediating role in balancing public and private concerns in the broadcasting and the telecommunications regime. As Canadian public broadcasting historian Marc Raboy comments:

Among Canada's policy particularities are the principles that communication infrastructures constitute a cornerstone of the national cultural heritage, that the main instrument for carrying out cultural and communication policy is a mixed system of publicly owned and publicly regulated public and private industries, and that the participation of social groups is a central part of the policy making process.[4]

However, the debates surrounding information policy in the 1990's deviated considerably from this pattern. The changing economic landscape demanded an increased emphasis on competition, privatization, and the rallying of pro-market forces. Governments responded with a significant withdrawal of funding and support for the social sector and a significant empowering of the private sector through deregulation and free trade agreements.[5] Given the changing role of government and the weakness of the social sector amid unstable social forces, intervention by public interest groups during this period of technological convergence (particularly with respect to the erosion of barriers between the telephone and cable industries) was both timely and important.

Among their many activities, public interest groups participated in, monitored and responded to government initiatives (notably the Information Highway Advisory Council and the hearings held by the Canadian Radio-television and Telecommunications Commission) designed to set the public policy agenda. The efforts of public interest groups in raising awareness on these public policy issues have been both proactive and provocative. Their (albeit limited) successes in keeping public interest issues on the agenda during a period of rapid deregulation are testament to the necessary functions these various groups assumed in this debate.

This article is divided into three sections which follow the chronology of events summarized below. Part one identifies the major participants in the information policy debate in the Canadian context. It provides a brief overview of the roles played by the Information Highway Advisory Council (IHAC), the Canadian Radio-Television and Telecommunications Commission (CRTC), and various public interest groups. Part two focuses on public interest attempts, through a series of universal access workshops, to develop a national access strategy. The article concludes with a brief assessment of public interest contributions over this formative period, and offers suggestions towards further public interest initiatives.

CHRONOLOGY OF EVENTS

Year	Access Advocacy Groups	Federal Government
1994	Coalition for Public Information (CPI) public consultation report: *Future Knowledge: A Public Policy Framework for the Information Highway.*	Information Highway Advisory Council (IHAC) formed
1995	Alliance for a Connected Canada: core groups – Public Interest Advocacy Council (PIAC), CPI, Telecommunities Canada (TC), (Information Highway Working Group (IHWG), Public Information Highway Advisory Council (P-IHAC)	Canadian Radio-television and Telecommunications Commission (CRTC) "Convergence" Hearings IHAC Final Report #1
1996	Electronic Public Space Steering Group (EPSSG) formulates *A Model for Electronic Public Space* Universal Access (UA) Workshop #1	*Building the Information Society* (official government response to IHAC Final Report #1)
1997	UA Workshop #2	IHAC Final Report #2
1998	UA Workshop #3: *Key Elements of a National Access Strategy* Canada – by Design lecture series	Throne speech – "Connecting Canadians" CRTC "New Media' hearings"
1999	Meetings between "access advocates" and Industry Canada & Canadian Heritage officials	

PART I: STAKEHOLDERS AND THE CONTEXT OF CANADIAN INFORMATION HIGHWAY POLICY

In recent years, the Canadian federal government and the CRTC have launched several major information policy initiatives, including the Information Highway Advisory Council (Parts I and II) and various CRTC hearings (including convergence, rate rebalancing, and new media). Inside and outside these fora, industry groups like Stentor (the now-defunct consortium of telephone companies), the Information Technology Association of Canada (ITAC), and the Canadian Advanced Technology Association (CATA), lobbied intensively to influence policy directions. They issued policy statements and press releases, held high-profile conferences,[6] and offered "partnership" opportunities for industry/public sector cooperation. Industry/government/school partnership activities were particularly popular.[7] This period of intense activity on the part of the IC industries is hardly surprising. There was a great deal at stake as industries lobbied to protect and expand their interests in the rapidly changing communications sector.

The extent to which these information policy initiatives attracted the attention of a new set of public interest groups is noteworthy. Very quickly, a variety of non-profit public interest advocacy groups (including ad hoc grassroots organizations and coalitions) formed in response to the lack of widespread public consultation on the important issues surrounding the changing IC infrastructure. These new groups sought to address the broader needs of the Canadian citizenry, particularly with respect to access, privacy, cultural content, and employment.

They included Canada's Coalition for Public Information (CPI), Telecommunities Canada (TC), the Alliance for a Connected Canada, and the Electronic Public Space Steering Group (EPSSG). As well, existing library and consumer associations (most notably the Public Interest Advocacy Centre) became active in dealing with the emerging public interest issues surrounding information and communications policy. Following is a summary of this very brief but significant flurry of activity.

Behind closed doors: the Information Highway Advisory Council (IHAC)

The Information Highway Advisory Council (IHAC) was established in April 1994 by Industry Minister John Manley. The Council was mandated to make recommendations to the Minister of Industry on a "national strategy to govern the evolution of Canada's advanced information and communications infrastructure respecting the overall social and economic goals of the federal government." [8]

The council addressed three main objectives of the government's information infrastructure strategy:
1. creating jobs through innovation and investment;
2. reinforcing Canadian sovereignty and cultural identity; and
3. ensuring universal access at a reasonable cost.

It was guided by five principles in formulating the strategy:
1. an interconnected and interoperable network of networks;
2. collaborative public and private sector development;
3. competition in facilities, products and services;
4. privacy protection and network security; and
5. lifelong learning as a key design element of the information highway. [9]

IHAC established working groups to cover five broad areas of interest: access and social impact; Canadian content and culture; competitiveness and job creation; learning and training; and research and development, applications and market development.

While IHAC Chair David Johnston, former Principal and Vice-Chancellor at McGill University, applauded the IHAC committee members for reflecting a "wide range of knowledge and expertise, as well as a broad perspective on linguistic, cultural and regional issues,"[10] the composition of IHAC was criticized by public interest advocates for being dominated by representatives of the primary stakeholders in the broadcasting, cable, and telecom industries; and for dismissing social issues, including equity, democratic participation, social justice, and particularly employment.

It was pointed out that this was an important departure from the usual practice. Until the 1990s, "any significant reworking of public policies in Canada has, by convention and common practice, been accompanied by extensive consultation processes with many groups in society."[11] With the IHAC process, however, "no public hearings were held and no unsolicited public interventions were invited. These elements alone were a significant break from practices of royal commissions or other panels or task forces in Canada."[12]

IHAC released its recommendations in September 1995 with little fanfare or media attention. As could be expected from such an industry-dominated group, the report called for a competitive strategy to be led by industry and the private sector. Access issues and the effects of new technologies on employment and work were not well addressed, although the report acknowledged that more studies were needed. Education, targeted early on by industry as one of the "killer apps," was identified as an important contributor to early adoption of the technologies. Community networks, it was suggested, could play a minor role in cases of "market failure."[13]

The lack of fanfare surrounding the final report may have been partly due to some dissension in the ranks. Labour representative Jean-Claude Parrot, Executive Vice-President of the Canadian Labour Congress, refused to sign on to the final recommendations, issuing a minority report instead. Parrot particularly objected to IHAC's assertion that market-driven solutions were the key to creating employment. Parrot recommended that the federal government, in partnership with provincial and territorial governments, industry, labour, and other stakeholders, form an information technology advisory board which would conduct widespread public consultations on workplace issues, including job creation, erosion of labour standards, telework and telecommuting, training and deployment, and privacy and electronic surveillance issues. This report stands out as the most progressive outcome of the IHAC exercise. In refusing to compromise on social issues, it offers a blueprint for a more comprehensive and inclusive approach to IC policy.

In mid-May, 1996, the federal government released its official response to IHAC's final report of September 1995. One of the issues that *Building the Information Society: Moving Canada into the 21st Century* identified as needing immediate attention was the development of "a national strategy for access to essential services: By 1997, the ministers of Industry and Canadian Heritage will develop a national access strategy involving policy, regulatory and other measures to ensure affordable access by all Canadians to essential communications services . . . developing this national strategy will involve widespread consultations with all interested parties."[14] This recommendation was reiterated in IHAC's final report issued in September 1997 and will be discussed later in this paper.

The CRTC offers public consultation

The CRTC regulates and supervises all aspects of the Canadian broadcasting system with a view to implementing the broadcasting policy set out in the Broadcasting Act. The Commission also regulates rates and other aspects of the services offered by telecommunications common carriers under federal jurisdiction. Until this time, the broadcasting and telecommunications sectors of the Commission had been able to function as completely discrete operations. The issues surrounding technological convergence in these previously distinct industries was certain to cause some crises of consistency for the Commission.

In 1994, the CRTC, through Order in Council P.C 1994-1689, proposed a public consultation on the "vision of competition" emanating from technological convergence. Rules regarding the regulation of the telephone and cable industries required reconsideration in light of technological innovations and industry pressures. The hearings considered issues surrounding convergence (should phone companies hold broadcast licenses and deliver movies over phone lines?); content (how can Canadian cultural content be protected?); access and competitive safeguards (how can universal access be achieved?); and broadcast definitions (how to meet the requirements of broadcasters, cable TV operators, and the telephone companies). Public presentations to this hearing began in March 1995, with the final report released in May 1995.[15]

A wide range of submissions was received from groups who usually responded to CRTC orders in council: telephone companies, cable companies, broadcasters, multi-media companies, entertainment companies, publishers, labour and consumer groups. But a unique feature of this hearing was the spontaneous flood of submissions from newly-formed public interest groups and activists frustrated until now by the closed-door process established by IHAC. A flurry of grassroots activity resulted in submissions and requests to address the Commission from numerous Canadians who had never before appeared at a hearing.[16]

The first day of the hearings was dominated by presentations from public interest groups. The *Ottawa Citizen* headline "Information Highway headed for dead end, CRTC hearing told," referred directly to the opening statement presented by an Internet communications for democracy advocacy group that publicly mocked IHAC by calling itself the Public Information Highway Advisory Council (P-IHAC). Stan Skrzesweski, CEO of the Coalition for Public Information (CPI), was quoted as saying: "The concept of cyberspace as public space is the best way to guarantee overall economic gain for Canada." The McLuhan Program in Culture and Technology called for a Royal Commission. Garth Graham, the volunteer Executive Director of Telecommunities Canada, told the Commission:

> A community network is electronic public space where ordinary people can meet and converse about common concerns. Like parks, civic squares, sidewalks, wilderness, and the sea, it's an electronic commons shared by all, not a cyberspace shopping mall. Government's role in cyberspace is to balance commercial use and social use of an electronic commons that belongs to everyone.[17]

Despite the unusually high level of public interest and activity seeking a unique national vision of the evolving IC infrastructure, the CRTC did not risk diverging from the official path established by Industry Canada, which, in the end, has the power to overturn any CRTC ruling.[18] The final CRTC report, *Competition and Culture on Canada's Information Highway: Managing the Realities of Transition,* echoed IHAC"s recommendations that a culture of competition be fostered, particularly between telephone and cable-TV companies:

> Increased and sustainable competition is fundamental to the development of the information highway. In an information economy, consumer demand for communications services will range from simple dial-tone service and Internet access to conventional television and multimedia applications. In the Commission's view, multiple suppliers, rather than monopolies, can best serve this diverse need. [19]

Some of the public interest concerns were addressed. With respect to ensuring community access to the information highway, the CRTC agreed with the view expressed at the hearing that "it is important to sustain the local in face of the global."[20] The CRTC also remarked that public access points within each community "are an important focus of governmental strategy in moving towards universal access."[21]

The British Columbia Electronic Highway Accord

While most of the provinces had yet to articulate their principles and strategies towards access to the evolving information infrastructure, British Columbia forged an exemplary policy statement. The *British Columbia Electronic Highway Accord* reflected the concerns of a wide spectrum of citizens and community groups, as well as industry, labour and government groups who worked together to define their objectives. The accord delineated a vision statement, principles to guide action, and specific objectives. One of its visions dealt with inclusive community-based participation:

> Participation depends initially on having affordable infrastructure in place, and then on the ability of individuals, businesses, and organizations to be involved. This characteristic underlines the importance of the community and its institutions as being there to assist, train, promote and create opportunities for the individual, taking into account particular circumstances and needs.[22]

Unfortunately, despite this head start on setting priorities with respect to information infrastructure, the initiative never moved beyond the vision statement. Without the will in government to move from ideas to action, the participants were unable to move the universal access agenda any further ahead at this time.

Tilting at windmills; public interest groups

Some, but not all, of the public interest groups that worked towards maintaining a public interest perspective are described below. In the context of what may be identified, in the future, as the "deregulation daze," these groups were determined, at a minimum, to leave a public record of opposition to the lack of consultation and lack of attention to the important role of communications and information in a democratic society. Many groups submitted lengthy papers to the CRTC hearings and addressed the Commission in person. Other activities included press releases, articles in newspapers and journals, online discussion groups, and face-to-face meetings when resources to do so could be found. Many of the written documents are accessible through the website created in conjunction with this volume.[23]

Coalition for Public Information

Canada's Coalition for Public Information (CPI) was founded by the Ontario Library Association as a national non-profit coalition of organizations, public interest groups, and individuals "whose goal is to foster broad access to affordable, usable information and communication services and technology." CPI's status within the library community gave it a more "official" status than some of the more ad hoc organizations that formed at the time. Although there were the usual financial woes, there was official government and industry recognition that CPI represented an interest group that could not be ignored.

Stentor (now defunct government relations arm of the telephone companies) lobbyist Brian Milton was a keynote speaker at the inaugural meeting of CPI, and CPI was invited to name a representative to the IHAC board. Liz Hoffman, former Ombudsman for the University of Toronto, gained the respect of industry lobbyists and public interest advocates for her tenacious and passionate support for public consultation and public interest issues. But CPI's participation was viewed by some as an example of co-opting one interest group to a forum dominated to such an extent by private sector interests that the public group allowed exclusive entry could have little impact.[24]

One important CPI contribution to the overall policy debate was a public consultation process that resulted in *Future-Knowledge: A Public Policy Framework for the Information Highway*.[25] This framework, which was presented to the CRTC "Convergence" hearings, outlined principles for Canada's emergent information infrastructure with respect to universal access and ubiquity; freedom of expression, pluralism, and intellectual freedom; privacy; intellectual property and copyright; public space; and employment and the quality of work. "The public needs a voice in the debates about who gets connected to the information highway, what the cost is, what kind of information is available and which rules apply," says the report.[26] This CPI document was one of the first to ask that a national access board be established which would oversee the establishment of public "lanes" and access points in the form of libraries and community networks.

Telecommunities Canada

When the members of the original IHAC committee were chosen, Canada already had a vibrant and growing community networking movement. This was recognized by the appointment of David Sutherland, one of the organizers of the National Capital Freenet, Ottawa's community network, to the Council. It was not until the IHAC deliberations were well underway that the community networking movement had an opportunity to form a national alliance. A national organization called Telecommunities Canada (TC) was formed at a meeting in Ottawa in June 1994. TC serves as the umbrella group for all the community networks in Canada.

Although TC is a registered not-for-profit national corporation, its formal organizational structure is very embryonic in that it consists of seven elected volunteer board members. Despite its extremely limited resources, TC has made significant contributions to the formal processes mentioned here and has played a key role in many of the coalitions and alliances noted.[27] Members of TC have also been involved with the Community Access Program (CAP), and other programs funded by Industry Canada under the "Connecting Canadians" agenda.

Alliance for a Connected Canada

Largely in response to the IHAC report of September 1995, CPI, TC, the Ottawa-based Public Interest Advocacy Centre, and other interested groups collaborated to form the Alliance for a Connected Canada. The mandate of the Alliance was to:

> represent the views of Canadians . . . promote public understanding, vigorous and open debate about [Canadian] . . . communications policies; [and] . . . influence the design and evolution of networks and services based on . . . social equity.[28]

The groups included, at one time or another, the Assembly of First Nations, Canadian Postal Workers Union, Communications, Energy and Paperworkers Union of Canada, Council of Canadians, Fédération Nationale des Associations de Consommateurs du Quebec, Information Highway Working Group, Information Policy Research Program, and McLuhan Program in Culture and Technology at the University of Toronto, National Library of Canada, P-IHAC, and the Telecommunications Workers Union of British Columbia. This alliance proved too diverse, unfocused and under-resourced to last for long. Its major contribution was a unified response to the report of IHAC II that reiterated the need to make access, affordability and employment the communications policy priority, and to allow the public access to the debate.[29]

The Electronic Public Space Steering Group (EPSSG)

In 1997, EPSSG, comprising representatives from the education, library and public-interest communities, and growing out of the Alliance for a Connected Canada, continued to work on a national access model. EPSSG defined electronic public space as:

> a shared learning space. It is the community that is the network, not the technology. The creation of a community network extends the idea of community into a shared electronic public space, a new not-for-profit transaction space where the impact on community values and social interaction is worked out in new ways.[30]

The EPSSG model emphasized local administration, with operation and maintenance of local space by a network of incorporated not-for-profit organizations, and elected boards featuring both not-for-profit community organizations and institutions, and individual citizen representatives. The mix of organizations would reflect the broad community interest, including existing community networks; community health organizations; education organizations; publicly-funded libraries; municipalities; labour organizations; volunteer and community services; and individual citizens. Such public space community networks would operate as not-for-profit services to facilitate "access to, and participation in, the creation and exchange of public information, content development and availability, broad social and formal education, learning, and training."[31]

As was the case with the BC Electronic Highway Accord, the vision was impressive. But the group lacked the resources to promote any model, and government had already announced its intentions to pursue a market model as closely as possible.

The Public Interest Advocacy Centre (PIAC)

The Ottawa-based PIAC is a non-profit organization which, since the 1970's, has provided legal and research services to various consumer groups wishing to intervene in public policy areas, particularly in the fields of telecommmunications, financial services, privacy, cable TV and broadcasting, e-commerce, and world trade. As well as preparing submissions to the CRTC on a variety of telecommunications issues, researcher Andrew Reddick has authored several reports dealing with consumer perspectives on the information highway, access issues and the digital divide, essential services, community networking, and local telephone pricing options.[32] Drawing upon its extensive contacts within the federal government, PIAC has played a pivotal role in policy discussions with federal officials. PIAC also provided the few resources that enabled the Alliance and the EPSSG to exist, however briefly.

Other players

Other groups active in deliberating and formulating policy initiatives include the Canadian Library Association (CLA), the Telecommunications Workers Union (TWU), the McLuhan Program in Culture and Technology, the Toronto Information Highway Working Group, the Internet Public Research Interest Group and P-IHAC (the Public Information Highway Advisory Council). Individuals like communications activist Mark Surman also participated in many activities. Papers, articles, submissions, research studies and other documents by the many public interest groups and concerned individuals who took an active interest in the evolution of communications policy during this period can be found online.[33]

PART II: TOWARDS A NATIONAL ACCESS STRATEGY

In 1996/97, three workshops were held at the University of Toronto to consider the challenges involved in implementing the ideal of universal access. The workshops were mainly funded by the federal ministries of Industry, Heritage and Human Resources Development, with their representatives participating in the discussions as observers. The first Universal Access Workshop focused on Canadian experiences in an international context.[34] The discussions were continued in the second workshop, "Developing a Canadian Access Strategy: Universal Access to Essential Network Services," held in February 1997[35] which drew upon the Access Rainbow model of information infrastructure.[36] Three key policy research issues surrounding access to essential services were examined:

1. Defining universal access to essential services: What core technical services should be provided: single-party telephone service, access to operator and emergency services, Internet access? What constituency-oriented services constitute essential services for various groups? What information is essential for education, public health, or public safety? How can more francophone and multicultural content be created to meet the diverse needs of the citizenry?
2. Proposing support mechanisms to ensure essential services are accessible: What information "safety nets" could be designed and established so that all citizens, regardless of their ability to pay, can partake of services? Should telecommunication carriers be required to contribute to a universal access fund?
3. Elaborating conceptions of "electronic public space": Given the commercial trajectory of the information infrastructure, there is a vital need to ensure that a vigorous public sphere is maintained. The creation and sustenance of a public sphere can allow for a broad range of citizens to partici-

pate in the benefits of the information infrastructure, thereby potentially ameliorating the distinction between the information "have's and have-not's", while at the same time extending and enhancing democratic practices. Governments and public interest groups alike have proposed creating community access points as a way for the public to gain access to the information infrastructure.

In defining universal access to essential services, it became apparent that what is considered essential would change over time, as would the amount and direction of funding and co-ordination needed to realize the access ideal. The tensions and potential co-operation between market forces, government, and citizens could only be resolved with the balanced combination of economic and legislative support, and equitable representative governance.

Position papers presented by participants and the resulting workshop reports offered valuable suggestions for policy. It was hoped that some of the recommendations would become part of the promised national access strategy.

Information Highway Advisory Council Final Report

IHAC's second report, *Preparing Canada for a Digital World*, was released in September, 1997.[37] It was encouraging that many of the recommendations issued by the IHAC Access Steering Committee echoed the recommendations emanating from the February 1997 Universal Access workshop and the interventions of public interest groups. The report urged the government to meet its commitment to articulate an access strategy before the end of 1997.

With respect to access to basic network services, IHAC asked the CRTC to monitor "trends in telephone penetration rates and affordability indicators, and to intervene when and if the principle of universality is threatened;" to address access to the Internet; and to monitor such access (through the federal government or the CRTC), with particular attention paid to people in remote areas and people with low incomes and disabilities. In addition, IHAC called on Statistics Canada to develop ways to measure access and collect and publish the relevant statistics. It called on industry, CANARIE (the Canadian Network for the Advancement of Research, Industry and Education), and public interest groups to monitor the deployment of high-speed Internet access and advanced video-based services on the World Wide Web.

Regarding public access, IHAC recommended that the "government and the CRTC work with industry to develop the means to make Internet access available without long-distance charges," so as to promote access in rural and remote regions; that industry proceed with the Advanced Satcom Initiative, which aims to provide Internet access to schools, libraries, community centres, and other local institutions via satellite; that an additional $30 million be allocated to an expanded Community Access Program (CAP), with the goal of establishing public access sites by the year 2000 in the 5,000 rural and remote communities with populations between 400 and 50,000, and that the CAP program be extended to urban neighbourhoods.

IHAC issued several recommendations on the issue of public space, urging governments, industry and public interest and consumer groups to "make community networks and public spaces sustainable on the Information Highway;" and further recommended "that the federal government develop policies and procedures to contribute financially to non-profit Internet access providers for the electronic provision of government services and information to the general public." Most importantly, IHAC recognized that, "while urging government to move to electronic provision of services and information, the Council emphasizes the continuing need for government to provide information and services in traditional forms to citizens without access to the Internet or public access sites."

Under the rubric of "digital literacy," IHAC recommended the continual funding and nurturance of SchoolNet; "the development of high-quality on-line tutorial and community-based instruction available via public access sites, community networks and the Internet;" and the provision of "resources to every publicly-funded library to support sustainable public access sites and learning of basic computer and Internet skills by people who would not otherwise be served."

With respect to content issues, IHAC recommended that "Canadian Internet access providers be encouraged to place Canadian reference points on their home pages;" that "the federal government resource existing programs, and develop partnership strategies with others, to develop more Canadian content, particularly in new media services;" that "governments . . . work closely with industry, and in cooperation with Francophone communities, to develop a critical mass of French-language content and services for the Internet."

Design issues were also considered by IHAC. The government should monitor Internet design developments, and "fund an award program to honour achievements in design of assistive devices and in application of universal design principles in communications products, systems and services," the report said.

Finally, IHAC, "while reluctant to create another advisory body," recommended the creation of a national access advisory committee, "reporting to the ministers of Industry and Canadian Heritage, to advise on emerging access requirements and what services will be essential in a knowledge society. The advisory committee should include balanced representation from industry and the non-profit sector."

In addition, IHAC stated that the operation of the advisory board "should be fully consistent with the constitutional and statutory responsibilities of the federal government and the CRTC." Public interest advocates were encouraged by what looked like progress toward a national access strategy. (For all quotes in this section please see note #37.)

Universal access: take 3

In the transition to a knowledge-based economy, the Government of Canada, through the Information Highway Advisory Council (IHAC), recognized universal access to essential network services as a principal policy objective. This sentiment was echoed in the final IHAC Report[38] and in the September 1997 Throne Speech, where the government declared its intention to "make the information and knowledge infrastructure accessible to all Canadians by the year 2000, thereby making Canada the most connected nation in the world."[39] Furthermore, IHAC recommended a national access strategy to ensure affordable access for all Canadians to essential communications services be developed by the end of 1997.

In support of this, in November 1997, the third Universal Access Workshop was held at the Faculty of Information Studies at the University of Toronto. It was assisted financially by Canadian Heritage, Human Resources Development Canada, and Industry Canada. The workshop included representatives of industry, academia, and public interest groups, as well as government observers. The workshop aimed to contribute to the formulation of the "national access strategy" the Canadian government committed itself to in *Building the Information Society*[40] by making recommendations to the drafters of the official government strategy and by outlining an alternative strategy that may differ from the official one. In doing this, it drew principally upon the recommendations of Chapter 4 of the IHAC Phase II report *Preparing Canada for a Digital World*[41] and the previous universal access workshops conducted at the Faculty of Information Studies.[42]

An access strategy, according to participants at this workshop, needed to articulate the following:

- a broad, positive vision of the role that information/communications infrastructure can play in Canadian society;
- general principles that can guide actions across a variety of situations during a period of rapid technological, economic, social and cultural change;
- clear, achievable objectives consistent with this vision;
- an integrated set of initiatives addressing objectives in both the short and long term; and
- an action plan that identifies concrete steps that are achievable within specified time periods.

The strategy developed at this workshop offers a significant extension and deepening of the government's 'connectedness agenda.' While this agenda is a valuable initiative in several regards, it is too narrow to constitute an adequate national strategy for access to the rapidly developing information/communications infrastructure. As announced so far, the connectedness agenda leaves serious gaps in terms of the conception of access, who is served, consultative processes, formative assessments, and governance.

Addressing these shortcomings, the strategy proposed by the workshops:

- articulates a more comprehensive and public-centred vision of the information /communications infrastructure;
- states clear objectives and guiding principles;
- offers a multi-faceted view of "access;"
- strengthens the role of grass-roots community initiatives;
- identifies an initial set of "essential network services:"

- proposes a "universal access fund" to support sustainable access;
- highlights the need for active public participation, research and consultation;
- promotes the creation of viable electronic public spaces;
- calls for the establishment of an on-going "National Access Council."

Rather than attempting to be comprehensive, this proposed strategy highlights key areas for immediate action. It thus offers a "skeleton" of a strategy to be fleshed out in the ongoing discussion of how Canadians can best develop and be served by the evolving information and communications infrastructure.

The initial federal response to the proposal was not favourable. Both Minister Manley (Industry) and Minister Copps (Heritage) rejected the central recommendation to establish a national task force on universal access when questioned publicly at the *Canada by Design* speaker series organized by Liss Jeffrey of the McLuhan Program for Culture and Technology. The government position was that, since 'Connecting Canadians' was well underway, there was no time nor need for further public discussion of an access strategy.[43]

Once more with feeling

The final text of *Key Elements of a National Access Strategy: A Public Interest Proposal*[44] was submitted to the federal government in August 1998. In early 1999, a series of meetings between federal government officials and public interest access advocates to discuss the proposal took place at the University of Toronto.[45] At these meetings, advocates emphasized that:

- There is a need for greater public participation in the information access policy process—the government has not held "the widespread consultations with all interested parties" that it committed itself to.
- There is a chronic imbalance in the policy process that seriously disadvantages public interest groups in terms of their ability to participate effectively.
- The main access program of the federal government (Connecting Canadians) is a useful start, but is too narrow to meet its broader access goals—"ensuring affordable access by all Canadians to essential communications services."

- Private sector initiatives and market forces generally are inadequate to meet public interest access requirements.
- Ongoing support by government is required for an effective public policy process, as well as the sustainable development of the information infrastructure in the public interest.
- Lack of resources alone is not the reason for government inaction, since a small proportion of existing programs would go a long way to enabling public participation in making these programs more effective.
- Government should make public much more detailed, timely information about its access related activities: e.g., program goals, funding allocations, problems encountered, results achieved.
- Government should develop an "access audit" capability, involving the ongoing tracking of an integrated set of quantitative and qualitative access indicators that can be used for setting government targets, reviewing legislative proposals, monitoring progress, and guiding development.
- While public access and cultural policies are indivisible, they are handled separately by Canadian Heritage and Industry Canada; they should be working more closely together and with the CRTC.
- Public interest groups are willing to work with the government in deepening its access programs and involving the public in the process— e.g., by developing partnerships between technology and disabled communities; by conducting integrated in-person and digital public forums (e.g., byDesign e-Lab based at the McLuhan Program in Culture and Technology).[46]

The response by Industry Canada officials was polite but discouraging. They recognized that the "Connecting Canadians" agenda was not enough to ensure universal access —that it was only a beginning and that the National Access Strategy proposal would be useful to them. However, they were not willing to provide long-term grants to support sustainability or public participation. They preferred instead service contracts with specified deliverables. The overall conclusion was that, while there was mild interest in continuing to discuss public interest access issues, the government takes little responsibility for the process or the outcome beyond what it is currently doing. The reaction by Canadian Heritage officials was slightly more positive in tone, in that they indicated more willingness to engage in longer-term discussion, but they lacked the resources to support it.

PART III: CONCLUSIONS

There has been significant progress in Canada in recent years in developing information and communication infrastructure initiatives. On the policy front, the Information Highway Advisory Council (IHAC) Reports, particularly Chapter 4 of *Preparing Canada for a Digital World,* offer a useful starting point for ensuring universal access to essential network services. On the practical side, there are already a great number of valuable access initiatives under way. These include the development of community networks and other community-based technology projects, as well as government initiatives under Industry Canada's "Connecting Canadians" agenda or the Office of Learning Technologies (OLT).

However, there is so far no comprehensive policy framework that would facilitate coordination among the various efforts and fill in the gaps they inevitably leave. The rise of public interest advocacy organizations, either acting alone or in concert through the ad hoc fora of the Alliance for a Connected Canada, the Electronic Public Space Steering Group and the three Universal Access workshops, clearly point to the need to establish a National Access Council as a critical next step in helping Canadians shape the emerging "knowledge-based economy/society" (KBE/S). Unfortunately, to date, despite the Canadian government's connectedness agenda, no national access strategy has been elaborated, nor has a mechanism for developing one been identified.

The record of public interest activities in attempting to influence IC policy during the years 1993-99 show a very Canadian response to a process that was clearly veering away from the historical experience in communications policy development. Access advocates have made concerted efforts to engage government policy-makers in conventional policy discourse. They have responded to government initiatives on its terms, participated in advisory bodies, developed their own public documents, appeared at official hearings, convened public events, and met face-to-face with officials, all producing a public record. There have been notable achievements.

These activities strengthened the connections between the groups. They have clearly articulated a broadly shared vision of what universal access in a networked world can mean and had some influence on the wording of official policy recommendations. However, there has so far been no discernible effect on actual policies or practices, and there is little prospect that further efforts in the same direction will change this situation.

Public access advocates have also learned some potentially useful lessons about the policy process. The active organizations are weak in resources and generally rely on the over-stretched energies of a few activists. Partly because of this and the complexities of the policy arena, they have not developed wider public understanding of the issues at stake. There is not yet a political constituency for universal access, which allows governments to dismiss its advocates.

This may be changing as the widening 'digital divide' comes into public prominence. It also reflects the immaturity of the field. Analogous to the state of ecological awareness 40 years ago, there are the first warnings of systemic malfunctioning, but little general concern or mobilization.

Finally, while there are individuals within government who see a continuing need for the government to play a strong public interest role in ensuring an open debate with balanced contributions of stakeholders, these people are in a minority. Increasingly, the government is pursuing an agenda that gives priority to private commercial interests over all others.

How does this experience of limited impact and lack of official recognition change the way Canadians might respond to such situations in the future? Principally, it highlights the need to move the debate to other fora. For some, this means shifting attention away from policy development *per se*, to more local efforts aimed at broadening access in practice—removing barriers and promoting inclusivity at a community level.[47] Also, public interest groups have recognized that governments in a globalized world do not function as independent entities. The battle to maintain a public voice in policy decisions of all kinds is now shifting to the level of super-governmental organizations—the WTO, World Bank, IMF, GATS, etc.

Activists have moved from presenting papers on their opposition to the New World Order to carrying placards demanding a halt to the increasing powers wielded by corporations and international bodies against citizens. Perhaps comparable to the beginnings of the environmental movement, these are the opening skirmishes in a lengthy struggle to counteract the acceleration of the progressively tighter but persistently inequitable global circuits of money, power and information access.

It is imperative that public interest groups stay actively engaged in the policy process. The vigorous public debate over the shape of Canadian society in the face of rapid information and communications developments is long overdue and more vital than ever.

NOTES

1   A version of this paper first appeared as "Kanadische Burgerinitiativen gestalten ein Netz fur alle," by Andrew Clement and Leslie Regan Shade in Leggewie, Claus und Christa Maar (ed). (1998). *Internet & Politik.* Bollman. pp. 354-365

2   Information and communication infrastructure encompasses the convergence of computer technology with existing techniques of broadcasting and telecommunications transmission. Popularly referred to in Canada as "the information highway" through media and policy formulation, it has also been referred to as "new media" by the CRTC, with the Internet increasingly seen as the central technology.

3   McDowell, Stephen D. and Cheryl Buchwald. (1997). *Consultation on Communications Policies: Public Interest Groups and the IHAC.* Toronto: Information Policy Research Program, Faculty of Information Studies, University of Toronto. Working Paper No.4. A modified version of this paper, "Public interest groups and the Canadian information highway," appears in the October 1997 issue of *Telecommunications Policy.* p.2-3.

4   Raboy, Marc. (1997). "Cultural sovereignty, public participation, and democratization of the public sphere: The Canadian debate on the new information infrastructure." in Kahin, Brian and Ernest Wilson (ed). *National Information Infrastructure Initiatives: Vision and Policy Design.* Cambridge, MA: MIT Press. p. 191.

5   Barlow, Maude, and Bruce Campbell. (1995). *Straight Through the Heart: How the Liberals Abandoned the Just Society.* Toronto: Harper Collins; Ralph, Diana, Andre Regimbold, and Neree St. Amand ed. (1997). *Open for Business, Closed to People: Mike Harris's Ontario.* Halifax: Fernwood; Buchwald, Cheryl. (1996). *Canadian Universality Policy and the Information Infrastructure: Past Lessons, Future Directions.* Toronto: Information Policy Research Program, Faculty of Information Studies, University of Toronto. Working Paper No. 3.

6   On February 1 & 2, 1994, a massive public relations event called *"Powering up North America; Realizing the Information Infrastructure for a Knowledge-based Continent"* was held in Toronto. This event was jointly sponsored by the Information Technology Association of Canada (ITAC), a lobby group representing 450 telecommunications and computer hardware and software industries and the Canadian Advanced Technology Association (CATA) representing advanced technology companies, investors and international enterprises. It was hailed as the conference of the decade for the information technology industry." The program emphasized that "convergence," the ability of different communications media to carry each other's signals, was not just a technological phenomenon. It was also a social and political phenomenon — involving the harmonization of regulatory and legislative regimes throughout the North American market.

7   Partnerships between the business and education sectors are a growing phenomenon in Canada. Although there are no precise figures available, the Conference Board of Canada estimates that there are as many as 15,000 to 20,000 such initiatives. In Ottawa alone, there are in the neighbourhood of 50 partnerships, up from about five in 1990. The Vancouver Board of Education's "Partners in Education" program includes over 80 businesses and government organizations. At the Etobicoke Board of Education in Ontario, partnerships with business and the local community have increased from 25 in 1992 to their current level of over 500. Provincial and territorial governments have also made partnerships a priority. A recent Council of Ministers of Education, Canada report on information technologies in elementary and secondary schools lists the formation of partnerships "to share equipment acquisition, networking, and resource development costs" as one of the key themes running through government vision statements on technology in education. (from "Gift horses and trojan horses: Why business-education partnerships to support educational technology are likely to proliferate."by Bernie Froese-Germain and Marita Moll. June, 1997. URL: http:/ / www.ctf-fce.ca/e/what/ ni/public/trojan.htm)

8   Industry Canada. (1995). *The Canadian Information Highway: Building Canada's Information and Communications Infrastructure.* Ottawa: Industry Canada. Spectrum, Information Technologies, and Telecommunication Sector. April. p. 33.

9   Information Highway Advisory Council. (1995). *Connection, Community, Content: The Challenge of the Information Highway.* Ottawa: Ministry of Supply and Services, September. p. vii, xxi URL: http:/ / strategis.ic.gc.ca/IHAC

10   Johnston, David. (1994). "Toward 2000: Public policy issues on the Information Highway" in *Policy Options/Options Politiques*. September. v.15, n.7: 5.

11   McDowell and Buchwald. (1997) p.14

12   Ibid.

13   Information Highway Advisory Council. (1995).

14   Industry Canada. (1996). *Building the Information Society: Moving Canada into the 21st Century*. May. Ottawa: Ministry of Supply and Services. p. 24. URL: http://info.ic.gc.ca/info-highway/society/toc_e.html

15   Canadian Radio-television and Telecommunications Commission (CRTC). (1995). *Competition and Culture on Canada's Information Highway: Managing the Realities of Transition*. May, 1995. p.11. URL: http://www.crtc.gc.ca/eng/highway/hwy9505e.htm

16   These and other presentation are available online. See URL: http://www.policyalternatives.ca

17   Graham, Garth. (1995) *A Domain Where Thought Is Free To Roam: The Social Purpose Of Community Networks*. A background paper supporting Telecommunities Canada's appearance, March 29 1995, at the CRTC public hearings on information highway convergence. URL: http://www.tc.ca/crtc.brief.html

18   In December 1995, an intensive lobby by the telephone companies resulted in the government's controversial reversal of a CRTC decision regarding service obligations attached to monthly telephone rate increases.

19   CRTC (1995).

20   Ibid. p. 45.

21   Ibid. P. 43.

22   British Columbia. Information, Science and Technology Agency. (1995) *British Columbia Electronic Highway Accord Document*. URL: http://www.ista.gov.bc.ca/Publications/accord.htm

23   See URL: http://www.policyalternatives.ca

24   Gutstein, Donald. (1999). *e.con: How the Internet Undermines Democracy*. Stoddart.

25   Canada's Coalition for Public Information. (1995). *Future Knowledge: A Public Policy Framework for the Information Highway*. URL: http://strategis.ic.gc.ca/SSG/ih01508e.html

26   Ibid. p. 1.

27   Graham, Garth and Leslie Regan Shade. (1996). "Rhetoric and Reality in Canadian Community Networking." Proceedings of INET 96 (The Internet Society). Montreal: June 25-28. URL: http://www.isoc.org and http://www.tc.ca/garth-net96.html

28   McDowell and Buchwald. (1997). p. 25.

29   "IHAC II, the sequel, better be for the public, Alliance demands." News release.
     April 30, 1996. Alliance for a Connected Canada. URL: http://www.tao.ca/con-
     nect/ihac2.html

30   Electronic Public Space Steering Group. (1997) *Community/Communications: A Model
     For Electronic Public Space*. URL: http://www.fis.utoronto.ca/research/iprp/ua/
     eps.html

31   Ibid.

32   Reddick, Andrew. (1995). *Sharing the Road: Convergence and the Canadian Informa-
     tion Highway*. Ottawa: PIAC;
     — (1996). *The Information Superhighway: Will Some Canadians be Left on the Side of the
     Road*. Ottawa: PIAC;
     — (1998). *Criteria for Defining Essential Services*. Ottawa: PIAC;
     — (1998). *Community Networking: Access Initiatives in Canada*. Ottawa: PIAC.

33   See URL: http://www.policyalternatives.ca/ICTpolicy/

34   Clement, Andrew, Joanne Marshall, Stephen D. McDowell, Vincent Mosco and
     Cheryl Buchwald. (1995). *Developing Information Policies for a Canadian 'Information
     Infrastructure': Public Interest Perspectives*. Toronto: Information Policy Research Pro-
     gram, Faculty of Information Studies, University of Toronto. Working Paper No. 1;
     URL: http://www.fis.utoronto.ca/research/iprp/clement.htm#paper1 ;Clement,
     Andrew and Leslie Regan Shade. Universal Access Workshop No. 1. (1996). *Defin-
     ing and Maintaining Universal Access to Basic Network Services: Canadian Experiences
     in an International Context. Final Report*. Toronto: Information Policy Research Pro-
     gram, Faculty of Information Studies, University of Toronto, April. An executive
     summary of this report can be seen at URL: http://www.fis.utoronto.ca/research/
     iprp/ua/estext.html; Clement, Andrew and Leslie Regan Shade. (1997). *What Do
     We Mean By 'Universal Access'?: Social Perspectives in a Canadian Context*. Toronto:
     Information Policy Research Program, Faculty of Information Studies, University
     of Toronto. Working Paper No. 5. August. URL: http://www.fis.utoronto.ca/re-
     search/iprp/workpap5.txt A version of this paper appeared in Proceedings of
     INET 96 (The Internet Society). Montreal: June 25-28, 1996. URL: http://
     www.isoc.org

35   David, Stephanie. (1997). *Universal Access Workshop No. 2. Developing a Canadian
     Access Strategy: Universal Access to Essential Network Services. Summary Report*. To-
     ronto: Information Policy Research Program, Faculty of Information Studies, Uni-
     versity of Toronto. URL: http://www.fis.utoronto.ca/research/iprp/ua/
     ua2summ.htm

36   Clement, Andrew and Leslie Regan Shade. (2000). "The access rainbow: conceptu-
     alizing universal access to the information/communication infrastructure," in
     Gurstein, Michael (ed). *Community Informatics: Enabling Communities with Informa-
     tion and Communication Technologies.* Hershey, PA: Idea Group Publishing. pp. 32-51

37   Information Highway Advisory Council. (1997) *Preparing Canada for a Digital World:
     Final Report of the Information Highway Advisory Council.* September. URL:
     http://strategis.ic.gc.ca/IHAC

38   ibid

39   Government of Canada. (1997). *Speech from the Throne to Open the First Session of the
     Thirty-Sixth Parliament* September 23, 1997. URL: http://canada.gc.ca/depts/agen-
     cies/pco/throne_e.html

40   Industry Canada. (1996)

41   IHAC. (1997)

42   Universal Access Workshops conducted at the Faculty of Information Studies. URL:
     http://www.fis.utoronto.ca/research/iprp/ua/

43   Canada by Design. Video and text transcripts of the March 12 and 26, 1998, ses-
     sions are available at http://www.candesign.utoronto.ca

44   *Key Elements of a National Access Strategy: A Public Interest Proposal.* Toronto: Infor-
     mation Policy Research Program, Faculty of Information Studies, University of
     Toronto, August 1998. URL: http://www.fis.utoronto.ca/research/iprp/ua/

45   See URL: http://www.fis.utoronto.ca/research/iprp/ua/nas.html

46   See URL: http://www.vitalspace.net// and http://www.bydesign-elab.net/
     index_nn4.html

47   Gurstein, Michael (ed.) (2000) *Community Informatics: Enabling Communities with
     Information and Communication Technologies.* Hershey, PA: Idea Group Publishing.

Privacy Then and Now: Taking Stock Since IHAC

Valerie Steeves

IN 1995, THE INFORMATION HIGHWAY ADVISORY COUNCIL'S ("IHAC") FINAL REPORT, *Connection, Community, Content,* devoted approximately three of 277 pages to the issue of online privacy. In some respects, one might consider it remarkable that privacy waHs mentioned at all, given the number of business interests that were represented on the Council. However, in retrospect, those three pages contain the core elements of a strategy that has limited, redefined and obfuscated the issue of privacy until the default position of legislators, bureaucrats and the private sector has become one of invasion.

I would like to think that this has been unintentional, but I am constantly reminded of a conversation I held, several years ago, with a colleague who works in the telecommunications sector. While discussing the distribution of privacy education materials, I suggested that we contact attendees at the 1997 National Public Consultation on Privacy Rights and New Technologies, conducted by the House of Commons Standing Committee on Human Rights and the Status of Persons with Disabilities. The committee's report, *Privacy: Where Do We Draw the Line?,* has become a touchstone for the privacy community, as it clearly defines the issues in the language of human rights and calls for the comprehensive protection of privacy. In dismissing the consultation, my colleague looked at me and said, "There are two approaches to privacy protection: the Charter approach and the e-commerce approach. We intend to crush the Charter approach."

DUELLING PRIVACY IDEOLOGIES: HUMAN RIGHTS OR COMMODITY

The "Charter approach" is based on the premise that privacy is a core human right that is central to individual autonomy and the democratic process. Privacy, from this perspective, is also a key social value that enables us to enter into relationships of trust with other people. It is hard to maintain either that autonomy or that trust when, for example, my employer can capture my online activities and fire me because I disclose I have cancer in an online support group. It is equally difficult to exercise my freedom of expression at a public protest when I know the video surveillance cameras covering the area can scan the faces in the crowd and identify me by name, all within a matter of seconds.

The "e-commerce approach", on the other hand, is predicated upon the belief that access to information is essential if we are to be competitive in the global information economy. In this model, unfettered access to, and manipulation of, a wide range of personal information will enhance corporate and government efficiencies and promote economic growth. And the Internet is a great source of that information. DoubleClick wants to watch our surfing patterns to create one-on-one advertising; drug companies want to watch our lifestyle habits so they can develop and sell more pharmaceuticals; and banks want to watch us so they can identify possible criminal behaviour in our banking patterns. From the e-commerce perspective, this secondary use of personal information is appropriate because it makes business—whether private or public business—cheaper, faster, and more efficient.

At the heart of the debate over privacy, in essence, is the philosophical conflict between these two very different paradigms. One paradigm purports to be quantifiable, practical, economically beneficial and morally neutral, while the other speaks to the more amorphous values of human dignity and autonomy. But let's be clear. Personal freedom, autonomy, democratic privileges, and other general human rights do not come to us *gratis*. Democratic societies are notoriously inefficient, but we accept those inefficiencies because democracy is the best way to maintain some degree of individual freedom.

To highlight the differences between these two paradigms of privacy, let's look at the implications in the context of a more firmly defined and familiar human right: the right to freedom of expression. Enshrined in Section 2 of the *Canadian Charter of Rights and Freedoms*, we generally recognize free expression as a social good that is inherently worthy of protection. The courts have jealously guarded free speech time and again, limiting it only so as to balance other, equally pressing social concerns. Free expression is valuable in part because it gives us dignity, and allows us to maximize our creativity and potential.

But consider for a moment how that would change if the right to free expression were framed only in the light of economic efficiency. In that context, free expression would be valued only so far as it facilitated commercial activity, and given only minimal protection in non-commercial circumstances. Inevitably, over time, the multi-coloured tapestry that we know as free expression would inevitably contract to a black-and-white mirage that excludes religious expression, anti-commercial or environmental ideas, and many forms of political dissent.[1] The very idea of free expression would be re-defined in much narrower terms, and protected only insofar as it was required for the effective operation of business. Ironically, as personal creativity and growth waned, economic creativity and growth would decline, and the short-term gains realized by limiting free expression would evaporate in the long-term world in which we live.

The Re-Definition of Privacy

In many respects, IHAC's final report signalled a similar re-definition by business and government with respect to the right to privacy and the information highway. By framing it in the context of e-commerce, the right to privacy has been subtly redefined as an issue of commercial security. The foundation of this re-definition was set out in IHAC's brief treatment of the subject:

> Rapid development of a PKI (public key infrastructure) is required *to ensure Canada's competitive position* and to accelerate the development of Canada's Information Highway. (Emphasis added.)[2]

And again, in Rec. 10.13 of the report:

> By furthering comprehensive privacy, confidentiality and electronic commerce support measures, Canada can *gain a competitive edge* in the global technology market. (Emphasis added.)[3]

From IHAC's perspective, privacy—essentially re-defined as the ability to engage in secured communications—is valued primarily for its ability to encourage consumers to engage in electronic commercial activity. The conceptualization of privacy as a good in itself, a fundamental human right, or indeed a right that is the foundation for many other fundamental human rights, is not part of the equation.

Now one could ask—and should ask—"What is wrong with this approach? Isn't secure communications an essential aspect of online privacy?" The answer, of course, is that nothing is wrong with encouraging secured communication as part of an overall strategy of privacy protection. Meaningful privacy depends in large part on the ability of parties to communicate with confidence that the communication will not be intercepted by third parties. The difficulty arises when security *becomes* the definition of privacy, rather than a component of it.

Electronic privacy is not the same thing as security. At a fundamental level, privacy is about the right to control who knows what about us—in other words, to determine what we keep within the confines of our personal lives. The trend towards 'privacy as secured communications' recasts privacy as an adjunct to commercial activity. Consider the consumer who connects to the Internet, and conducts a secure, encrypted online purchase from a commercial web site. During the course of the transaction, the consumer provides personal information for the purposes of completing the purchase. Once the immediate transaction is ended, the secured aspect of the transaction is at an end. The privacy implications, however, are just beginning. What happens to the consumer's personal information? How will the website use it? What will prevent the website from mining that data, and adding it to other personal information to create a highly personal picture of the consumer? Who gets to see that picture? What happens if the information is used to embarrass or harm the individual? How will the fact that the sale was conducted over encrypted channels prevent the website from selling it to a third party marketing database or providing it to the government?

It won't, and it hasn't. The intimate details of our online transactions—those highly personal portraits of our private lives—are now being collected, perused and shared by the government and the private sector alike. Our privacy, once an integral part of our human dignity and autonomy, has become simply a commodity that can be bought, sold or bartered—most often behind the scenes without the informed consent of the consumer-citizen.

This commodification of privacy is not a necessary result of new communications technologies. The open nature of online community is not inimical to privacy just because everyone can see what everyone else is doing. We have always been able to place our neighbours under surveillance, but we have developed social norms and laws that have restricted snooping because those restrictions protect our autonomy and dignity.

Being known is part of human community, and the online community is no exception. Indeed, it is the open architecture of the Internet that has enabled a self-actualizing online community to develop and thrive. Like the proverbial small town, where everyone can see what everyone else is doing, the Net has enabled individuals to develop self-regulating norms of social behaviour. In the early days, online privacy was protected by a form of voluntary zoning; if you didn't want to see online pornography, for example, you didn't have to go to sites that display or discuss it. Individuals who used the Net to impose unwanted material on an online group quickly learned better, as the technology itself gives each group the power of censure. However, that censure was not undemocratic because there is nothing to stop the censured individual from flowing into another online community where his or her views could be expressed.

Privacy Since IHAC—Cause for Concern

What has changed since the public and the private sectors have joined the online world is the extent to which we know what they are doing with our information. Privacy is built on reciprocity and transparency. Knowing what is done with our online information once it has been collected, and having reasonable control over those uses, is in the end more important than whether that information was initially collected in a secure environment.

To date, online collectors of personal information have not been transparent about their collection or their usage. Websites targeted at both adults and children have used any number of imaginative ways to cajole visitors to hand over personal information that can be sold or used to market other products or manipulate consumers into future purchases. One touchstone for popular complaints, Colgate, used the friendly image of the tooth fairy to collect children's personal information until a popular outcry led to a change in policy. Nevertheless, online clubs, memberships and product discount enrolment schemes allow companies to collect personal information and use it in ways the provider of that information never anticipated. Data mining,[4] secondary uses of personal information,[5] the use of electronic cookies,[6] data shadows,[7] and other forms of electronic surveillance are all practices that have grown in frequency and sophistication. Each is justified by the internal logic of commercial efficiency.

Similarly, employers, buoyed by court decisions ruling that e-mail and office systems are legitimate targets of monitoring and review, have stepped up online surveillance of their employees. For real humans, working in the real world, the workplace cannot be divorced from their personal lives. Yet private conversations or family-related messages, sent by phone or e-mail, are now potential targets for interception by an employer concerned about the productivity of workers. In the world where privacy is a commodity, employers are granted a window into the private lives of their employees in the name of economic efficiency.

The response of virtually all governmental jurisdictions to the changing nature of privacy invasion has been disappointing. Under the banner of "technological determinism," governments have made clear policy choices supporting the re-definition of the right to privacy as the right to secured communication. They have steadfastly refused to recognize privacy as a human right, or to create the over-arching privacy legislation which would address emerging invasive practices in a cohesive manner.

Bill C-6—Help Or Hindrance?

The Personal Information Protection and Electronic Documents Act (Bill C-6) is a good example. In essence, the bill requires that organizations must obtain an individual's consent before his or her personal information can be collected, used or disclosed. So far, so good. However, the bill also makes it clear that the purpose of the legislation is to promote electronic commerce to ensure that Canada will be competitive in the emerging global information economy. The discussion paper which preceded the bill states:

> Legislation that strikes the right balance between the business *need* to gather, store, and use personal information and the consumer need to be informed about how that information will be used . . . is an important element of building the *consumer trust* and the *market certainty* needed to make Canada a world leader in electronic commerce.[8]

It is also worth noting that the discussion paper uses the word "citizen" 10 times, as opposed to a total of 78 occurrences of "consumer," "business" and "industry," collectively.

The market language used in Bill C-6 echoes the perspective outlined in the IHAC report. Bill C-6, as the logical next step of the e-commerce paradigm, is designed to ensure that the flow of personal information *continues*. Accordingly, under Bill C-6, organizations can *imply* an individual has consented to the collection of his or her personal information because an obligation to obtain express consent in many cases would unduly hamper the flow of commerce. There is also no recognition in the Bill that information providers and collectors have no equality of bargaining power.

It is unlikely that a consent requirement will protect my individual choice when my employer, bank, insurance company or health clinic asks me for my health history, for example. If I refuse to disclose the information, chances are, like Mr. Christie, I'll be shown the virtual door.

Laws which have confused business efficiencies and human rights have caused trouble for us in the past. In 1939, for example, the Supreme Court of Canada, in the case of *Christie v. York Corp.*,[9] held that tavern owners must have the freedom to transact their business as they see fit. Individual rights, the Court argued, must be balanced in a way that does not unduly hamper commerce. That balancing meant that the owner of the tavern in the Montreal Forum was legally justified when he refused to serve Mr. Christie a beer after a Canadiens game simply because Mr. Christie was black. Perhaps refusing to serve a black man a drink made good business sense in 1939, but it made bad law, not because it was inefficient, but because it was wrong.

Privacy is no different than any other human right. It requires three elements to remain vibrant and alive: public recognition, government protection, and judicial vigilance. Today, privacy is under attack as never before from commercial and governmental ideology that would treat it as both a commodity and a secondary adjunct to business activity. And it has been weakened by judicial decisions that have framed it in economic or utilitarian terms.

Whether privacy will survive in our society as a human right will depend on the third element: public recognition and activism. If citizens are prepared to trade their right to privacy for economic efficiency, they will find willing allies in government and business. By the time we, as a society, realize what has been lost, the proverbial genie will have flown the bottle. But, if they are willing to insist on recognition of their personal autonomy and the enshrinement of privacy in a general, over-arching human rights law, Pandora's box can be closed before its contents escape. The choice, in the end, is one of political will, not technological determinism.

NOTES

1   Oprah Winfrey, for example, was sued for slander of food when she agreed with a guest who argued that beef is not an environmentally-friendly food product. Beef producers argued that her free speech should be restricted because her comments would hurt their ability to sell their product.

2   Canada. Government of Canada. (1995, September). *Connection, Community Content: The Challenge of the Information Highway. Final Report of Information Highway Advisory Council.* Ottawa: Minister of Supply and Services. p.145 URL: http://info.ic.gc.ca/info-highway/ih.html.

3   Ibid.

4   The practice of assembling personal information in a database to provide a blueprint of an individual's personal likes, dislikes, habits, hobbies, buying patterns, opinions, medical conditions, financial status and lifestyle. Specific information can then be sold or utilized by third parties.

5   The collection of personal information for one legitimate and authorized purpose, and then later used for another, unauthorized or illegitimate purpose.

6   Small data files sent to your computer by a web site to help the web site identify you and your previous web-surfing activities. Cookies are used legitimately to enhance site performance and illegitimately to track visitor activity

7   The electronic "tracks" made by online use, such as sites visited, information posted, etc.

8   Industry Canada/Justice Canada. Task Force on Electronic Commerce. (1998, January). *Building Canada's Information Economy and Society: The Protection of Personal Information.* Ottawa. pp. 2-3.

9   Christie v. York Corporation (1940). I.D.L.R. 81. (S.C.C.)

The Media Cluster: Communalizing Intellectual Property While Socially Appropriating the Media Conglomerate

Jesse Hirsh[1]

T HE DRIVING FORCE OF OUR CURRENT ECONOMY IS THE ARTIFICIAL SCARCITY OF INTEL-
lectual property (IP). The atomization and disenfranchisement of labour,
culture and art enables the organized forces of capital to create and govern a
virtual reality commonly called the global market. The mission of the market is
to employ mechanisms of control and commodification that serve to contain
human society within a structure of competing, cooperating, and interlocking
corporate conglomerates.

Taken at face value, this 'state' is both 'artificial' and 'virtual,' thus there
is no reason for us to accept or allow it to continue as it is. How do we take that
which surrounds us, subvert it, and then reclaim it as our own— not just as a
means of survival, but also as part of the ongoing efforts to build a new society
within the shell of the old?

AMERICA ONLINE

It is increasingly safe to say that one can describe or call the Internet
'America Online'. For that's what you find when you traverse the nets: a whole
lot of America, all of it (even too much of it) online, making like the almighty
mall in the mind's eye. It all fits together. Where do many people in the world
want to go? They want to go to America! They want jobs, they want capital,
they want products, and some even go to America looking for freedom. More
and more people want to go to America, and they are doing it online.

The big myth of the Internet was always the facade of the consumer as producer. Anyone can publish a web site, they say, and striking it rich is supposedly as easy as opening a store on the Web. E-commerce has become the pyramid scheme of pyramid schemes, the atomized economy that allows anyone to have the arrogance and illusion of innovation and financial success.

The reality, however, is that the Network of Networks is more about economies of scale than it is about individual empowerment. The magic words (and worlds) of convergence and synergy have made mega-mergers the real means of production, at least as far as capital is concerned. Convergence really is about a black hole, a collapse of gravity, that has sucked us all into some strange mix of social space, outright hallucination, and emerging economy.

The rush to circle the wagons, to secure the IP, and to create the corporate media conglomerate has left the rest of us with this sprawling and seemingly endless (AOL) mega-mall with 'lamers' as the model consumer. The name of the game is containment, and it is the mechanism of the market that commodifies and captures the attention and imagination of the society.

Have we sacrificed our sensibilities and our understanding of the system just to get user-friendliness? The personal computing revolution was largely fuelled by closed and proprietary systems that looked pretty and were easy to use. Out of this culture was spawned the 'Monster Media Corp' that also operates using closed and proprietary systems, which are then used to make said monster look pretty and thus make it easy for us to be used.

LOCALIZED ANESTHETIC

The network computing revolution, however, has the potential to reverse this trend. One of the core by-products of the Internet has been free and open source software. Increasingly, the speed and stability with which free and open code can be developed is showing the potential to make proprietary software obsolete. Instead of paying for the software, people will pay for the configuration, support, and servicing of the software. This localizes the economics involved to the operations of the facilities and spaces necessary to move and exchange data with the networks.

In many respects, it is not surprising to find that the free market loves free software. At the turn of the millennium, it is the free software firms that are becoming the darlings of the market, setting records for surges in stock, and ludicrous market valuations that create paper-thin heavyweights whose only economic power is in the all-stock mergers and acquisitions.

So, even in the free and open software world, the established pattern continues. The substantial amount of capital that's being sunk into free software (commonly under the 'Linux' brand name) really speaks to the notion of economies of scale, and the market's need for control. After all, one of the main functions of power is the ability to integrate and appropriate, and in the case of free software, the stakes are just too high to leave it to chance.

Yet the larger social question is whether money can really buy loyalty (to the market)? Or are these young coders just taking whatever money they can get, regardless of where it comes from? Age and youth are definitely a key factor in the dynamic of this economy. It's important to recognize that, for the bulk of (the middle half of) this century, technology, explicitly communications technology, was really the domain of the military. Politically speaking, communications is the central nervous system of any empire or governing structure. Yet, what makes our current period in time so paradoxical is the fact that our communications technology is increasingly being developed and led by children.

The kids are the ones most involved in innovation. They are the driving force of this economy in that they are creating the conditions in which the Network of Networks becomes autonomous and genuinely self-regulating. The parental and patriarchal figures are obviously not too comfortable with this, although they are careful about what they say since they know the kids control the technology.

Yet what the patriarchs still control is the intellectual property. It doesn't matter how free the software gets, nor how young and radical the innovators become, whoever controls the property within the capitalist system makes and breaks the rules because the market will flex its muscles to appear strong (when really weak) and in so doing, offer (financial) security to those (kids) who want that type of protection (racket).

INTELLIGENCE IN ABUNDANCE

The concentration or accumulation of media into corporate or governmental structures has generally been the rule for the duration of human civilization. Harold Innis wrote extensively on the role and presence of 'monopolies of knowledge' within empires and political economic structures. These were and are a direct result of the 'biases of communications' that are active within the dominant modes of information. With every (cultural) tendency that pushes toward decentralization, there is a counter-tendency that pulls toward (political and economic) centralization. The Internet, as this paper will illustrate, has demonstrated this seemingly contradictory tension rather poetically.

Five years or so ago, I found myself studying Innis in university, while also seeing this same story of empire play itself out for the public. The Internet at this time was just giving birth to the Web, and quite rapidly the attention of all gravitated toward the Network of Networks. The mythology of the time effectively depicted the Internet as the Messiah that was supposedly manifesting for this manic of millenniums. It was clear then, as it is now, that the real message of this medium was the politics of monopoly. So, despite the mania and euphoria of the culture, the seeds of resistance were there. What we needed was the movement.

The Media Collective, which was started in Toronto in 1997, was one of the first grassroots expressions of the politics and practice of culture jamming. It can best be described as an eclectic articulation of what is now blossoming into the movement for and of independent media. Originally, it served as a pool of resources, labour, ideas, and inspiration. It quite literally sought to circumvent the artificial scarcities imposed by the regime, and instead wove a social network of artists and activists that have since become their own Internet (Network of Networks).

As an organized expression of network-based political and cultural movements, the Media Collective was itself a synthesis of two divergent yet similar underground cultures: hip hop music and computer hacking. These two genres have distinctively energized and catalyzed our culture, in many instances contrary to intellectual property laws, and in effect contributing to an alternative and vibrant society.

What's remarkable about these two areas is that, while they are vilified by the powers-that-be, they have completely revolutionized the areas in which they are active. The sampling and production techniques found within hip hop music have, in and of themselves, spawned whole new music genres, and dramatically altered the nature and focus of the music industry as a whole. Similarly, the techniques and culture found within traditional computer hacking have served to define the ethos and character of the Internet, as well as to provide the unofficial training ground for present and future network engineers and system administrators.

In both instances, hip hop and computer hacking represented a means by which those producing and consuming the music/code could communicate directly, free of the constraints and controls of intellectual property.

Explicitly, the Media Collective[2] organized around the model of 'open source intelligence' that was and is the promise of these network environments. With this form of organizing knowledge, one finds it all too easy to defy the state of intellectual property. Popular examples include the publication of 'zines, web sites, and other do-it-yourself media, which are produced using whatever resources and recycled ideas are available at the time. This in itself serves to reinforce the natural inclination to sample, steal, and distribute any piece of the culture you can get your hands on.

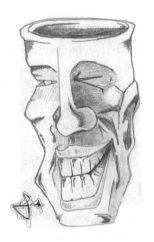

However, as time went on, the meme of the Media Collective continued to infect more and more people. Thus the ability for the collective to maintain coherence or foster democratic control (of the means of production) declined. It seemed that, in our zeal to freely share and gleefully appropriate the culture, we neglected to build and secure a structure for our own defense. In the end, the Media Collective dissolved, in large part due to our own inability to retain the gains we had achieved via our struggles. It seemed that, while we could quite easily and successfully disbelieve in intellectual property, the rest of the society still held rather tightly onto the security and promise of IP, and in doing so consistently undermined our efforts towards long-term social change.

This is why I am now trying to articulate the media cluster and the need for communalized intellectual property. Unlike the Media Collective, the cluster is less of an organization, and more of an organizational model. It is the social appropriation of the media conglomerate, serving as a means by which communities and social networks can communalize intellectual property. This is undertaken in the face of—and in spite of—the converging corporate conglomerates.

THE MECHANISMS OF THE MARKETING MACHINE

E-commerce is deeply indebted to, and hence relies heavily upon, the myth of the virtual community. As not much more than 'the better mouse trap,' the virtual community is the term used for whatever is the best containment mechanism at any specific time. E-commerce arose out of the normalization of the computer-based social network, which, while not being a normal community (of humans living together) can vacuously be called a virtual (almost but not quite) community.

This functionally describes what is now called 'marketing.' Identifying and organizing a set (social network) of people who may be buyers, suppliers, consumers, distributors, investors, or hackers, it doesn't really matter, as long as they are identified and classified within the system. In this regard, containing a market is that which ensures mo' money now, and mo' money in the future. It is also the engine of the so-called 'new' or Internet economy that sinks capital into so many 'dot-coms.'

Within the networks, surveillance mixed with feedback and programming resources yields an environment in which data trails converge into avatars and composite database identities. As many have understood since day one, this is the political economy of the e-commerce model: communications, control, and command.

However, as with all things, there are counter-effects and sub-cultures that exist and flourish, regardless. Thus the promise of participatory environments is the obsolescence of marketing and advertising. While the big brands are organizing at the top to corral any and all they can into their virtual communities, the rank-and-file are appropriating the tools and creating their own worlds, products, economies, and societies. One could invert the three c's and say the counter-cultural effect of e-commerce is: context, contradiction, and conflict.

The initial openness and transparency of the emergent networks affords almost any observer the distanced perspective that nurtures an ongoing contextualization of events in and of space and time. This perspective thereby opens up the contradictions that are resident and relevant in the system, from which the source of present and future conflicts are derived. An interesting example of this is the current state of labour relations and working conditions in the high-tech sector. While the salaries and stock options are in largesse, so too is the overtime, stress, and all-around monotony. The road to high clergy has always been a path of (self) sacrifice, even if paved with (self) indulgence.

The question then returns to facilities and intellectual property, and what resources are available to organize networks that transcend the market realities. Is it enough to just organize against the mainstream and the big labels? Or is it not also important to occupy the positions of power to practise hands-on demonstrations of democracy via participation?

Certainly, that was the other angle of the myth: that participation was meaningful, and that the economy genuinely reflected the views of its participants. Instead, the reality that is the economy reflects the views of its owners. Interestingly enough, the owners are obsessed with our children.

THE THUNDER AND LIGHTNING OF YOUTH

The nature of the network pedagogy is one in which the open mind of the child moves like lighting and listens like thunder. The ability for the young to intuitively grasp and deconstruct the open networks speaks to the power they hold in the value of their inherent intellectual property. It is no wonder, then, that a huge amount of attention and resources are now being invested in 'children's programming' and the 'youth market.'

The successful model of 'music television' with its 24-7 stream of non-stop advertisements speaks to the cliché of the participatory environment as the better-built mousetrap. The viewing and purchasing habits of the audience supposedly determine what is carried, but the actual economy that produces the content and products on the channel is still out of the hands of the kids consuming. Again, the central thing that prevents anyone from setting up their own music channel is the current intellectual property regime that regulates the centralization and oligopolization of this particular sector of the economy.

One still has to wonder, however, if there is potential in the participatory network-based environments that are housed or based in non-market facilities? Furthermore, could tools be developed in non-market participatory environments that could then be used within the market to make it more of a level playing field by massively appropriating large scores of intellectual property? Effectively, the political play would be to initiate a process of communalizing intellectual property as a counter-force to the market-based model of IP.

Democracy is most effective and awe-inspiring when it is direct and involves as much participation as possible from as diverse a range of perspectives as imaginable. The open networks offer this type of opportunity, but in order to engage in this type of activity and organizing, we must secure our own facilities. In so doing, we can create funnels into the economy, and bring the public's attention to a new host of meta-economies, a Network of Networks that can counter the hierarchy of hierarchies that is America, Online.

THE PRODUCT IS THE PROCESS

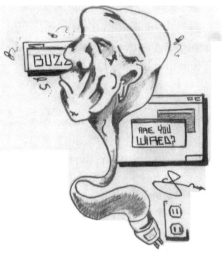

The non-linear interconnected nature of the networks facilitates an accumulative model of organizing. This is perhaps the greatest character of the mega-mergers. The combination of intellectual property and market-based valuation meant that the act of the merger is almost in itself profitable. The logic of the system is to develop via combination and conglomeration. In this regard, every product is not an end, but a means to a better product.

What is produced matters less than how you actually produce it. In this, it doesn't matter what you know, but instead what it is you are learning, since everything is changing so quickly. Even more to the point, however, it's whom you know, since they can always help you learn and keep connected with the ebbs and flows of the nets. As you learn how to do things, you're also learning how to work with various types of other people.

The process that facilitates all of this is what is of real value: the means by which the networks self-organize are central to the character and behavior of the economy. Identifying and expanding who is involved, while also understanding the logic of network self-organizing, contributes towards a greater program of distributed political action and power.

The social agent in this world is the consumer: an alienated anti-member of the society, who is constantly trying to buy his/her way back in. Nobody belongs, but access will be granted to anyone with the right amount of 'credit' or the right combination of identity and intellect. Thus the value of this consumer is largely based on their relationship to, and possession of, intellectual property.

Yet herein lies the paradox, if not breathing contradiction within our emergent economy: Intellectual property is inherently infinite, in the same way that our imagination knows no limits. The world of computing is really the world of cognition. We would be fools to continue thinking 'within the box.' Instead, we must allow our own minds as bodies to explore the vast wilderness of the open networks. Clearly, this involves some form of appropriation or redefinition of IP.

The 'con' or 'sell' of intellectual property as an artificial scarcity exists only because we allow it to. We have within our power and culture the ability to share and give freely the ideas, inspiration, knowledge, wisdom, and imagination that are inherent to our humanity. However, we find ourselves surrounded—or worse, contained—by a set of corporate conglomerates that claim ownership of the very thoughts and feelings we seem to spontaneously sense, see, hear, and have.

The model of distributed network-based cognition is that which, perhaps unconsciously or otherwise, deliberately created the Internet. As an organizing model, it has the potential to liberate us from our existing oppressive political and economic relationships. However, it also has its own tendencies that work to enslave us in new and perhaps even more insidious relationships of oppression, violence, and abuse.

Perhaps participatory environments mixed with distributed networks will allow us to create a culture of self-defense that rejects the new forms of the same old tyrannies? When created as workshops outside of the market, they could possibly provide the tools to counter the comparable environments that were constructed to contain us.

WuWei Productions

WuWei Productions[3] is a current attempt to address these concerns and move towards actualizing some of the concepts discussed above. The name WuWei is Chinese for 'Non-Action.' However, when translated contextually, it means something along the lines of 'appropriate spontaneity' or 'improvisational consistency.' The production aspect of this project relates to the byproduct of distributed network facilities that our culture employs when appropriating the surrounding technological environment.

Beginning with the assertion that the Internet does not exist, WuWei productions maintains that, instead, what is commonly referred to as the Internet is really a complex and multi-layered network of networks that constantly reconfigures itself. Thus, if the Internet is to exist at all, **we** are the Internet. We, the inhabitants of the system, are the system, even if (and thus because) the sum of its parts is greater than the whole.

WuWei Productions sees the Internet as an extraordinary organizing and production tool that facilitates the analysis, collection, and distribution of knowledge. Traditional convergence strategies see the migration of television to the Internet on the assumption that it is where the delivery mechanism will be. Instead, WuWei recognizes that TV is already an effective delivery mechanism, and instead the Internet has to migrate to the world of broadcasting, bringing with it the potential for democratization and transparency.

Our first project with WuWei is titled *TV Eats the Internet*. It seeks to bring together the two formats of late-night talk television and user-driven network news. Using a mix of discourse and performance, we seek to disarm the culture of anxiety that surrounds technology. We seek to draw coherence (via television) out of the discordance of the networks (Internet). We will facilitate the demystification of the Internet using television; we will show people the myriad of flows that make the nets what they are.

We will bring convergence to the audience, instead of waiting for the audience to come to convergence. The Internet is the content and television is the delivery mechanism. The stage and studio audience exist nowhere and anywhere. Humour and relaxation allow us to speak to the belly and the brain, bringing the laugh before the language. With this we will occupy the centre, surround ourselves with difference, and demonstrate what diversity can do, while showing what the Internet really is: the network society.

The narrative of the networks is about collaborative story telling. The origin of the networks is social agency. When television eats the Internet, culture subsumes the determinism of technology, and the immediacy of live performance attracts and retains the animate audience.

When the culture of hacking is brought back to the street level, pop culture becomes direct action, and the distributed organizing modes of the net facilitate youthful and original expression. A new playground enables the exploration of new democratic demonstrations of politics, economy, and society. WuWei Productions seeks to build and maintain that playground as an initial garden for an emerging media cluster.

NOTES

1   With drawings by Crysys
2   Although the media collective is defunct, and has been removed it from the web, TAO Communications (www.tao.ca) was a direct derivative of the media collective.
3   www.wuweitv.net

Information Highway Policy, E-commerce and Work

Gregory J. Walters

T HE PURPOSE OF THIS ESSAY IS TO ASSESS THE STATE OF THE PUBLIC INTEREST WITH RE-
spect to work and workers during the two main phases of Canadian information highway policy and subsequent e-commerce strategy developments.
The goal of the economy is meant to serve the basic goods and well-being of
workers, and not vice versa. This aim begs the question of how best to serve
human dignity and human rights through information technology (IT) development, and whether or not IT is in fact a 'jobs killer'.

This has been one of the most hotly debated questions during the past
decade of information policy development, and the question turns back on
both empirical data and substantive ethical concerns. We will begin with an
exposition of the three main phases of information policy. Two competing moral
visions of the Internet emerge from policy developments: A vision of the information highway as a space for e-commerce, versus the ideal of an electronic
commons. Highlighting key elements of the Canadian and American policy
debates, I argue that there are empirical and ethical problems with the argument that IT is leading to the 'end of work.' A cultural shift is needed that
embraces a view of work based on productive human agency.

INFORMATION HIGHWAY POLICY AND E-COMMERCE STRATEGY

Industry Canada (IC) is mandated to foster "the development of Canadian business, by promoting a fair and efficient Canadian marketplace and by
protecting, assisting and supporting consumer interests."[1] On January 18, 1994,
in the Speech from the Throne, the Government of Canada announced the de-

velopment of its information highway strategy. In March 1994, IC Minister John Manley created an Information Highway Advisory Council (IHAC) to assist the federal government in developing and implementing a strategy for the Canadian information highway.

The Council addressed 15 policy issues ranging from competition and job creation, to Canadian content and culture, to human and social impacts (including access, illegal and offensive content, privacy, security, and employment and workplace issues), information technology (IT) learning and training,[2] research and development, and applications and market development. Its three key policy objectives—creating jobs through innovation and investment in Canada, reinforcing Canadian sovereignty and cultural identity, and ensuring universal access at reasonable cost[3]—roughly corresponded to the parallel yet overlapping interests of industry, the state, and civil society.

Four principles guided the development and implementation of the Canadian I-way as an 'interconnected and interoperable' network of networks, a 'collaborative public and private sector development,' marked by 'competition in facilities, products and services,' and 'privacy protection and network security.'[4] A fifth principle, 'lifelong learning,' was added later. David Johnston chaired the 29-member council,[5] with 26 *ex officio* members reflecting a wide range of knowledge and expertise, including diverse perspectives on linguistic, cultural, and regional issues. From the outset, however, communications scholars and national public interest groups spokespersons worried that the council was dominated by primary stakeholders in the broadcasting, cable, and telecom industries, and that issues concerning equity, democratic participation, social justice, and employment could be compromised by council member interests.

In the first policy phase, the 'information highway' denoted the advanced information and communications infrastructure seen as essential for Canada's emerging information economy, and included both the means of information conveyance (or carriage) and content.[6] This new 'network of networks' would link Canadian homes, business, governments and institutions to a wide range of interactive services from entertainment, education, cultural products and social services to data banks, computers, electronic commerce, banking and business services.[7] The network of networks referred to the converging of cable and satellite television, digital and traditional airwave radio, broadband, narrowband and cellular telephone, local area networks (LANs), wide area networks (WANs), and databases.

Policy initiatives expressed an optimistic view of the information highway as essential for Canada's economic success. While the early I-way metaphor did not completely ignore the role of individuals and communities,[8] it did so with an economic hitch. In September 1995, IHAC released *Connection, Community, Content: The Challenge of the Information Highway.*[9] Success on the I-way depends on establishing a competitive framework that will unleash 'creativity, innovation and growth,' exploiting the economic and cultural potential of IT, and preserving values as a society. Under the policy rubric of 'competitiveness and job creation,' the goal is to set a regulatory and policy framework that encourages investment, competition, growth, and jobs, and where the marketplace determines 'winners' and 'losers'. Because financing is mainly a private sector responsibility, individuals and firms who provide venture capital and take on the financial risks should reap the market's rewards. Foreign investment policies should keep pace with the decline of national ownership of globally dispersed operations, and outdated and unnecessary regulatory barriers should be removed.

Two divergent approaches emerged with respect to the role and responsibility of the government and private sectors on employment and work issues. The policy debate reveals the classic clash between full employment as a central policy goal of the state, versus a laissez-faire market driven approach. IHAC maintained that the state ought to play a minimalist role as 'facilitator,' rather than central actor in the informational economy. The Minority Report by Canadian Labour Congress Vice-President Jean-Claude Parrot rejected their assumption that the private sector should build and operate the I-way or that competition should be its driving force. Free trade, deregulation, privatization and cuts to social programs and public services are the symptoms of the subordination of governments to markets. *Full employment* ought to be the central policy goal, along with government and employer-sponsored training programs, work sharing, phased-in retirement, and facilitation of worker mobility.

IHAC followed up with a National Forum on the Information Highway and Workplace Issues, February 21-22, 1997,[10] discussing the impact of the I-way on the workplace, new approaches to work, worker protection, with a policy paper that was prepared by the 'Committee on Workplace Issues and Lifelong Learning.' Both business and labour contributed to a discussion on non-standard forms of work (e.g., part-time work, contingent or contract work, 'telework,' hours of work and the distribution of work time, self-employment, polarization of income and opportunities, education, training and skills development). Predictably, business and labour perspectives concerning the impact of IT on employment were at odds.

The *business view* states that technological change can either be exploited for its opportunities and adjusted to in order to mitigate costs, or technology can be resisted while policy tries to protect old paradigms that will eventually be overwhelmed by IT change. The traditional definition of 'non-standard' work is any type of work that deviates from a full-time, permanent job with 9-to-5 hours. This is an entirely negative definition of work at a time when new standards are coming online. Part-time work, contingent/contract work, and telework are not necessarily bad. Such alternative work arrangements may in fact help retrain workers, provide opportunities for gaining specific work experience, or give individuals the ability to choose the most optimal place and time to work. There exists no increasing polarization of incomes or shrinking of the middle class. Rather, technology 'enables' individuals by increasing their skills and earnings, and the most appropriate response, therefore, is to increase access to training as the best policy framework for closing the gap between information haves and have-nots—not to create government or state-managed work programs.

The *labour view* presents a view of technology that assumes a weak link between economic growth and job creation because of the negative impact of IT on work. In the policy debates over whether or not to prioritize job creation or job security, job creation invariably wins out over the value of security. High unemployment and fierce global competition is radically different than technological changes of the 1950s-1970s. New technologies are not limited to one industry or form of commerce, but impact all labour related activities and effect the demand for and supply of labour.

The excesses of market forces need to be constrained in order to deal with the negative short term impact of technological change by means of collective bargaining and legislative reform. Legislated minimum standards are necessary to check the downward pressure of market forces that seek merely to improve the 'bottom line.' The labour perspective acknowledges that part-time work is a reality that is neither inherently superior or inferior. The problem is that there are a significant number of individuals who are involuntarily underemployed for whom part-time work is not 'lifestyle.' They fear that they will not be able to put bread on the table and meet other family responsibilities. In addition, part time workers do not have access to equal pay and employment benefits, such as health care and pension plans, and they often work extremely variable hours.

This policy phase promotes the advantages of 'telework' for workers, business, and society, but it is important to distinguish telework from telecommuting. *Telecommuting* is a phenomenon that affects skilled professional workers and often does entail less travel, less on the job stress, and more access to the labour market for individuals with disabilities and women with children. *Telework*, by contrast, tends to be low status, low paid work, with few of the protections that on-the-job workers have, including proper equipment, regular breaks, health and safety protection, and visibility.

Most business discussions of telework erroneously describe it as if it were telecommuting work, when it is actually referring to telework.[11] We should not assume that everyone will be doing telecommuting or telework in the future, nor that either type of work will necessarily be beneficial, especially to women.[12] Empirical evidence suggests that the ways in which work gets decentralized vary enormously from country to country and region to region, and depends upon the prevailing organizational culture, government regulation of the labour market, population density, family structure, income levels, and the availability of IT infrastructure.[13] Despite the policy struggles between business and labour, there did exist some common ground with respect to roles for education, training, and skills development.

The second phase of the policy mandate began in June 1996. Its aims were to advance earlier policy, and to report on Canada's actual progress in the transition to a knowledge-based society.[14] The creation, manipulation, and sharing of information and knowledge is the essential human imperative:

No longer will distance pose an obstacle to economic development, social intercourse, learning, voluntary action, adequate health care, business success or full participation in society and Canada's national cultural dialogue. Knowledge will become increasingly available to everyone, allowing us all to make wiser decisions [sic] in all aspects of our lives—from business to government to health care to education to work to our everyday existence. Everyone will be not only a consumer of knowledge and content, but also a creator. Canada's national cultural dialogue and political discussion will take on a liveliness and depth that will strengthen national, regional and local communities.[15]

We must set aside analysis of the presuppositions undergirding these three promises. Suffice it to say that phase two policy recognizes a 'seamless interdependence' between the economic, social, and cultural dimensions of the I-way. If the first phase focused on access and *physical infrastructure*, this phase emphasizes IT *use* to meet individual and collective goals. The shift in emphasis partially reflects a response to public interest critiques of technological imperative and optimism. "We have always recognized that technology is *not an end in itself, but only a means* to realize traditional Canadian goals and values."[16]

Moreover, the second phase is far more circumspect about the negative impact of IT on unemployment, and makes explicit reference to the human rights challenges of I-way policy. By this time, networks, telecommunications, broadcasting, and computer communications had become increasingly integrated. Telephone companies entered the broadcast distribution market in January 1998, pursuing the policy principle of so-called 'technologyneutrality.' In this view, market forces are to determine what technology is appropriate for the provision of particular services, while government and the Canadian Radio-television and Telecommunications Commission (CRTC) should merely provide frameworks for fair and sustainable competition.

By 1997 the information highway had become the Internet. I-way policy has never compromised the view of e-commerce as Canada's top economic priority. In fact, it believes that the creation of a legal and policy environment that promotes e-commerce on the Internet is the only way to ensure that the economic promise of information highway policy can be realized. Surveys of Canadian employers and workers show that they acknowledge the revolutionary economic changes occurring as a result of technology.[17] By 1998, $13 billion in goods and services were purchased through the Internet and the market is expected to grow to $73.7 billion by the year 2001. About 75% of Canadian businesses expect to buy and sell on the Net, and some estimate that business-to-business markets will swell to $327 billion by the year 2002.[18]

Innovation, ideas, and information drive growth and now overshadow physical goods and services; but the behaviour of interacting markets in the production, distribution and consumption of information goods is far from clear in a world where day-traders enact far-reaching global currency trades in seconds that impact entire national economies. What is clear is that traditional economic theories about market behaviour don't really seem to fit the informational economy and that "low employment can weaken demand, decrease output and cause further declines in the demand for labour."[19]

Policy entered a third phase on September 22, 1998, when the Prime Minister announced Canada's Electronic Commerce Strategy with the goal of making Canada a world leader in the development and use of e-commerce. E-commerce includes "any kind of transaction that is made using digital technology, including open networks (the Internet), closed networks such as electronic data interchange (EDI), and debit and credit cards."[20] The strategy entails four action priorities: (1) Building trust via security/encryption, protection of personal information, and consumer protection; (2) Clarifying marketplace rules surrounding the legal and commercial frameworks, financial issues and taxation, and intellectual property protection; (3) Strengthening the information infrastructure by increasing network access and support for open networking standards; and (4) Realizing opportunities through the development of digital skills and awareness, with governments acting as model users.

The e-commerce policy debate poses a host of ethical questions. Because the Internet knows no international boundaries, how will governments tax digital products such as software, music, videos and services rendered over the Internet from another country? Will this be an opportunity for governments to increase their tax revenues, or an opportunity for transnationals to find tax shelters? Won't businesses tend to set up their virtual shops where tax law is lenient and rates lower?[21] While smaller players may be able to enter the market as a result of e-commerce, this does not change a host of traditional business ethics issues concerning competition and fair play.[22] Regulatory issues surrounding access, privacy and security continue to be debated.

There is surely merit to the argument that companies and organizations that fail to adapt to e-commerce may be in danger of losing a competitive position or missing opportunities. But whether or not e-commerce among rapidly growing companies will help create jobs, except for those with high-technology skills, is a moot question. Peter Drucker believes that only 30% of future workers will be part of the so-called knowledge worker class. The productivity of the non-knowledge services worker will be the greatest social challenge of the digital world. But the nature of non-knowledge services work and how it will be compensated is not merely a social challenge. It also signals a profound change in the 'human condition.' What this social challenge means— "what are the values, the commitments, the problems, of the new society—we do not know. But we do know that much will be different."[23] While the industrial revolution was labour-intensive, the present revolution is 'restructuring' workers at an ever-increasing rate.

Competing Moral visions: E-Commerce vs. E-Commons

Two competing moral visions of the Internet have emerged: A vision of the I-way as a space for e-commerce versus the ideal of an electronic commons. The commerce or 'jobs-agenda' vision has led a variety of individuals, organizations, and special interest groups to criticize the government policy as a market-driven, top-down approach—an information equivalent of trickle-down economics. In this view, the global commodification of information is having negative implications for social control and power over community and cultural forms.

'Commodification' refers to the transformation of use value into exchange value in which objects and ideas are stripped of their intrinsic, moral, aesthetic, and utility values and replaced by market values, or what an object or idea will bring in economic trade.[24]   This is leading to an ever-widening gap between the rich and the poor, between wealthy information 'haves' and poor information 'have-nots.' Critics of IHAC policy point to the negative impact of IT on employment, equity, leisure and social cohesion.[25] They suggest that the e-commerce vision of the Internet is really about increased transnational corporate power, the blurring of national identities, the breakdown of human solidarity and community, and a neo-liberal policy agenda of privatization, deregulation, and user-pay that is leading to the collapse of public space and education. This is an information world of in-your-face-capitalism where one loses a job one day, the ex-employer's stock prices rise the next day, and the telecommunications CEO—already boasting a seven-digit salary— gets a fat raise or stock options on the third day.

Such developments are not mere fantasy, but have emerged in the context of corporate mergers and acquisitions and growing societal divisions and unemployment. Over 19% of Canadians appear to have no ties or commitments to mainstream economic life, while 22% are living on government programs with no alternatives. In short, 41% of Canadians no longer felt connected to mainstream society in the nascent information economy.[26] In this view, e-commerce is really 'e-con,' with corporate propaganda blurring Canadian national interests with business interests, collapsing the public interest into private interest, and whittling away public information access and democracy.[27] The I-way is being used not to serve the goal of participation and social justice in the electronic commons, but rather as a palliative for a vulner-

able time of social and economic transition.[28] The electronic commons vision
of the information highway wants to guard against the logic of technocratic
and economic polarization. It holds out a view of electronic democracy that
can be to the benefit of all citizens, male and female, in the electronic polis.

Is Information Technology A "Job Killer"?

Economies are meant to serve human beings, not vice versa. This begs
the question of how best to serve human dignity and rights through IT development and whether or not IT is, in fact, a jobs killer.[29] The question turns back
on empirical data. The Conference Board of Canada entered the policy debate
in 1997 with the publication of *Jobs in the Knowledge-Based Economy*. Lafleur
and Lok[30] conclude that the adoption of IT does not lead to an overall loss in
employment. Firms that both purchase and use IT intensively have actually
created more jobs in the long run than those that do not, even though IT's
impact across industries and occupations is not uniform. High IT-intensive
industries (e.g., commercial services, electrical power and gas distribution, electrical products, and construction) experienced significant employment growth
during the period from 1986-95, while low IT-intensive industries (forestry,
mining, furniture and fixtures, textile products) saw employment fall.
There are, however, a number of important factors that effect the impact
of IT on employment. A great deal seems to depend on how much IT investment occurs, how quickly the technology is diffused, the extent to which labour productivity is increased, how wages and product prices respond, and
the time frame under consideration. Much also depends on the point in the
economic cycle at which new IT is introduced, governments' policy reaction,
the flexibility of labour markets, the skill mix of the workforce, domestic and
international competition forces, and the specific regulatory environment in
which a firm operates. In the long-run, they conclude, price, income and investment benefits compensate for short-term employment loss.
The Conference Board's macroeconomic forecasting model charts the flow
of economic activity arising from new IT in terms of productivity impact and
investment impact. With respect to productivity impact, the Board admits that
the extent to which productivity increases depends on whether IT replaces
workers, the speed at which workers can do their jobs, the proportion of work-

ers or workers' hours affected by IT, and the 'diffusion' rate—the rate at which the full potential of the new technology is realized. Diffusion rates, in turn, are affected by the training and education of the workforce and how well institutions adapt to change and innovation.

The assumption here is that as productivity increases there is initial employment loss. However, if cost savings are passed through to prices, then output increases and net employment gains result. On the other hand, if firms do not pass on the cost savings resulting from diffusion to consumers, then there is no real increase in output and the initial job losses result in net employment losses. With respect to investment impact, the authors assert that investment creates jobs independently of the productivity effect. More investment dollars raises production in IT industries and positively impacts on other industries through income and consumption.

THE "END OF WORK"?

The Canadian policy debate follows on the heels of the American debate launched by Jeremy Rifkin's controversial book *The End of Work* (1995). Rifkin argues that the 'apostles and evangelists' of the information age presuppose that the Third Industrial Revolution will succeed in creating more new job opportunities than it forecloses. The promised increases in productivity will be matched by elevated levels of consumer demand and the opening up of new global markets to absorb the flood of new goods and services that will become available. Rifkin does not deny IT productivity growth so much as challenge its implications for a right to participation and a government-guaranteed income:

> In the debate over how best to divide up the benefits of productivity advances, every country must ultimately grapple with an elementary question of economic justice. Put simply, *does every member of society, even the poorest among us, have a right to participate in and benefit from increases in productivity brought on by the information and communication technology revolutions?* If the answer is yes, then some form of compensation will have to be made to the increasing number of unemployed whose labor will no longer be needed in the new hightech automated world of the twentyfirst century.[31]

We are set on a firm course to an automated future and a near workerless era, if not in the service sector, then at least in the manufacturing sector. Globalization and automation will permanently idle hundreds of millions of workers. Unused human labor will be the overriding reality of the 21st century. If human talent, energy, and resourcefulness are not redirected to constructive ends, then civilization will sink into a state of destitution and lawlessness. The middle class finds itself buffeted on every side by technological change, reduced wages and rising unemployment. More and more individuals are looking for quick solutions and dramatic rescue from the market forces and technological changes that are destroying former ways of life.

In Rifkin's view, the Third Industrial Revolution is spreading quickly to the Third World. Capital-intensive, highly automated production has now been successfully transplanted. Because the wage component of the total production bill has shrunk in proportion to other costs, the cost advantage of cheap Third World labour has become less important. Advances in technological innovation have made the advantage of human labour over machines a thing of the past. Between 1960 and 1987, "less than a third of the increase in output in developing countries . . . came from increased labour," while "more than two-thirds [came] from increases in capital investment."[32] Whether the context is the *maquiladoras* or Japanese-looking plants in Brazil, machines are replacing workers. The polarization of incomes for the élite knowledge workers and growing long-term unemployment for millions of others has led to labour unrest in Bangkok, China, India, and the United States. Rifkin's prognosis is not good:

> Between now and the year 2010, the developing world is expected to add more than 700 million men and women to its labor force– a working population that is larger than the entire labor force of the industrial world in 1990 .... Worldwide, more than a billion jobs will have to be created over the next ten years to provide an income for all the new job entrants in both developing and developed nations. With new information and telecommunication technologies, robotics, and automation fast eliminating jobs in every industry and sector, the likelihood of finding enough work for the hundreds of millions of new job entrants appear slim.[33]

The problem, in short, is that new information technologies are bringing us 'near workerless production' at a time when world population is surging to unprecedented levels. The problem is exacerbated by the influx of immigrants into poor communities who are competing for a smaller slice of the economic pie, thus giving rise to neo-Nazi youth gangs as well as neo-fascist movements in France, Italy and Russia. Rifkin's practical solution is to build up the 'Third Sector' and renew communal life. Instead of a market economy based solely on economic productivity, which is amenable to the substitution of machines for human input, he advocates a new social contract and economy centered on human relationships, feelings of intimacy, companionship, fraternal bonds, and stewardship.

His alternative vision to the utilitarian ethics of the marketplace with its materialistic cornucopia and resource depletion includes a 'shadow wage' for volunteer work given to legally certified tax-exempt organizations, and a government provided 'social wage' as an alternative to welfare payments and benefits for permanently unemployed. A social wage would build trust and shared commitment to community-building tasks. It would be extended to management and professional workers whose labour is no longer valued or needed in the marketplace. He also proposed grants to nonprofit organizations to help recruit and train the poor for jobs in their organizations.

In addition to public-works projects and corporate tax credits for hiring welfare recipients and high subsidies in the form of direct payments and tax breaks, he wants a greater expansion of community-service programs for impoverished communities. The shadow and social wages could be paid for by replacing current welfare bureaucracies with direct payments to individuals performing community-service work, discontinuing costly subsidies to corporations that no longer invest at home, cutting unnecessarily bloated defence programs, and, most importantly, by enacting a value-added tax (VAT) on all nonessential goods and services, which would tax consumption rather than income. The VAT would also be targeted and levied on IT goods and services, the entertainment and recreation industries, and advertising, thus hitting the 'symbolic analyst' class the hardest and asking them to help those cast aside by the high-tech global economy.

EMPIRICAL AND ETHICAL PROBLEMS WITH THE "END OF WORK" THESIS

I am extremely sympathetic to Rifkin's heartfelt concern for human dignity and the renewal of human and social community ties, but there are two
main empirical problems with the 'end of work' thesis related to unemployment data and the productivity paradox.

First of all, unemployment is now a relative concept which, at least under U.S. definitions, requires that one is looking for work. If you have given up
looking for work, you don't count. From a historical perspective, unemployment is very low when compared to standards of the past 30 years. In January
1998 the average U.S. unemployment rate was 4.7% compared to 7.0% over a
108-year average, and 5.6% in the post-WW II period. In fact, 64.2% of the
adult population was working. The so-called broad unemployment rate stood
at 9.3%. This rate includes those employed part-time for economic reasons,
such as those who want full-time work but can only find part-time work, and
those 'marginally attached' or those who want to work but have hopelessly
given up the search.[34]

The U.S. Bureau of Labor Statistics lists 30 occupations with the greatest
projected growth between 1994-2005.[35] Of the top 30 categories, only 7% fall in
the class of 'symbolic analysts' with a 13% projected growth by 2005. Indeed,
"engineers, computer professionals, and associated technicians together now
account for about 3% of total employment and under 7% projected growth."[36]
The data stands in sharp contrast to those like Noble[37] who see rising unemployment as proof of the thesis that all technological developments sooner or
later manifest themselves in job losses and rising unemployment.

In Canada, the picture appears more mixed. Osberg et al.[38] have analyzed
the shrinking number of opportunities for blue-collar and white-collar workers in various sectors of the economy. In the Maritimes and Nova Scotia, the
role of technology has altered jobs or reduced them altogether in the coal mining industry. The nature of the production process has fundamentally changed,
with productivity now depending primarily on coordination of jobs and cognitive and social skills, not on individual physical effort. The common de-
nominator in the mining, fishing, construction and farming industries is that
they all employ fewer workers today than they have in the past. Between 1989
and 1992, 338,000 jobs in manufacturing in Canada disappeared, a decline of
16% in employment.

The textile and forestry industries were particularly hard hit by the North American Free Trade Agreement. In sharp contrast to textile and forestry industries, the aerospace industry has flourished with "highquality technology and flat, egalitarian team management." While there are opportunities opening up in the service and information industries, these new jobs are not being created fast enough to replace the old ones. In the early days of the telecommunications and computer revolution, "there was a degree of technological optimism about the possibility that telecommunications could also work to encourage a diffusion of jobs from the city to the country." Technology 'diffusion' has scarcely happened, even though IT has 'delayered' levels of management with more broadly diffuse supervisory roles.[39] In the years between 1994-96, Canada's unemployment rate was roughly even at 10%, 9.8% and 9.8% respectively.[40] Early in the year 2000, Statistics Canada reported the jobless rate at 6.8% down from the 8.3% of 1998.[41]

Even the experience of developing countries does not support the 'end of work' thesis. To be sure, Third World unemployment grew in the second half of the 1980s in the midst of what most of the developed world experienced as a major economic expansion. In many favoured developed countries, the boom of the 1980s ended with unemployment at a higher level than at the end of the previous cyclical expansion. The recession of 1990-93 brought unemployment levels to politically dangerous levels in countries like Britain, France, Spain, Germany, and Italy. The 15th edition of the Organization for Economic Co-operation and Development (OECD) *Employment Outlook* notes that there are 36 million unemployed individuals in OECD countries.

Over the 1990s there have actually been structural unemployment declines in Ireland, the Netherlands, New Zealand and the United Kingdom, but increases in Finland, Germany, Spain and other countries. Workers' perceptions of job insecurity have certainly risen sharply, but "on average, jobs last just as long now as in the 1980s."[42] There would appear, then, to be no real long-term structural change in the relationship between economic growth and employment growth in the OECD countries.

This is not to suggest that global underemployment and unemployment are not serious problems; they are. The ILO called the global employment situation 'grim' in its *World Employment 1996/97* report. "Nearly one billion people around the world, approximately 30% of the entire global work force, are unemployed or underemployed in industrialized and developing countries alike".[43] The ILO calls for renewed international commitment to *full employment* in order to reverse global unemployment and underemployment. Current levels of unemployment and 'jobless growth' make no economic sense, and are neither economically nor socially sustainable. And yet, the ILO sees no evidence that globalization, technological change, or even corporate downsizing are bringing about an 'end of work.' Indeed, Kari Tapiola affirms that "the information technology revolution is a key element in globalization" and that "nations, enterprises and individual workers who are able to acquire, transform and use information productively and imaginatively will benefit from the technological advances now set in motion."[44]

At the same time, *full employment* is both feasible and highly desirable and should not be abandoned at a time when trade and investment flows are being integrated into the world economy. The problem with developing countries is that workers "are engaged in low-productivity work that is often physically onerous but yet yields only meagre earnings." While full employment is a long-term objective, it nonetheless "provides a useful framework for the formulation of employment policy."[45]

THE PRODUCTIVITY PARADOX

A second empirical problem with the 'end of work' thesis stems from the assertion that the cause of work disappearing is productivity gains, whereby machines are replacing labour. What Industry Canada, the Conference Board, and Rifkin's work all reveal is that expert economic opinion is solidly divided on the question of the impact of IT on productivity. The apparent contradiction between the deceleration in measured productivity growth rates in most industrial countries since 1973, and the extraordinary growth of IT during the same period, defines the so-called productivity paradox. As Solow[46] asked, why can you "see the computer age everywhere but in the productivity statistics"? The productivity paradox in Rifkin's view 'suddenly disappeared' in 1991.[47]

Some American and Canadian analyses of productivity directly counter Rifkin's thesis. Drawing upon U.S. Bureau of Labor Statistics data, Doug Henwood has argued that there is no U.S. productivity miracle. Labour productivity in all private U.S. non-agricultural industry is growing under 1% per year. While manufacturing productivity is growing more quickly, computers are not making human workers obsolete, nor does the Bureau's capital productivity series support any empirical evidence of fundamental change. Despite the conceptual and practical difficulties surrounding the measurement of capital productivity[48] Henwood states that the 'output per unit of real capital' is in a 40-year downtrend.

Sharpe notes that, between 1992 and 1995, investment in office computers in the Canadian service sector rose 64.2% in real terms, but total factor productivity advanced a meagre 1.2%.[49] Even more significant is the fact that service industries with the highest percentage of total investment seem to have experienced the worst total factor productivity growth. So what accounts for this paradoxical behaviour of productivity growth?

Sharpe advances three basic hypotheses to account for the apparent productivity paradox. The first hypothesis argues that 'the benefits of IT are already here,' but statistical agencies underestimate increases in real or inflation-adjusted output arising from computerization, especially in the service sector. Variations on this hypothesis are that the benefits of IT cannot be captured in output statistics—for example, benefits resulting from greater customer service—and that slow demand growth acts as a negative influence on underlying productivity growth.

A second major explanation is the 'lag hypothesis.' This hypothesis takes electricity as its main historical analogue. Just as it took 40 years from the time the first dynamos were introduced for the diffusion of electricity to result in faster productivity growth, so too the productivity effects of IT take a long time because we humans take a long time to adapt organizational structures in to gain the full benefits.[50] An MIT study by Brynjolfsson and Hitt[51] published productivity data for more than 380 giant U.S. firms between 1987-1991. Their conclusion is that computers added a great deal to productivity, but also contributed to downsizing. The lag in productivity gains was a result of outdated organizational structures, or the wrong use of IT, but not with new information technologies per se. We must also place Industry Canada and the Canadian Conference Board Report in the 'lag hypothesis' camp. The latter's macroeconomic forecasting model assumes a time frame from 1990 to 2015:

[Canadian IT] growth in productivity fell from 1.84 per cent in 1990 to 1.66 per cent in 1996. Under status quo conditions, it is forecast to continue to fall, reaching 1.26 per cent in 2015. With the introduction of new IT spending, however, productivity growth is expected to increase gradually over the forecast period, reaching 1.72 per cent in 2015.[52]

The Conference Board's model assumes an IT investment average of 6% per year between the period 1997-2015, and under status quo conditions.

A third hypothesis stresses the 'exaggerated benefits' of IT. There is no productivity paradox because one shouldn't expect it given IT's total investment in the economy. A variation on this thesis is that in many economic areas, IT doesn't basically alter production and improve productivity. In fact, many computer applications such as spread sheets, graphics and presentation programs, e-mail, and web sites may create little value, and games are often a productivity sink. Similarly, it is also argued that the costs of IT are greatly underestimated. Hardware and software upgrading, technical support, employee training and retraining, and the substitution of expensive labour and machines for cheap labour actually reduces the net benefits of IT. The year 2000 conversion problem cost $600 billion to correct[53] and this is a permanent feature of IT use.

Each of the above hypotheses may capture aspects of the productivity paradox. To be sure, based on quantifiable indicators of output such as, for example, ATM transactions processed, IT has increased productivity. But when IT does not fundamentally affect the nature of the production process, as may be the case in many managerial and professional activities, IT does not directly increase any quantifiable indicator of output. Sharpe concludes that the strongest case can be made for the mismeasurement of and exaggerated benefits of the lagged benefit hypothesis. Thus, in his view what we need to do is give priority to the development of better output and performance measures and indicators for the service sector, and provide tougher approval criteria for IT investment decisions in the private sector.

Despite the empirical problems with the 'end of work' thesis, we must not minimize the increasing harshness of economic life as a result of downsizing and technological change. Even if there is no general disappearance of work, it is difficult to dispute rising wage polarization, the decline of middle-income jobs, the loss of fringe benefits, overwork, job insecurity, rising stress levels, and much alienation in our present historical situation.[54]

The ethical objection to the 'end of work' thesis is tied to the concern for social and economic rights, including full employment policy. Is there really no need for work? It is often objected that the protection of human dignity and well-being can be achieved without individuals having to work. Let us assume for the sake of argument that the first and second hypotheses regarding the productivity paradox noted above are correct. In this view, tremendous IT productivity is real, or will be realized in the short- or middle-terms of the 21st century. The argument is that such productivity now makes it possible for modern technology to supply all individuals' basic needs without working.

Moreover, and assuming a 'natural' rate of unemployment,[55] full employment policies are outdated modes of thinking in this view. The conclusion to be drawn from these putative IT developments has been called 'the no-work solution'—in other words, that "income should be separated from work; individuals, including those capable of working, should be enabled to live at leisure while drawing an 'unconditional basic income' set 'at the highest sustainable level'."[56] If we call 'loafing' the opposite of working, then the ethical problem with the 'no-work thesis' is that potential 'loafers,' living off the work of others without contributing anything, would violate the moral requirement of *mutuality* at the heart of a proper view of human rights and responsibilities.

Basic income policy entails a legal right to receive at least subsistence. However, if a 'loafer' has a positive right to subsistence, then other individuals have a positive duty to provide the subsistence by working, including any loafers who are in a position to fulfill the subsistence needs of other individuals. The exemption from working proposed by the 'no-work solution' is contradictory, since the 'loafer' is not exempt from the generalization to which they are logically committed in claiming their own right to receive subsistence.

Instead of a 'no-work solution' based on the wrong assumption that IT will render work unnecessary, a more realistic and feasible response would be to reduce the hours of work and aim for a full employment policy. I do not imply that Rifkin's pragmatic proposals for work in the voluntary sector do not fit the 'no-work solution.' His suggestion that government tax credits be issued for voluntary work with not-for-profit organizations strikes me as a creative proposal. A full employment policy could provide private and public sector retraining of workers and shortened work weeks. In addition, one can envision tax credits to employers who hire previously jobless workers, as well as direct public sector employment for all those able and willing to work on various publicly funded projects.

What is additionally needed is a cultural shift that embraces a view of work based on productive human agency. What I have in mind is not 'workfare,' which points in the right direction but incurs factual and moral problems. Rather, I am thinking of 'productivist welfarism' that focuses on distributing and fostering personal productive abilities and responsibility, as well as economic and political democracy, in developed and developing countries alike.[57]

Most theories of distributive justice involve dependence and passive welfarism where individuals are dependent recipients of money or economic goods produced by others. In contrast, productivist welfarism doesn't revolve so much on distributing products, but rather helping individuals to develop their own capacities for producing goods or commodities, including their own effective sense of personal responsibility, so that they can dispense with help from others to secure their basic well-being. The notion of a right to productive agency is both in keeping with the spirit of Rifkin's concerns, as well as the United Nations Development Program's notion of human development. Fulfilling the right to productive agency is crucial, given the growing importance of information and knowledge skills for human development in the 'informational economy.'[58]

CONCLUSION

The social, economic, and cultural revolution brought about by the IT paradigm means that 'a new game is starting, and the older rules no longer apply.' Have the new rules of the game been defined fairly, and do they involve the participation of as many players as possible? The gap between information haves and have-nots has widened, and the pay gap between CEOs and workers is obscene. The ratio of top executive to factory worker pay has exponentially increased during the decade of the 1990s. If the average production worker's pay had risen as rapidly as CEO pay, then a worker would be making $110,000 a year today, instead of the $29,000 a worker actually makes. Put another way, the minimum wage today would be $22.08 an hour, rather than the $5.15 it actually is.

The average CEO pay was $10.6 million in 1998, a fivefold increase from the $1.8 million of 1990. CEO pay rose 36% compared to only 2.7% for the average blue-collar worker.[59] Much of the CEO increase came from the robust

performance of the stock market, and because most corporations offer generous stock options. Defenders of corporate largesse argue that tremendous competition for talent drives compensation packages in a way analogous to free-
agent sports stars. These gaps may widen even further in the future, since no
economic decision is devoid of 'the market value system,'[60] now transformed
by automated trading systems and the informational economy.

The keys to unlocking the genetic code for long-term, functioning, sustainable democratic national institutions and international development may
be an 'elusive.'[61] The challenges of the Canadian and global informational
economy are as much existential and ethical as they are technological, economic and political, for they require new institutions and a community of rights
based on informational foundations. Future empirical data may resolve the
productivity paradox. The new libertarian wave and utilitarian contention—
that the well-being of some individuals may be sacrificed through their being
unemployed if this leads to the greater good on the whole—is difficult to accept as morally justified policy in rich nations. National or global policies, in
which millions of individuals are subject to pervasive poverty or the trauma of
unemployment for the purpose of maintaining a general level of well-being in
which they do not share, cannot be ethical. It remains to be seen whether the IT
revolution will lead to an analogous revolution in human care and global solidarity for the so-called losers in the informational economy. Surely, we are all
'losers' in a world where basic human rights are not met, and poverty and
unemployment remain non-virtual.

NOTES

1   Ferguson, Mary, ed. (1994). *Canadian Federal Government Handbook. A Guide to Dealing
    with the Federal Government*. Toronto, Ontario: Globe Information Services.

2   Industry Canada. (IC). (1994). *Providing New Dimensions for Learning, Creativity and
    Entrepreneurship: Progress Report of the Information Highway Advisory Council/Source
    de nouvelles dimensions pour l'apprentissage, la créativité et l'esprit d'entreprise: Rapport
    d'étape du Comitéé consultatif sur l'autoroute de l'information*. Ottawa: Minister of Sup-
    ply and Services Canada.

3   Industry Canada (IC). (1994a). *The Canadian Information Highway: Building Canada's
    Information and Communications Infrastructure/L'autoroute canadienne de l'information:*

Une nouvelle infrastructure de l'information et des communications au Canada. Ottawa: Minister of Supply and Services Canada; Industry Canada (IC). (1994).

4   IC. (1994a).

5   Johnston, David, Johnston, Deborah and Handa, Sunny. (1995). *Getting Canada Online: understanding the Information Highway*. Toronto: Stoddart.

6   Angus, Elizabeth and McKie, Duncan. (1994, May). *Canada's Information Highway: Services, Accessibility and Affordability*. A Policy Study prepared for the New Media Branch and Information Technologies Industry Branch, Industry Canada.

7   IC. (1994a).

8   At times, policy captured a communicative vision of the I-way being not so much "about information as it is about *communication in both its narrowest and broadest senses*.... not a cold and barren highway with exits and entrances that carry traffic, but a series of culturally rich and dynamic intersecting communities, large and small, north and south, east and west, populated by creative thinking people who reach out and enrich one another.... *a personalized village square* where people eliminate the barriers of time and distance, and interact in a kaleidoscope of different ways" (IC, 1994a, 3; emphasis added).

9   Industry Canada (IC). (1995). *Connection, Community, Content. The Challenge of the Information Highway: Final Report of the Information Highway Advisory Council/Contact, Communauté Contenu. Le défi de l'autoroute de l'information: Rapport final du Comité consultatif sur l'autoroute de l'information*. Ottawa: Minister of Supply and Services Canada.

10 Industry Canada (IC). (1997a). *The Impact of the Information Highway on the Workplace: A paper to further the discussion of issues related to the introduction of information technology and its effects on Canadians at work/Les incidences de l'autoroute de l'information sur le milieu de travail: document visant à alimenter le débat sur les questions relatives à la mise en application de la technologie de l'information et à ses effets sur la maind'oeuvre canadienne*, February/Février. Ottawa: Industry Canada.

11 Wheelwright, Geoff. (1997). "Survey finds telecommuting brings benefits." *IT Monthly: A Special Report on Information Technology* (15 November): IT27.

12 Shade, Leslie Regan. (1998). "A gendered perspective on access to the information infrastructure." *The Information Society* Vol.14:33-44.

13 Home-based telework is common in the US, UK, Canada, and Australia where between 5-7% of the working population [are] working from home with a link to the employer. In Scandinavia, there are similar levels of telework, but the working conditions and culture are different. Those who work from home are trusted

by their employers to work wherever it is most convenient for them. In southern Europe, levels of telework are much lower because of higher telecommunications costs, extended family structures, and a work culture that places a premium on face-to-face communication. In developing countries, where the costs of IT are greatest and out of reach for all but the rich, telework is for the privileged few. Telematics have made it possible to shift work to many parts of the world, such as data processing outsourced to the Caribbean, Philippines, or other low-wage regions using satellite links to retransmit results to a parent company. Call centres are being concentrated in declining industrial regions such as the North of England, New Brunswick, Canada, and Tasmania, Australasia. In Europe, operators in call centres work across national boundaries, automatically routing calls to an operator that speaks the appropriate language for the region where the call originated. A campaign to unionize the United Parcel Service call centre in Dublin, Ireland, actually originated among German speakers who had been recruited to work there. The Germans were used to collective bargaining or 'social dialogue' wherein every workplace has a work council with trade union representation. The Germans were apparently shocked by the lack of consultation with workers under the lax Irish system (Huws, Ursula. (1999). "Teleworking & telematics." *Women's Space*, Vol.4, No.1:10-13.)

14   Industry Canada (IC). (1997b). *Preparing Canada for a Digital World/Préparer le Canada au monde numérique: Final Report of the Information Highway Advisory Council/Rapport final du Comité consultatif sur l'autoroute de l'information.* Ottawa: Industrie Canada.

15   IC. (1997b) p. 2

16   IC. (1997b) p. 7, (my emphasis)

17   OECD. (1996). *Technology, Productivity and Job Creation.* Paris: OECD; Reid, Angus. (1996). *Workplace 2000: Under Construction: Survey of Canadian Employees.* Toronto: Royal Bank of Canada.

18   Aly, Shala. (1997). "Surfing for dollars." *Financial Post 2000: Report on the Nation- Internet Commerce*, (11 October): 8-9,12.

19   IC. (1997b) p. 81

20   CECS. (1998). *The Canadian Electronic Commerce Strategy.* Industry Canada/ Industrie Canada. Electronic Commerce in Canada, the web site of the Task Force on Electronic Commerce. Available at: http://e-com.ic.gc.ca.

21   The international accounting firm KPMG has prepared one solution to the problem. The idea is to have the European Commission set up virtual bonded warehouses holding computer-controlled inventory at strategically located sites around

Europe. Goods would be tracked by one central bonded warehouse and could be audited by customs officials using the Internet (Powell, Johanna. (1997). "Flight to tax havens." *The Financial Post, Tax Planning: A Special Report, 22*, November, 48)

22 The primary goal of strategic information systems (SIS), interorganizational systems (IOS), and information partnerships is to provide organizations with a sustainable competitive advantage or leverage over competitors. This is done by raising entry barriers for the industry, building in switching costs, changing the basis of competition, and changing the balance of power in supplier relationships. In fact, a popular IOS can lead to industry restructuring by compelling smaller players to exit the market if they cannot afford to link up with the industry-wide system (Johnston, Russell and Vitale, Michael. (1988). "Creating competitive advantage with interorganizational information systems." *MIS Quarterly* (June):153-65.) Empirical studies suggest that between 50 and 80% of all strategic business alliances fall apart because of poor communication across companies where one does not really know the other company's structure or direction. Poor communication leads to a lack of trust which translates into noncommital relationships (Shaw, Andy. (1997). "Myths and realities of partnerships." *Computing Canada* 23/23 (November 10): 17-18.)

23 Drucker, Peter. (1994). "The age of social transformation." *The Atlantic Monthly*, November, 53-80.

24 Babe, Robert E. (1995). *Communication and the Transformation of Economics: Essays in Information, Public Policy, and Political Economy*. Boulder, Co.: Westview Press; Mosco, Vincent. (1995). *The Political Economy of Communication: Rethinking and Renewal*. London: UK: Sage; Yerxa, Shawn W. and Marita Moll. (1995). "Commodification, communication, and culture: democracy's dead end on the infobahn." *Government Information in Canada/Information gouvernementale au Canada*, Vol.1, No.3 (Winter/Hiver).

25 Forrester, Viviane. (1996). *L'horreur économique*. Paris: Fayard; Menzies, Heather. (1996). *Whose Brave New World? The Information Highway and the New Economy*. Toronto: Between the Lines.

26 EKOS. (1996). *Rethinking Government*. Ottawa, Ontario: EKOS Research Associates, Inc.

27 Gutstein, Donald. (1999). *E.con: How the Internet Undermines Democracy*. Toronto: Stoddart Publishing Company.

28 Franklin, Ursula. (1994). *The Real World of Technology*. Concord, Ontario: Anansi; Turkle, Sherry. (1984). *The Second Self: Computers and the Human Spirit*. London/ Toronto/ Sydney/ New York: Granada.

29   The argument of this section is developed in greater length, particularly the inter-
     national economy and global context of the question, in Walters, Gregory J. (1999).
     "Information technology, work and human development: a human rights per-
     spective." *Canadian Journal of Development Studies* XX, No. 2:225-245.

30   Lafleur, Brenda, and Lok, Peter. (1997). *Jobs in the Knowledge-based Economy: Infor-
     mation Technology and the Impact on Employment.* Ottawa: Conference Board of
     Canada.

31   Rifkin, Jeremy. (1995). *The End of Work: The Decline of the Global Labor Force and the
     Dawn of the Post-Market Era.* New York: G.P. Putnam's Sons. (my emphasis)

32   Rifkin. (1995) p. 204

33   Rifkin. (1995) p. 206

34   Henwood, Doug. (1998). "Unemployment." *Left Business Observer* Overview, May
     24. Available at: http://www.panix.com/~dhenwood/Stats_unempl.html

35   These 30 occupations include cashiers, janitors and cleaners, retail salespersons,
     waiters and waitresses, registered nurses, general managers and top executives,
     systems analysts, home health aides, guards, nursing aides, orderlies, attendants,
     secondary school teachers, marketing and sales supervisors, teacher aides and
     educational assistants, receptionists and information clerks, truck drivers, secre-
     taries (except legal and medical ones), clerical supervisors and managers, child
     care workers, general utility maintenance repairers, elementary teachers, personal
     and home care aides, special ed teachers, licensed practical nurses, food service
     and lodging managers, food preparation workers, social workers, lawyers, finan-
     cial managers, computer engineers, and hand packers and packagers (Source
     Monthly Labour Review, November 1995, cited in Henwood, 1996b).

36   Henwood, Doug. (1996). "Work and Its future." *Left Business Observer*, #72, April.
     Available at: http://www.panix.com/~dhenwood/Work.html.

37   Noble, David F. (1995). *Progress Without People: New Technology, Unemployment,
     and the Message of Resistance.* Toronto: Between the Lines.

38   Osberg, Lars, Wien, Fred, and Grude. (1995, Jan.). *Vanishing Jobs: Canada's Chang-
     ing Workplaces* Toronto: James Lorimer Publishers.

39   Osberg. (1995).

40   ILO. (1996). "World employment report: global unemployment crisis continues,
     wage inequalities rising." *World of Work* 18: 4.

41   Statistics Canada/Statistique Canada. "Labour force characteristics for both sexes,
     aged 15 and over." February 2000. Available at: http://www.statcan.ca

42   OECD. (1997). *Employment Outlook,* July. Available: http://www.oecd.org/els/
     publicatio/labour/eoblurb.htm

43 ILO. (1996) p.4

44 ILO. (1997). "Will the information age mean a virtual revolution in employment? ILO Symposium on Multimedia Convergence. *World of Work*, No.19, March.

45 ILO. (1996) p.3

46 Solow, Robert M. (1987). "We'd better watch out." *New York Times Book Review*, July 12, p.36.

47 Rifkin. (1995) p. 91

48 Henwood, Doug. (1996b). "How jobless the future?" *Left Business Observer*, #75, December. Available at: http://www.panix.com/~dhenwood/Jobless_future.html.

49 Sharpe, Andrew. (1998). "Solving the Productivity Paradox: The Mysterious Link Between Computers and Productivity." Centre for the Study of Living Standards. Available at: http://www.csls.ca/finpost2.pdf.

50 Davenport, Paul. (1997). "The Productivity Paradox and the Management of Information Technology." Conference on Service Sector productivity and the Productivity Paradox. Sponsored by the Centre for the Study of Living Standards, Chateau Laurier Hotel, Ottawa, Canada, April 11-12. Unpublished manuscript; David, Paul. (1990). "The dynamo and the computer: an historical perspective on the modern productivity paradox." *American Economic Review* 80, No.2:355-361.

51 Brynjolfsson, Erik, and Hitt, Lorin. (1993). "Is Information Systems Spending Productive? New Evidence on the Returns to Information Systems. Cambridge, Ma.: Sloan School, MIT, WP#3571-93, June 4.

52 Lafleur. (1997) p.12

53 Jones, Capers. (1999). "The Global Economic Impact of the Year 2000 Software Problem." Burlington, MA: Software Productivity Research, Inc.

54 Osberg, Lars and Sharpe, Andrew. (1998). "An Index of Economic Well-being for Canada." Paper Presented at the CSLS conference on the State of Living Standards and Quality of Life in Canada, October 30-31, 1998, Chateau Laurier Hotel, Ottawa, Ontario.

55 Friedman (1968) argues that the natural rate of unemployment is the level of unemployment at which inflation indeed exists but is not accelerated. Unemployment below the 'natural' level accelerates inflation. Unemployment above that level accelerates deflation. The policy implication is that unemployment should be held at this 'natural' rate. In the US, this is about 4% to 7%, with each percentage point representing about one million workers. See Friedman, "The role of montary policy." *American Economic Review*, Vol.58 (March 1968):1-17, pp. 7-11.

56   Gewirth, Alan. (1996). *The Community of Rights*. Chicago & London: The University of Chicago Press, p. 229.

57   Space constraints do not allow me to develop the action-based philosophical analytical framework that informs this response, but see further Walters, 1999, "Information technology, work and human development: a human rights perspective." *Canadian Journal of Development Studies* XX, No.2:227-231.

58   Castells, Manuel. (1996). *The Information Age: Economy, Society and Culture. Vol.I, The Rise of the Network Society.* Oxford, UK and Malden, Ma.: Blackwell Publishers, Ltd.

59   These pay figures are cited in U.S. dollars. In the words of AFL-CIO research analyst Chris Bohner, "People are just beaten down, hearing year after year how good things are, seeing top leaders take home healthy increases, while they get little or nothing....Whichever economist you listen to and whatever rationale – pro or con – you buy into, the facts are that the pay of chief executives is in the stratospheric range today, while the real, spendable earnings of the average worker are stagnant or sinking." Cited in "Pay gap becoming Grand Canyonesque," *International Operating Engineer*, Vol.142, No.5 [October-November 1999]:8.

60   McMurty, John. (1998). *Unequal Freedoms: The Global Market as an Ethical System.* Toronto: Garamond Press.

61   Conley, M. and Livermore, D. (1996). "Human rights, development and democracy: the linkage between theory and practice," *Canadian Journal of Development Studies*, Special Issue, pp.19-36; (Livermore, 1996)

Learning A Living

As I WRITE THESE INTRODUCTORY NOTES, I AM READYING MYSELF TO APPEAR AT A RALLY before the Ottawa Carleton School Board District protesting the Board's recommendations to close nine inner-city schools. The rationale for the proposed closures is that Ottawa won't receive any provincial grants to create new schools in the suburbs unless they close inner-city schools. This, despite the increase in population brought about by Ottawa's growing reputation as "Silicon Valley North," and despite the demographic trend known as "the doughnut effect," in which families flee urban areas for the suburbs, creating a decay of the downtown core.

Protesters were planning to bring doughnut holes to the rally. But I think it will take more than stockpiling doughnut holes from Tim Hortons and pelting them at Queen's Park. It's going to take political will and activism to staunch the decline of our public spaces.

Neoliberal policies, the rise of Mike Harris and Stockwell Day, deficit reduction, and the increased emphasis on competition, privatization, and the rallying of pro-market forces have wreaked havoc on our public institutions. Health care, education, and public libraries have been struggling to stay afloat. The panacea of privatization and technological fixes pervades the discourse on how to make Canada more "competitive" in a global economy.

This section looks at the fate of libraries, education, and unions in our current dot.com delirium. Sandra Smeltzer considers the fate of the public library, where public support and resources are dwindling, even though the library is well positioned to serve as one of the more viable public spaces for citizens to access information. What happens when the library becomes the recipient of private funding—in this case, from the Bill and Melinda Gates Foundation? Is this just free corporate PR, or disguised altruism—even if the end result is increased commodification?

The public school as the site of ideological battles between pro-market forces and public defenders is focused in Marita Moll's paper. She looks at the tensions between government programs that promote new technologies in the classroom, at the expense of other valuable programs, such as music and art, which are becoming endangered species.

It is telling that one of Nortel Network's recruiting slogans is "The Internet Revolution is led by great minds following their hearts." This probably only applies to those highly educated workers who are also endowed with great stock options. Those stuck in call centres in New Brunswick or in lower-status telework need not apply. Marc Bélanger argues that, as technology pervades the workplace, unions are now more important than ever. He offers valuable suggestions for creating a popular technology organizing movement which would, among other things, promote people-oriented technological designs and lobby for publicly-controlled technological inquiries.

Gated Communities or Public Spaces? The Future of the Public Library

Sandra Smeltzer

SINCE THE 19TH CENTURY, THE MANDATE OF THE NORTH AMERICAN PUBLIC LIBRARY has been "to ensure that people had access to essential information, and that their opportunities to participate in political, social, and economic activities were not determined by their ability to pay for books and other information."[1] Although the Canadian public library system has played an important role in fulfilling citizens' informational needs over the past century, and is currently the most frequently used of all government-supported institutions in Canada,[2] recent trends in the privatization of public space have jeopardized its objectives.

As Herbert Schiller has argued, increasingly public libraries are being brought into the corporate sphere, "either through financial dependence or the transformation of information into a salable good."[3] Unfortunately, this process has been exacerbated by recent government budget cuts. The dismantling of the welfare state in countries such as Canada has acted as a catalyst for institutions like the public library to seek out other forms of financial livelihood.

Since human resources account for such a large portion of a library's annual budget, staff layoffs are one of the first steps taken by many Canadian libraries in order to stay afloat. At the same time, the introduction of various information and communication technologies into the library system has caused an even greater strain upon dwindling librarian human resources. Many libraries have also resorted to reducing their hours of operation in order to cut human resource costs, as well as imposing user fees for additional services and/or increasing already existing fees.[4] Charging fees for services, as Andy Reddick explains, "is a reasonable expectation to account for resources used arising from demands on the system." However, as he rightfully points out, "some user fees risk being a barrier to those who could benefit most from these services."[5]

In this era of budget cuts, there are also numerous examples of Canadian libraries turning to the private sector for financial assistance. One of the most notable sources of private funding for public libraries is the Gates Foundation. The Bill and Melinda Gates Foundation, established in June 1997, "provides funding to public libraries throughout Canada and the United States to narrow the gap between those who have access to technology and those who do not."[6] In the United States, the Foundation's "plan is to help close the growing digital divide between rich and poor by donating money for public-access computers to libraries in all 50 states by 2003."[7]

The Gates's munificence has seeped into Canada as well. In February of 2000, for example, it was announced that 376 Ontario libraries will share "$8.4 million in grants and services from the Bill and Melinda Gates Foundation to ensure that everyone, regardless of income, has access to the Internet and the latest information technologies."[8] Although a private company is the benefactor of these funds, the Gates proposition is appealing, considering that the grants are directed towards libraries that serve low-income communities. However, Microsoft Canada also provides software to all of the libraries that receive Foundation grants. In Ontario, Microsoft Canada is intending to supply software with a retail value of $3.2 million to those 376 libraries who will share in the grant money.[9] This software is considered to be "a separate donation." All told, the Gates Foundation will contribute $26,030,949 (Canadian dollars) for 762 libraries across all the provinces, the Northwest Territories, and the Yukon.[10]

In his book *E.con: How the Internet Undermines Democracy*, Donald Gutstein argues, rather successfully, that the Gates Foundation is a "Trojan Horse" which, "once inside the library, spreads Internet Explorer, Microsoft Windows, and Microsoft Office and BackOffice into every nook and cranny of North America. Eventually, libraries will become dependent on Microsoft products, and once programs like Network 2000 are up and running, Gates and Microsoft will benefit handsomely from his minimal largesse."[11] Of note, Gutstein makes a distinction between the Carnegie tradition of benefaction to public libraries and the motto of the Gates Foundation: "Philanthropy spurs business expansion and provides publicity a company just can't buy." [12]

In this era of Gatesism, privatization of information has expanded and databases have increasingly become available only to those who have purchasing power. According to political economy research, commodification is the "process of taking goods and services that are valued for their use . . . and transforming them into commodities that are valued for what they can bring in the marketplace."[13] Critical skeptics would argue that data and information have become such marketable commodities. Schiller, for example, has asserted that, in a "world where raw material and manufacturing commodities are no longer the centerpieces of economic growth and profit, information takes on growing significance," causing a shift away from the notion that information is a public good.[14]

This is of direct relevance to libraries because they are "being pushed out of their traditional role as owners of materials . . . [and] are now simply owners of equipment that can access materials."[15] Moreover, libraries face difficulties in fulfilling their role of providing free access to information because they have become more dependent on information providers who operate according to a corporate mandate, not a public interest one.[16]

There is also the concern that libraries are becoming increasingly business-oriented, often undertaking marketing strategies and public relations campaigns with the assistance of private sponsorship.[17] This new business model is not only a product of budget cuts, but it is also a result of having to compete with private sector companies. The mega-bookstore *Chapters Inc.*, for example, is a private company that (according to its mandate) provides an "environment which is conducive to extended browsing and *which becomes a part of the local community* . . . Chapters superstores are designed to make customers comfortable and encourage browsing for extended periods. They feature wide aisles, comfortable seating, warm lighting, soft colours and maple or cherry wood accents. Floor plans partition the stores into manageable areas and lead customers to popular categories such as "fiction", "children's" and "multimedia".[18] Recently, Ottawa public libraries have allowed private coffee shops to operate within their 'public' walls. For example, the main library branch in Ottawa recently installed a private coffee shop (*The Original Coffee Bar Company*) because it provides additional revenue for the library and offers 'clients' a comfortable setting while visiting the library.[19]

Our public library is not the only public space facing impinging privatization and commodification (education is also a huge target). As many scholars have demonstrated, the emergence of the Internet was initially met with an optimistic belief in the democratic power of the technology's horizontal, non-hierarchical structure.[20] As Lawrence Lessig notes, the Internet and cyberspace seemed to promise "freedom without anarchy, control without government, consensus without power."[21] In an era of declining democracy and civic engagement, new information and communication technologies like the Internet seemed to offer remarkable solutions to old debates on the public sphere.

However, as the Internet evolved throughout the 1990s, much of the initial enthusiasm regarding the Internet's democratic abilities began to dwindle—in large part owing to issues of access to and ownership and control of the Internet, which effectively limit the technology's democratic potential. As Peter Golding remarks, "[t]he corporate takeover and commercialization of the Internet can lead easily to a weary fatalism, accepting that another potentially liberating technology has been engulfed by the still rampant forces of the 'free market'."[22]

One of the first indicators of the Internet's privatized future came in 1995 when the United States government decided to turn over its share of the Internet's backbone to seven private companies.[23] Since this time, the Internet has continued to move further away from its initial freenet archetype to one that is subsumed under the umbrella of capitalism—a move that is supported by the Canadian federal government.[24] In his 1999 *Response to the Speech from the Throne*, Prime Minister Jean Chrétien stated that one of the government's main goals was to capture "5% of the world share of e-commerce for Canada by the year 2003—and do over $200 billion of business in this way."[25]

In order to be a world leader in online technology (a goal directly related to its industrial policy), the government has also struggled to 'connect' the Canadian population. Canada has always prided itself on being a world leader in the field of telecommunications, and a recent push to get Canadians online over the past few years appears to be a result, in large part, of a fear of being 'left behind'. In the 1999 *Speech from the Throne*, the Governor General of Canada stated that "[w]e have to brand Canada, at home and abroad, as a dynamic and skilled knowledge-based economy. And we must do these things faster than our global competitors—*because speed wins!* "[26]

Thus, the Canadian federal government has embarked on a number of initiatives to improve its world standing in connectivity. In 1995, it created one such initiative called the Community Access Program (CAP). This program falls under the federal government's Connecting Canadians strategy, which was created in 1997 on recommendations from the government's Information Highway Advisory Council (IHAC). The strategy is designed "to make Canadians the most Internet-connected people in the world."[27] In order to help fulfill this goal, the objective of CAP is to "provide Canadians with affordable public access to the Internet and the skills to use it effectively."[28] The Ministry of Industry Canada expects that the program will be able to help establish access sites in 5,000 rural and remote communities (defined as having a population of less than 50,000), and up to 5,000 access sites in urban communities by March 31, 2001. Under the CAP program, public sites such as libraries, as well as local schools and community centres, act as "on-ramps" to the 'information highway' and provide support on how to make the best use of the Internet.

Certainly, the CAP program is a valuable initiative: one that has been emulated in a number of other countries.[29] The program offers a means for citizens throughout Canada to go 'online' from a number of locations if they are unable to do so at home, at work or at school. However, CAP has been criticized for failing to include an effective evaluation mechanism of the programs. The evaluations that have been conducted to date consist primarily of 'success stories' of various CAP sites.[30] As Ellen Balka and Brian Peterson argue, however, there is a need to conduct empirically-based evaluations that utilize participant observation and survey methods in order to find out for what purpose people actually use public Internet sites.

As they explain, "[e]mphasis on securing access to the information highway has obfuscated questions about how new information technologies in general, and the Internet in particular, are being used."[31] These are the questions that need to be asked in order to understand how the Internet effects, or fails to effect, citizen engagement, democracy and social cohesion in our country. Through their study on Internet sites in a Vancouver public library, Balka and Peterson found that "the field of dreams philosophy (build it and they will come) does not translate into internet use for many under-served populations."[32] Moreover, "[a]lthough library Internet terminals are in constant demand . . . our observations of Internet users suggest that, for the most part, Internet users in public libraries are not engaging in activities related to the broad goals of citizenship."[33]

Balka and Peterson's library case study illustrates the importance of distinguishing between having access to a specific technology and actually using it. Physical access to technologies such as the Internet is only part of the challenge of connectivity. Despite various government efforts to mitigate the growing gap between the information "haves" and the "have-nots" in Canada, for some sectors of the population access remains a persistent problem. Various axes of marginalization may include gender, language, socio-economic status, disabilities, geographic location, education, ethnicity and age.[34]

In addition to these traditional forms of marginalization, individuals who face classic literacy difficulties[35] as well as auxiliary computer, digital and information literacy adversities may also experience significant barriers to Internet usage.[36] Moreover, individuals may feel that they do not have the ability to use a technology like the Internet, or may decide that they have no interest in it. Recent statistics from a 34-country Angus Reid survey indicate that "hundreds of millions of citizens have no immediate intention of going online . . . in fact, four in 10 survey respondents—representing about 340 million people worldwide, or the equivalent of the population of the United States—were aware of the Internet but had no intention of using it in the next 12 months, with the majority citing a lack of interest, knowledge and relevance to their lives."[37] Thus, in spite of the tremendous growth in Internet usage over the past several years, it is dangerous to assume that everyone will eventually be online.

The Internet has been lauded for its potential to enable people from marginalized groups to participate more effectively in society. However, it is sadly ironic that these people are also hampered by their very marginalization in accessing and using new technologies. What's more, this marginalization may be intensified in a public place like the local library where, for example, citizens may not feel comfortable using a technology that is new to them. Balka notes that women often fall into this category if they lack a "willingness to compete with others (often young, male teenagers) for access to network facilities, and an inability to obtain adequate assistance from (frequently male) staff maintaining facilities."[38] Thus, even though sites in public locations such as libraries do provide 'on-ramps' for people who may not have access to or usage of the Internet from a home or work location, a build-it-and- they-will-come mentality does not ensure the connection of all Canadians.

The point of discussing issues of access to and usage of the Internet in these broader, more social and cultural terms is to illustrate that the market alone cannot provide. The neoliberal mentality that pervades contemporary society suggests that the market allocates resources efficiently. Yet, the objective of neoliberalism is economic growth regardless of the resultant inequalities in the distribution of income. Arguably, Canadian policy-makers created the Community Access Program with the intent of facilitating greater access to the Internet, in large part because such a market-driven method could not and would not provide for all citizens. Although the program is a worthwhile and laudable endeavour, principles of equality must extend beyond the mere physical provision of new technologies, and even beyond the provision of librarian assistance to transfer technical skills and technological know-how to Internet users.

As Karim et al. explain, "up until the present day, the focus of public policy in enhancing the use of online technologies has largely been on extending infrastructure, developing content, and broadening the market... a mechanistic, supply-side model which assumes that the mere provision of technology and training will produce online access is bound to produce limited results."[39]

The Canadian federal government appears to support such a mechanistic and consumerist approach to the 'information highway,' as exemplified by the fact that, although the Connecting Canadians strategy (under which the CAP program falls) is technically a government-wide horizontal initiative, Industry Canada is spearheading the entire agenda. Assuredly, Industry Canada is more than capable of providing physical access to new technology, which is an important aspect of connecting citizens since 'cost' repeatedly tops most surveys as a barrier to accessing the Internet. However, as the name of the department implies, the mandate of Industry Canada does not take into consideration some of the more social and cultural issues discussed above. The department's mission is to "foster a growing competitive, knowledge-based Canadian economy. The department works with Canadians throughout the economy and in all parts of the country to improve conditions for investment, improve Canada's innovation performance, increase Canada's share of global trade and build a fair, efficient and competitive marketplace. Program areas include developing industry and technology capability, fostering scientific research, setting telecommunications policy, promoting investment and trade, promoting tourism and small business development, and setting rules and services that support the effective operation of the marketplace."[40]

Of note, this clash between economic concerns and social/cultural concerns has consistently plagued the Canadian policy-making process. In international forums, Canadian policy has supported the cultural side, as evidenced by the Bill C-55 split-run magazine debacle and the continual efforts to achieve cultural exemptions in bilateral, multilateral and international treaties. In fact, the Canadian government has recently pursued a New International Instrument of Cultural Diversity (a temporary title) to ensure that culture and cultural industries are not treated as products or commodities.[41] However, on the home front, a department based on *industry concerns* leads the future of new information and communication technology.[42]

A Public Sphere?

The above discussion on the privatization and commodification of both the Internet and the public library should provide ample evidence that neither of these spaces can be considered 'public'. In order to be true public spheres, according to Jürgen Habermas, they would have to be institutionally independent of the state and society's dominant economic forces.[43] Although a separation of political and economic forces from these spheres is idyllic and not entirely possible, the prospect of even a partial partition appears to be diminishing. Thus, what we find on a surface level is a supposed public sphere (the Internet) inside another supposed public sphere (the public library) via programs (such as the Community Access Program) that are lauded for enhancing democracy and connecting Canadians. Yet both the public library and the Internet have become increasingly commandeered by private interests and driven by capitalist principles and an equality of voices in these public spaces is notably absent. Thus, neither represents the public sphere that much policy rhetoric and utopian academic discourse suggests.

As Armand Mattelart's *The Invention of Communication* documents, throughout history communication technologies have been propelled along a path created at the behest of dominant groups within society.[44] Of concern, however, is that we the 'public' believe that these developments happen in a "sphere of high visibility, whereas in fact the major stakes of the new mode of communication are not necessarily decided there."[45] Thus, we must strive to bring the Canadian policy-making process into the sphere of visibility by examining how a public institution such as the library and a new technology such as the Internet have become increasingly privatized and commodified.

Moreover, we must critically examine government initiatives like the Community Access Program to determine if they are, in contrast to their stated mandates, only amplifying an Athenian democracy in which, to quote Peter Golding, "neither women nor slaves got much of a political look-in."[46]

NOTES

1   Gutstein, Donald. (1999). *E.con: How the Internet Undermines Democracy.* Toronto: Stoddart. p. 24.
2   Canadian Association of Public Libraries (CAPL). (1997). *DIVIDENDS: The Value of Public Libraries in Canada.* URL: http://www.cla.ca/top/CAPL/fintext.htm#canada
3   Schiller, Herbert I. (1989). *Culture Inc.: The Corporate Takeover of Public Expression.* New York: Oxford University Press. p. 4.
4   Gutstein. (1999). pp. 51-52.
5   Reddick, Andrew. (1998). *Community Networking and Access Iinitiatives in Canada,* Ottawa: Public Interest Advocacy Centre, pp. vii-viii).
6   Gates Library Foundation (2000). URL: http://www.glf.org/
7   Hafner, Katie. (February 21, 1999). "Gates's library gifts arrive, but with windows attached." *The New York Times* (Sunday), A1.
8   Ottawa Public Library (OPL). (2000). URL:http://www.opl.ottawa.on.ca/english/news/index.html
9   Ottawa Public Library. (2000).
10   Nolen, Stephanie. (June 26, 2000). "Bill's Canadian adventure." *The Globe and Mail,* R1.
11   Gutstein (1999). p. 42.
12   Gutstein (1999). p. 44.
13   Mosco, Vincent and Andrew Reddick. (1997). "Political economy, communication, and policy." In Bailie, Mashoed and Dwayne Winseck (Eds.), *Democratizing Communication? Comparative Perspectives on Information and Power* (pp. 11-32). Cresskill, N.J.: Hampton Press. p.19.
14   Mosco, Vincent. (1989). *The Pay-Per Society: Computers and Communication in the Information Age. Essays in Critical Theory and Public Policy.* Toronto: Garamond Press. p.79.
15   Gutstein. (1999). pp. 55-56.

16 Gutstein. (1999). p. 68.

17 This business mentality is also represented by business-like staff designations, as exemplified by Barbara Clubb, the Chief Librarian and *CEO* of the Ottawa Public Library.

18 Chapters, Inc. (2000). URL: http://www.chaptersinc.com/corpdesc.htm

19 Désormeaux, Monique. (2000). Manager of Service Planing & Communications, Ottawa Public Library. Personal communication, April 24, 2000.

20 Barney, Darin. (2000) *Prometheus Wired: The Hope for Democracy in the Age of Network Technology.* Vancouver: UBC Press; Clift, Steven. (1998, August). *Democracy is online.* URL: http://www.e-democracy.org/do/article.html; McChesney, Robert W. (1999). *Rich media poor democracy: Communication politics in dubious times.* Chicago: University of Illinois Press.

21 Lessig, Lawrence. (1999). *Code and Other Laws of Cyberspace.* New York: Basic Books, p.4.

22 Golding, Peter. (1998). "Worldwide wedge: division and contradiction in the global information infrastructure." In Thussu, Daya Kishan (Ed.), *Electronic Empires: Global Media and Local Resistance* (pp.135-149). London: Arnold, pp 139-140.

23 Herman, Edward S. and Robert W. McChesney. (1997). *The Global Media: The New Missionaries of Corporate Capitalism.* London: Cassell, p. 118.

24 An apt example of this process of privatization and commodification is the Internet Corporation for Assigned Names and Numbers (ICANN). ICANN, physically located in California and composed of primarily private companies, allows the market to allocate cyberspace by doling out domain names and addresses. Following in the footsteps of the United States model, Canada has created a method to allocate its ".ca" domain via a private sector led initiative (Mosco, Vincent. *Public Policy and the Information Highway: Access, Equity and Universality.* Report to the National Library of Canada. Ottawa: Carleton University, February 2000. p.69)

25 Canada, Prime Minister. (1999, October). *Response to the Speech from the Throne.* URL: http://pm.gc.ca/cgi-win/pmo_view.dll/ENGLISH?1085+0+NORMAL

26 Canada, Governor General. (1999, October). *Speech from the Throne.* URL: http://www.pco-bcp.gc.ca/sft-ddt/doc/fulltext_e.htm

27 Canada, Industry Canada. (2000). URL: www.ic.gc.ca.

28 Canada, Industry Canada. (2000).

29 For an overview of how Canada's ICT strategy has been adapted, in, for example, a Flemish and Dutch setting refer to d'Haenens, Leen (Ed.) (1999). *Cyberidentities: Canadian & European Presence in Cyberspace.* Ottawa: University of Ottawa Press.

30   A notable exception is the work performed by Andrea Görgeç, Shirley Lew, and Ann Curry at the School of Library, Archival and Information Studies at the University of British Columbia. They completed a study entitled "An analysis of internet use in the public library" and are currently in the beginning stages of a sequel study. Their work, however, only examines transactional log analysis of data from web server logs in public libraries, which registers which Internet sites are accessed (Görgeç, Lew, and Curry, 1999). URL: www.schoolnet.ca/ln-rb/e/about/ubc/index.html

31   Balka, Ellen and Brian J. Peterson. (1999). *Jacques and Jill at VPL: Citizenship and the Use of the Internet at Vancouver Public Library.* (Draft paper) Presented at "Citizens at the crossroads: Whose Information Society?" (October 21, 1999). London, Ontario. p. 1.

32   Balka, Ellen and Brian J. Peterson. (1999), p. 15.

33   Balka, Ellen and Brian J. Peterson. (1999), p. 14.

34   Dickinson, Paul and Ellison, Jonathan. (1999). Getting connected or staying unplugged: The growing use of computer communication services. In *Services indicators - 1st quarter* (pp. 33-50). Ottawa: Statistics Canada

35   16.6 percent of the Canadian population is considered to be functionally illiterate. United Nations Development Programme. (1999). *Human development report 1999.* UNDP. p. 149

36   In her book, *Literacy in a Digital World,: Teaching and Learning in the Age of Information.* Kathleen Tyner explains that a traditional notion of literacy "does not seem to take into account the glut of information available to people, or the amount of electronic information they use, or the new interactive nature of mediated experience, or converged/multiple modalities, or the confluence of digital media forms and content" (New Jersey: Lawrence Erlbaum Associates, 1998, p. 62).

37   Angus Reid. (2000, March). *Face of the web study pegs global Internet population at more than 300 million.* URL: http://www.angusreid.com/media/content/displaypr.cfm?id_to_view=1001

38   Balka, Ellen. (1997). *Viewing Universal Access Through a Gendered Lens.* Information Policy Research Program, Faculty of Information Studies, University of Toronto, Working papers. No. 4. URL: http://www.fis.utoronto.ca/research/iprp/va/gender/balka.html

39   Karim, Karim H. et al. (1999). *On-line Access and Participation in Canadian society.* SRA Reports. Ottawa: Canadian Heritage, p.16.

40   Industry Canada. (2000).

41 Scoffield, Heather. (1999) "Ottawa seeks global deal to end cultural trade wars." *Globe and Mail.* October 20. p. A1.

42 Also, the Canadian Radio-television and Telecommunications Commission (CRTC) decided not to regulate the Internet in Canada in large part because it was "concerned that any attempt to regulate Canadian new media might put the industry at a competitive disadvantage in the global marketplace." (*CRTC won't regulate the Internet,* May 17, 1999. URL: http://www.crtc.gc.ca/eng/news/RELEASES/1999/R990517e.htm

43 Habermas, Jürgen. (1989). *The Structural Transformation of the Public Sphere: An Inquiry into a Category of Bourgeois Society.* Mass.: MIT Press.

44 Mattelart, Armand. (1996). *The Invention of Communication.* Minneapolis: University of Minnesota Press.

45 Mattelart, Armand. (1996). p.xvii.

46 Golding, Peter. (1998). p. 143.

Pianos vs. Politics: Sustaining Public Education in the Age of Globalization

Marita Moll

FROM POLITICIANS TO PUBLICISTS, FROM PARENTS TO PUNDITS, THE URGENT APPEAL TO enter the 21st century with schools fully "wired" to the emerging global communications network has been unrelenting. Access to this network will make students smarter, businesses more competitive, workers more collaborative, and citizens more active, says the rhetoric. If critical thinking is one of the outcomes of education, as a well-educated nation we have certainly failed to apply critical thinking to these claims for new technologies.

Mr. Holland's Opus is a popular movie on video-rental shelves. Mr. Holland is a teacher who tries to save his school's music program, about to be closed down because of budget cuts. He rallies the students and the community in a valiant attempt to rescue the program. In the end, he doesn't succeed, and viewers are saddened because they have a feeling that Mr. Holland is right. There's more going on than meets the ear as students prepare this year's version of *When the Saints Go Marching In*. Music education is a valuable part of basic education. Looking at the research, the feeling turns out to be well supported.

In June 1996, Kenneth Whyte, then the editor of *Saturday Night*, described how his attitude changed from supporting a total ban on music in schools, believing the time would be better spent on science, to becoming a strong supporter for the reinstatement of music into the curriculum. "Music is the most scientific of the arts," he writes. "Pythagoras . . . considered it a mathematical discipline along with arithmetic, geometry and astronomy."[1] The research he considered included a study at the University of California in which preschoolers who received daily music lessons scored 80% higher on tests of spatial intelligence than did those who did not receive such lessons. Spatial reasoning is essential for complex tasks in math, science and engineering.

There is a growing body of research evidence that supports the long-term value of music and arts education. The February 1994 issue of *Phi Delta Kappan,* a prestigious education journal, reported that 66% of students who had majored in music and then applied to medical school were accepted, while only 44% of those who had majored in biochemistry were successful in their applications. A U.S. College Entrance Examination Board study found that students who took more than four years of music and arts scored 34 points higher on the verbal sections of the SAT (Scholastic Aptitude Tests) and 18 points higher on the math sections than students who took these subjects for less than a year.[2] The arts have long been acknowledged contributors to creativity, critical and lateral thinking, team building and problem solving—common goals expressed for education by a wide range of business and public interest groups.

So why does Mr. Holland's story sound so familiar? If music supports the current educational "holy grail"—the development of math and science skills—why were such programs the first to disappear in the educational budget squeeze of the late '90's? In the March 1998 issue of *Quill and Quire,* Lesley Krueger notes that "In New Brunswick, the local branch of the Coalition for Music Education in Canada has been fighting deep province-wide cuts to school music programs brought in under a back-to-basics curriculum introduced by former premier Frank McKenna . . . At the Toronto Board of Education . . . a visual arts coordinator hears rumors that her entire department may disappear during the provincially ordered amalgamation . . . of the five Toronto-area school boards. Meanwhile, [they] are facing the loss of even private sector support for the arts."[3]

With all the evidence to support the educational value of integrating music and arts education into the curriculum, companies should be lining up to donate musical instruments and art supplies to schools in financial difficulty. Companies, often with the help of government programs, are certainly lining up to donate computers and related high-tech equipment to schools. Governments across the continent have established special funding programs for new technologies in schools (see Appendix A). New partnerships between the high-tech industry and a school or school district or a ministry of education are reported daily.

Clearly, the education system is being re-engineered on a grand scale to accommodate expensive high-tech equipment which is said, without much supporting evidence, to promote creativity and critical thinking, team building and problem solving—skills which research has shown quite clearly are common outcomes of the much cheaper, much more inclusive, much more personally and culturally ennobling arts programs. "To be illiterate in the arts is to be blind, mute and deaf at a most fundamental level," says John Bradmas in *Growing up Complete: The Imperative for Music Education.* [4]

Industries acknowledge that their interest in placing computers in schools is part of a market building strategy. Governments, recognizing that the initiative is worthless without teacher training and curriculum integration, are trying to put these in place. Any initiative on this scale would build markets. If every classroom had a piano and every teacher had basic music training, and every curriculum had a compulsory music component, the numbers of musical instruments in homes would soar. So would the sale of sheet music, and the number of music teachers, and the number of piano tuners, maintenance people, concert goers, etc. A whole sector of the economy would flourish around it.

But nobody is lining up to donate pianos or any other instrument of music and arts education to classrooms. There is something else at work here—something beyond education and market building. The real explanation for the current emphasis on using new technologies in the classroom is to be found in the larger world of politics and economic change.

THE POLITICS OF ARTIFACTS

In the Winter 1980 issue of *Daedalus: Journal of the American Academy of Arts and Sciences*, Langdon Winner asks: "Do artifacts have politics?"[5] He points out that, throughout history, tools have been created, used and promoted by existing power structures to maintain and expand their power. The horse was a technology of warfare long before it became a technology of agriculture. The promoters of the private automobile sometimes actively opposed public transportation systems. Following this pattern, the agenda to connect schools to new technologies also enables a particular power structure.

Stories abound about how e-mail exchange projects open classrooms up to the world, and how electronic mentor projects can give students access to

international experts. Less often are stories written about how these same connections can facilitate the delivery of standardized curriculum and the accompanying imposition of standardized assessment procedures, centralized control over school budgets, and extensive gathering and storage of information
about teachers and students. Rarely is it mentioned that these technologies
make it possible for education to become commodified like never before, with
mass-marketed, off-the-shelf curriculum projects designed by Disney and
Microsoft waiting to fill the gap created by the steady erosion of public funds
for local and regional curriculum development.

The idea of connecting all schools to the Internet originated in the market expansion needs of the predominantly U.S.-based information, communications and entertainment industries. Deregulation and free trade initiatives
were already well under way around the globe when the "challenge to connect
schools, hospitals and libraries" emerged in a January 1994 speech by then U.S.
Vice-President Al Gore.[6] The speech was not about education. It was about
easing regulations limiting the ability of these industries to operate in each
other's markets. There was no evidence offered about the educational value of
connecting schools. There was no discussion of what such an initiative might
cost. Connecting schools was just an idea that, as they say in the media world,
"had legs"—except that this one had jet-propelled fuel packs. Before one could
say "APEC, NAFTA, OECD," every developed country in the world was prom-
ising school connectivity—and putting substantial public funds behind that
promise.[7]

In Canada, Industry Canada's SchoolNet was the main promotional ve-
hicle. It was a program fuelled by generous federal funding and extensive
promotion of partnerships with the information and communications industries.[8] Within two years, SchoolNet evolved from a 1992 Master's degree project
created by two Carleton University engineering students to a full-fledged national program with a 30-45- member board of public/private "partners." The
initial goal of the project was to see that all schools in Canada were connected
to the Internet. But it quickly gained momentum. SchoolNet Phase II plans to
ensure that every classroom has at least one computer (250,000 computers).
Phase III, announced in 1999, raised the bar to include "increased access to
high-speed Internet service . . . [to] "stimulate the production of Canadian
multimedia learning content and applications."[9] Money spent so far, according to the *Ottawa Citizen* is about $13 million a year between 1995 and 1998,
and up to $25 million a year between 1998 and 2001."[10]

Industry Canada understands and plays by the rules of globalization where everything is weighed on the scales of commerce. "Education should be a producer (not just a consumer) in the economy" is the common rationale.[11] At the federal level, it has so far had a stranglehold on both the development and the implementation of the policy to "wire" classrooms. Other federal departments, including Heritage Canada, whose mandate includes the cultural sector and the Canadian Broadcasting Corporation (CBC), and Human Resources Development Canada, whose interest in continuing education and job training seems relevant, have not been actively engaged in the process.

Wiring schools, whatever the eventual educational impact, never grew out of an educational need. Computers are artifacts that speak the language of the highly privatized and commercialized post-industrial society. The agenda to wire schools grew out of the perceived need to privatize and commercialize one of the last and largest unexploited markets in the world. Investment consultants Merrill Lynch see a two-trillion-dollar global education and training market. In the U.S., they predict that "10% of the publicly-funded K-12 school market will be privately managed 10 years from now, implying a market of over $30 billion in today's dollars." Technology plays a significant role. "Technology and specifically the Internet will 'democratize' education, providing greater access at lower cost," says Merrill Lynch.[12] Who will get greater access and to what is, of course, an unanswered question.

CUTTING TO THE BONE

Despite the disappearance of traditional art and music programs as public spending on education is reduced, the public wallet seems always to be open for new technologies in schools. "Our walls are falling down, but we'll have computers into the next century," says Justin Millette, a student trustee for the Ottawa-Carleton District School Board. "It's kind of strange what they spend their money on."[13]

No one knows exactly how much money has been spent on new technologies for schools by various levels of government, but there is no doubt that the amounts have been considerable. According to Alison Armstrong, Canadian journalist and author of *The Child and the Machine*,[14] "between 1992-1995, Ontario alone spent an estimated $150 million (Canadian)."[15] The Quebec gov-

ernment recently set aside $380 million over five years to fund technology ini-
tiatives at the elementary and secondary levels.

The federal government has invested through projects like SchoolNet,
TeleLearning, which funds research into effective use of technologies in education, and CANARIE, a non-profit corporation which distributes large amounts
of federal funds to support product development. Creative use of various fed-
eral-provincial transfer programs has also been a source of funds. A $62.1 mil-
lion "information technology initiative" under the Canada/Nova Scotia Cooperation Agreement on Economic Diversification targeted $35.3 million to
hardware, software, support and training in the public schools.[16]

This generous funding is all the more remarkable because of its timing.
Throughout the 1990s, politicians were consumed with reducing public spending to bring down deficits and reduce taxes. Taxes increase production costs.
In the globalization juggernaut, areas with high production costs lose out to
low- or no-tax zones. The new global marketplace demands a level playing
field.

A close look at the damage these funding cutbacks have inflicted on local schools reveals an educational "Guernica" of dismal proportions.

> [In Ontario] the number of teachers in the province's schools has de-
> clined by 11,399 in the past six years, while enrolment over the same
> period has jumped by more than 59,000, according to People for Edu-
> cation, a parents' group. Urban school boards are hurting the most. In
> 1998, their local taxing powers were stripped away and replaced with
> a new funding formula. By 2003, when the formula will be fully im-
> plemented, the Toronto District School Board alone expects it will have
> slashed $362 million from its budget. It plans to shut as many as 30
> schools by 2002. Across the province, 137 are slated to close this year
> and next . . . Signs of cutbacks are everywhere: vocational subjects
> have been scaled back, and increasingly, parents are being asked to
> raise money for such basics as classroom maps, sheet music and teach-
> ers' resources.[17]

During this period, the benefits of private over public service delivery
models were broadcast from every possible vantage point. The privatization
subtexts of new technologies made them acceptable beneficiaries of public

funds. Governments sharpened their pencils instead on libraries, music and art programs, teachers and everything else that was generally viewed as part of traditional public spending. Some programs were nearing the "endangered" status. At its 1996 Annual Meeting, the Canadian Home and School and Parent-Teacher Federation passed an emergency resolution urging all education stakeholders to support the continued role of music and fine arts education as a fundamental part of public schooling.[18]

Recently, Industry Canada Minister John Manley and British Prime Minister Tony Blair have raised concerns publicly that their own children were spending too much time interacting with a computer. This is a curious comment from two men who have spent the last few years actively promoting both the benefits of privatization and the use of computers in the one place where its use might be appropriately restricted pending further study. Even at this level, or perhaps especially at this level, the degree of disconnect between new technologies and their impacts is as profound as it is alarming.

GOING GLOBAL

Global education policy has become an increasingly important subject of discussion for international bodies like the WTO, OECD and APEC. APEC's Working Group on Human Resources, for example, issued the following "broad principles and expectations of a school system that integrates business practices" in a strategy paper for the 1997 meeting in Vancouver:

- A school system should have an integrated framework on education based on standards and expectations set by a society.
- Students should acquire a breadth of knowledge, skills and attitudes necessary for adjustments into work environment.
- All students are expected to develop work ethics and attitude appropriate for a working life.
- Schools should provide a comprehensive skills-based achievement record to better inform the employers of a student's social skill development level and width and depth of a student's knowledge and skills. This will aid the employers to better select and recruit workers.[19]

These kinds of decontexualized economic agendas which hijack public services for private purposes are increasingly provoking angry responses. Tired of being ignored by their elected representatives in their fight against the increasing powers vested in organizations and mechanisms beyond the reach of democratically elected governments, demonstrators have taken to the streets. Intense lobbying and demonstrations against the OECD-initiated MAI (Multinational Agreement on Investments) resulted in a withdrawal of that agenda at the OECD level. Recent demonstrations in Seattle, Washington and Windsor show an escalating level of suspicion about the closed-door activities of these supergovernmental organizations. Demonstrators are especially concerned about secret negotiations towards deregulation and free trade in the services sector, including health and education.

In the current round of talks, the WTO is aiming to expand the General Agreement on Trade in Services (GATS) to cover public services such as education and health. The Canadian government's position, which claims that public education will not be part of any trade agreements while at the same time promoting trade in educational products and services, is an untenable position according to public education advocates. "If the GATS is expanded to include education, it would have disastrous consequences," according to British Columbia Teachers' Federation President David Chudnovsky. "Canada could lose sovereign control over many crucial educational issues." Chudnovsky said teachers are very concerned that under WTO rules, Canada could be compelled to:

- provide the same subsidies or loans to private foreign-owned institutions as are provided to Canadian public schools;
- relinquish the authority to determine standards in teacher training and certification;
- open up curriculum development to private, foreign, for-profit firms;
- allow foreign-owned institutions to set up in Canada, without requiring local involvement in hiring, ownership or governance; and
- offer foreign-owned institutions the same degree-granting authority as Canadian ones.

"Education is a public trust," says Chudnovsky. "When we permit corporate bureaucrats to make fundamental decisions that ought to be made democratically by communities, then we betray that trust. Public education is too important to be bought and sold as a commodity."[20]

Our social, economic and political systems are undergoing a period of intense change. The first key to using the current change cycle to protect fundamental public services is careful analysis and broad understanding of the various change agendas unleashed by the current deregulation/free trade environment. These forces do not tolerate the social safety nets which have evolved, often through bitter struggles between workers and factory owners, to cushion the extremes of the industrial society. If the world is indeed on its way through another economic revolution, new ways must be found to ensure that health, education and social services are available to all. Ricardo Petrella, professor at the Université Catholique de Louvain (Belgium) says:

> We must go to Seattle . . . We must tirelessly repeat our message: education is not a commodity. The same applies, of course, to water, to health . . . These are not "goods" like, say, bananas or wrist-watches. Apart from Seattle,

> [We must] contribute to devising and developing a *new discourse on society and the world* at large—a discourse which is different from, and represents an alternative to the current emphasis on globalization based on a capitalist, liberalized, deregulated, privatized and competitive market economy.

> [We must] turn *education into an area* for teaching and promoting the *common good* and finding and testing ways of "living together."[21]

A blueprint for doing just that can be found in the UNESCO- sponsored International Commission on Education for the Twenty-first Century report called *Learning: The Treasure Within*.[22] This report seeks to guide education systems through turbulent times by providing a clear vision. "Education must, as it were, simultaneously provide maps of a complex world in constant turmoil and the compass that will enable people to find their way in it."[23] We can keep our bearings on this journey, says the report, by recognizing that education throughout life is based on four pillars: "learning to know; learning to do; learning to live together; and learning to be" (see figure 1). Each of these pillars must be given equal value, says the Commission.

Learning: The Treasure Within is a document that stands in stark contrast to the utilitarian education statement released by APEC. Skills that are needed in a well-functioning society are not confined to those that register immediately on the economic scale. "A broad, encompassing view of learning should aim to enable each individual to discover, unearth and enrich his or her creative potential, to reveal the treasure within each of us. This means going beyond an instrumental view of education, as a process one submits to in order to achieve specific aims (in terms of skills, capacities or economic potential), to one that emphasizes the development of the complete person,"[24] says the report.

Creating A Public

In Canada, health, education and social services are all public projects to which everyone contributes and from which everyone benefits. Equal access to a broad range of services in each of these sectors is a fundamental principle. But the demands of globalization, the pressures of privatization, and the hype of commercialization push us away from this principle. It would be a sad outcome indeed if equal access to generous social programs in general, and comprehensive public education in particular, became a casualty of the late 20th century.

Neil Postman has said that the business of schools is not to serve the public, but rather to create a public, and that no one has invented a better way to create a public than through a public school system.[25] In Western nations, it is the schools that reinforce the social and cultural myths fundamental to our way of life—the principles of democracy, the rights and responsibilities of citizenship, the belief that all citizens, with appropriate education and motivation, will be able to find gainful employment and share in the wealth of society.

Will a "user pay" system, in which comprehensive services are available only to those with sufficient financial resources, create the kind of public that holds to such egalitarian social and cultural myths? Many prominent thinkers are doubtful. Canadian philosopher John Ralston Saul says that public education is the single most important element in the maintenance of a democratic society. "That a private system may be able to offer to a limited number of students the finest education in the world is irrelevant. Highly sophisticated élites are the easiest and least original thing a society can produce. The most difficult and the most valuable is a well-educated populace."[26]

FIGURE 1

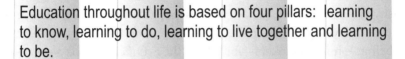

Education throughout life is based on four pillars: learning
to know, learning to do, learning to live together and learning
to be.

Learning to know, by combining a sufficiently broad general knowledge
with the opportunity to work in depth on a small number of subjects.
This also means learning to learn, so as to benefit from the
opportunities education provides throughout life.

Learning to do, in order to acquire not only an occupational skill but
also, more broadly, the competence to deal with many situations and
work in teams. It also means learning to do in the context of young
peoples' various social and work experiences which may be informal,
as a result of the local or national context, or formal, involving courses,
alternating study and work.

Learning to live together, by developing an understanding of other
people and an appreciation of interdependence -- carrying out joint
projects and learning to manage conflicts -- in a spirit of respect for the
values of pluralism, mutual understanding and peace.

Learning to be, so as better to develop one's personality and be able to
act with ever greater autonomy, judgement and personal responsibility.
In that connection, education must not disregard any aspect of a
person's potential: memory, reasoning, aesthetic sense, physical
capacities and communication skills.

Formal education systems tend to emphasize the acquisition of knowledge
to the detriment of other types of learning; but it is vital now to conceive
education in a more encompassing fashion. Such a vision should inform
and guide future educational reforms and policy, in relation both to contents
and to methods.

Source: Delors, Jacques (Chairman). *Learning the Treasure Within: Report to
UNESCO of the International Commission on Education for the Twenty-first Century.*
Paris: UNESCO Publishing, 1996. P.97.

With this in mind, we must challenge the agendas of government and corporate interests when their policies and practices threaten to erode the public education system. And we must encourage a reinvestment in public education and the processes that have been shown to be effective and efficient in achieving broad educational goals. Among these are the teaching of fine arts like music, drama, and art. "[These studies are] about more than the learning of fractions or developing discipline. [They are] about fulfilling our destiny as human beings—human makers—for whom the act of creation is a species-defining experience."[27]

NOTES

1   Whyte, Kenneth. (1996, June). "Why Johnny can't sing." *Saturday Night.* p.13-14.

2   "The arts in education." (Theme issue) *Phi Delta Kappan.* February 1994.

3   Krueger, Lesley. (1998, March). "The surprising benefits of music lessons." *Quill and Quire* p.75.

4   Bradmas, John. (ed.) (1991). *Growing Up Complete: The Imperative for Music Education.* Reston, Va.: National Commission for Music Education.

5   Winner,Langdon. (1980) "Do artifacts have politics?" *Daedalus: Journal of the American Academy of Arts and Sciences.* Winter.

6   White House. (1994, January 11). *Remarks by Vice-President Al Gore.* Remarks given to Royce Hall, UCLA, Los Angeles, California.

7   For more detail see Moll, Marita. (1996, June). *Supporting or Subverting the Public Interest: A Critical Look at the Agenda to Connect all Schools, Hospitals and Libraries to the Information Highway.* Paper presented to meeting of INET 96 (The Internet Society) in Montreal. Available : http://www.iif.hu/inet_96/e3/e3_3.htm.

8   Moll, Marita. (1997). "Canadian classrooms on the information highway: making the connections," in Moll, Marita (ed). (1997). *Tech High: Globalization and the Future of Canadian Education.* Ottawa: Canadian Centre for Policy Alternatives.

9   Canada, Governor General. (1999, October). *Speech from the Throne.* URL: http://www.pco-bcp.gc.ca/sft-ddt/doc/fulltext_e.htm

10   Wake, Bev.(2000). "Computers versus classrooms." *Ottawa Citizen.* Sept. 11 F3.

11   Informal remarks by an Industry Canada employee

12 Merrill Lynch (1999, April 14). *The Book of Knowledge; Investing in the Growing Education and Training Industry.* In depth report by Merrill Lynch & Co., Global Securities Research and Economics Group. p.3.

13 Wake, (2000).

14 Armstrong, Alison and Charles Casement. (1998). *The Child and the Machine.* Toronto: Key Porter.

15 Armstrong, Alison.(2000, Apr. 14). "Suffer the children." *Globe and Mail.*A16.

16 "Technology agreement 'step in the right direction'." *The Teacher.* Nova Scotia Teachers' Union. 36:9. June 1998. p.1.

17 Schofield, John (2000, May 17). "A season of strife: bitter disputes between teachers and governments threaten to turn schools into battle grounds." *Macleans.*

18 Canadian Home and School and Parent Teacher Federation. (1996). "Emergency resolution: music and fine arts." Annual General Meeting.

19 Asian Pacific Economic Community. Human Resources Development Working Group, (1997). "The Provisional Themes for the 2nd APEC Human Resources Development Ministerial Meeting (part I) Main Theme: The Strategy for Developing Human Resources under a New Environment and Challenges. Republic of Korea." [http://www.vcn.bc.ca/summit/edkor1.htm].

20 "Public education is not a commodity." News release. British Columbia Teachers'Federation. Nov. 30, 1999.

21 Petrella, Riccardo. (1999, October 25). "Education: challenges and prospects for the public sector. Four pitfalls to be avoided." General introductory presentation to the International Conference of the leaders of the trade union organisation "Education International." Tokyo.

22 Delors, Jacques (Chairman). (1996). *Learning the Treasure Within: Report to UNESCO of the International Commission on Education for the Twenty-first Century.* Paris: UNESCO.

23 ibid, p.85

24 ibid. p.86

25 Postman, Neil.(1995) *The End of Education; Redefining the Value of School.* New York: Alfred A. Knopf.

26 Saul, John Ralston. (1995) *The Doubter's Companion; A Dictionary of Aggressive Common Sense.* Toronto: Penguin Books. p. 115-116.

27 Gough, Pauline. (1994) "The art of being." *Phi Delta Kappan* February p.1.

APPENDIX A
PROVINCIAL GOVERNMENT FUNDING PLANS FOR NEW TECHNOLOGY IN SCHOOLS

• ALBERTA

Framework for Technology Integration in Education

Goals: help students acquire future employment skills
increase teachers' use of technology as a learning resource
share information
facilitate connectivity

Program to upgrade computers in classrooms School boards to match grant	$45 million Sept.'96-Dec.'98
Network Access grant	$5 million

Enhancing Alberta's Adult Learning System through Technology

Goals: integrate technology into adult learning system	$30 million Sept.'96-Dec.'98

• BRITISH COLUMBIA

School Technology Fund

Goals: to improve computers to student ratios by turn of the century one computer/3 students (secondary) one computer/6 students (elementary)	$100 million over 5 yrs. (announced in 1995)

• SASKATCHEWAN

Telecommunications Enhancement Fund

Goals: helps schools and colleges buy the wire and cable needed for connectivity.	$934,000

• MANITOBA

Renewing Education: New Directions

Goals: to set up community-based infrastructures for the design and delivery of educational programs.

To connect 70 Manitoba high schools in interactive television clusters and data interconnection linkages.	$8 million
• QUEBEC	
Vision and goals for technology in education are being formulated on the basis of two events: - "Conférence socio-économique sur l'utilisation des technologies de l'information et des communications en éducation" - Quebec Estates General on Education	
In June 1996, the Quebec Ministry of Education announced its action plan designed to increase the use of information and communications technology in elementary and secondary schools — the goal is one computer for every 10 pupils. It will spend $41.5 million/yr. for five years on capital expenditures and an additional $4.3 million in funding operations; the capital budget makes up 70% of a shared-cost program (between government and school boards), with school boards contributing $17.8 million annually; total expenditures will amount to $318 million over 5 years.	$318 million over 5 years (announced in 1996)
Private sector involvement includes Vidéotron ($3 million), Bell Canada (funding for content development), Québec Tél (won't charge long distance fees for schools in its territory).	
The Estates General recommended technological training and professional development of staff and the creation of suitable cultural products; to this end, $5 million over 5 years will go to training teachers and educational researchers in the new information and communication technologies as part of the university sector plan (announced in 1997); and approx. $2 million will go to help faculties of education upgrade their equipment.	$5 million over 5 years $2 million
• NEW BRUNSWICK	
One of the Dept. of Education's strategic goals is to exploit technology to enhance learning through: - the availability and applicability of technology in the schools; - the integration of technology into the curriculum; - the utilization of technology in the classroom by teachers.	$15.8 million over 3 years (announced in 1993)
UNITE-MER (Using Networks to Integrate Technology with Education-Mise en réseau) Project — a three year initiative that began in the 1992-93	

school year to install LANS in schools and link schools to the Internet; objectives are to support writing across the curriculum, support research, and support telecommunications.

Long-term partnerships with the private sector have been established — this includes Apple, IBM, Microsoft (on-line "virtual campus").

• NOVA SCOTIA

Under the Canada-Nova Scotia Cooperation Agreement on Economic Diversification program, the province has put approx. $3 million into computer systems, networks and software for nearly 50 junior high schools.	approx. $3 million

Computers in Schools — by Sept. 1996, Industry Canada's Computers in Schools program had put over 1,700 computers in the provinces classrooms; in addition to Industry Canada, Nova Scotia Dept. of Education and Culture, NovaKnowledge, Nova Scotia School Boards Association, and Telephone Pioneers, private sector partners include Maritime Tel & Tel and All Cities North American VanLines.

Goal: one computer for every 5 students by the year 2005.

• PRINCE EDWARD ISLAND

Technology in Education (TIE) project

PEI schools and educators are involved in a variety of initiatives to promote sound use of technology in education, including: - creation and testing of Internet curriculum; - a unique teacher professional development model for improving IT skills — 2 full-time facilitators provide training sessions tailored to teacher needs and skill levels in the teachers' setting; the Educational Technology Centre provides teacher training and support in addition to other services; - establishing a comprehensive web site for education (*Links for Educators and Students to Educational Resources*, or LESTER, set up by the PEI Department of Education); - Community Access sites in schools.	approx. $3 million

Local Area Networks have been installed in most junior high schools and half of the elementary schools (a total of 46 of 65 schools are networked); all schools have new computer workstations, multimedia computers, and department-mandated curriculum; Internet access for all schools will be achieved through partnerships with government and industry.

Technology Strategy Standing Committee — committee recently established
to develop a vision and mandate for information technology in PEI schools.

* NEWFOUNDLAND AND LABRADOR

STEM~Net — Internet connectivity is provided through STEM~Net; in 1995
became first province with full Internet access in all schools; STEM~Net is
working with Cable Atlantic to provide broad-band links to approx. 140
schools; Newfoundland is also a major participant in SchoolNet, including
the SchoolNet Rings projects, testing of the Direct-PC satellite downlink
technology identified in the SchoolNet-Stentor project, and digitization
projects.

Community Access Program — 9 pilot sites established with 17 more sites
approved for funding.

Teacher training — in addition to the establishment of a Professional
Development Centre, regional training centres are being set up to deliver
information technology training to teachers. A number of teacher in-service
training projects have taken place.

* ONTARIO

Ontario Royal Commission on Learning identified the use of information
technology as one of four "engines of learning".

Roundtable discussions — a series of roundtable discussions on technology
in education are taking place (beginning in Dec. 1996) to consult with
educators and the private sector to design the development of a comprehensive vision for the use of leading-edge technology in K-12 classrooms, a five
year plan to achieve the visions, and an investment plan to support it; in
conjunction with private sector, Minister of Education has indicated he hopes
to spend $500 million on classroom technology.

Grant Eligible Microcomputer Systems — school boards receive funding
through the General Legislative Grant tagged for the purpose of Grant
Eligible Microcomputer Systems (GEMS); Ontario also participates in
Computers for Schools program; up to 35% of the funds that boards receive
for the acquisition of computers can be spent on the professional development of teachers; up to 10% of the computers purchased can be allocated
to teachers for administrative and instructional use, the balance being used
for instructional purposes.

Ontario Education Highway — schools boards and schools are being linked to the Ontario Education Highway, the government's province-wide network announced in June 1994; Ministry of Education and Training contributed $5 million in start-up funding; as of Dec. 1995, approx. 70 of 168 boards were connected to this network.

Technology Incentive Partnership Program (TIPP) — through TIPP, the Ministry of Education and Training has allocated $40 million in seed funding to school boards for partnership projects to bring computer technology into classrooms; grants can cover up to half of project costs; this funding is matched by the school boards and their private sector partners who have put in approx. three dollars for every two dollars of government money for a total investment over two years of over $100 million; 36 new projects were announced in late March that focus on grades 1-3 and involve 94 school boards and over 200 private sector partners; these partners include IBM EduQuest, Computer Curriculum Corporation, Scholastic Canada Ltd. and Apple Canada.

$40 million

Education Network of Ontario — a telecommunications initiative used by educators throughout the province for professional development and administrative purposes; Ministry of Education in partnership with the Ontario Teachers' Federation.

• YUKON

YESnet (Yukon Educational Student Network) — designed to provide Internet access to Yukon schools in conjunction with YukonNET and NWTel (Northwestel) telephone company; Yukon Dept. of Education has established a coordinated procedure to assess and plan implementation of networking needs, prior to the building and remodelling of Yukon schools.

Important issues include equality of access and ongoing teacher training.

Education Technology Committee — established for the purposes of planning and public consultation.

• NORTHWEST TERRITORIES

People: Our Focus for the Future

NWT Depart. of Education, Culture and Employment set up North of 60 in 1992, a bulletin board system for education across the territory; now covers more than half of NWT schools; in 1995 the bulletin board was

augmented by an Internet-based educational resource system
(learnnet.nt.ca) now available in 7 communities.

In conjunction with Industry Canada's Community Access Program, the
department is in the process of establishing 14 community access sites
to be located either in a school or implemented in conjunction with a
municipal network linking a school to the community access site.

(sources: Council of Ministers of Education, Canada. "The Use and
Teaching of Information Technologies at the Elementary and Secondary
Levels. Summary of Questionnaire Responses", July 1996; CEA
Newsletter, "Technology Plans (An Update on Recent Initiatives", March
1997)

---

[1] Moll, Marita and Heather-jane Robertson (1997). "Backwash from the
technological wave; critical perspectives on the impact of information
technology on public education." Paper prepared for the annual meeting
of the Canadian Society for the Study of Education (CSSE), St. John's,
NFLD.

Technology Organizing and Unions

Marc Bélanger

U NIONS WERE CREATED IN RESPONSE TO AN INDUSTRIAL REVOLUTION WHICH IS NOW IN its death throes. Should we be preparing shrouds for our unions? Or will unions still exist in a hundred years?

This essay suggests that they *could* exist—not that they will —if we refresh our ways of thinking about technology and do what we do best as unionists: organize! It looks at the new computer communication technologies being implemented and some of the effects those technologies are inducing. Then it discusses a context in which unionists could operate to leverage their current talents and capabilities, while maintaining their core values to participate aggressively and effectively in the *design* of the new electronic world being born. Its premise is that unionists need to face the emerging technological world with a new set of thinking tools, a new vocabulary, and a new method of participating in technological change.

The technological maelstrom buffeting us as we head into the 21st century is just the edge of the storm front. There are hurricanes of technological change coming our way. Think of being in Gutenberg's shop just as people were learning how to print books—and what was to come after. Think of being in Edison's laboratory as electricity was being used to light bulbs or create sound recordings—and what was to come after. Now think electronically— and what will come.

What comes after the introduction of electronics—and its use in computer communications—is of course difficult to predict. But electronic communication technologies have general tendencies and direct effects which can be considered as we think about what is going to happen to our workplaces, homes and communities.

THE GENERAL TENDENCIES OF COMPUTER COMMUNICATIONS

The *general* tendencies include: decentralization, customization, deterioration of hard linkages, universal software translation, and the development of a biological paradigm.

Decentralization means (in the first instance) that computer communications will put pressure on organizations, including unions, to decentralize their operations. Organizational centres were built to contain filing cabinets and the staff to put paper into the filing cabinets. But now that information is not paperbound, it can be accessed from anywhere, or copies of it can be put anywhere. There is no need for a large number of people in one centre. With computer communications an organization could be a collection of many centres. Not only *could* it be a collection of many centres, but the use of computer communications will put pressure on the organization's leaders to *make* it a collection of many centres. That does not mean all organizations will decentralize—but those that do will be the ones to survive.

The forces of decentralization will affect individuals as well. The trajectory of computer communications is aimed at reaching any individual, anywhere in the world, at any time with text, graphics, sound, video, and even smell. The goal is to make the presence of the sender virtually real for the receiver, and vice versa. One result will be greater pressure to decentralize work to the home.

A second general tendency of computer communications is customization. Services and products will be customized for individuals and organizations. Levi's is customizing jeans for particularly-shaped buttocks. General Motors, Ford and Toyota are all starting to custom-create cars for individuals at regular car prices. Where these companies go others will follow, not only because they control galaxies of suppliers around them, but because they serve as models for other sorts of manufacturers. Clients, users, union members and others will begin to *expect* customized treatment.

Another general tendency of computer communications will be to make people think of linkages as fragile and temporary. The Industrial Revolution produced hardware such as trains and toilets—things made up of parts which connected in physically hard ways and were disconnected with difficulty. This encouraged people to think of linkages as hard and permanent. Employees, for example, were considered as linked to the machines, and over time became permanently attached to the work. Today, however, many of our dominant products are software creations with bits and bytes which can be easily and quickly disconnected. Employees can be seen, and are being seen, as easily disconnected from one project (or company) to be used in another project (or company). Think of linkages (parts to assembly lines; people to organizations) and consider them dissipating and you will be able to better predict what will happen around you.

An additional general tendency of computer communications is that *everything* is being translated into software: the chair you are sitting in, the paper you are reading, and even you. What used to be important about a chair was how a crafter chose the particular kind of wood, moulded the legs, and curved the seat. What is important now is how much of the chair's description has been put into a software program so it can be manipulated to optimize it for fast production or customization.

Even people are being translated into software. Not literally, of course, but there are software descriptions of people in databases which put together would produce a clear picture of the individual's health, purchase patterns, reading habits, financial situation, political leanings, and more. If a company searched all the databases that included information about you and put that information together, it would have a better picture of your behaviour than you do.

Thinking about fragile linkages and universal software translation may seem strange, and, to the practical mind of many unionists, fantastical. But remember: ways of thinking have revolutionized how we organize ourselves, our communities and our workplaces. Newton's greatest "Aha!" moment did not come when he saw the apple fall. It came when he looked at the inner workings of a clock and said: "That's how the universe works: like clockwork. There must be mechanical-like laws which determine how the universe operates." The scientific methods developed to find those laws led to the industrial production, which led to unions. Ways of thinking are important to consider as we develop software programs which mimic human thought.

We no longer see the universe as a mechanistic contraption with a master blueprint. Instead, the metaphor we use is biological. Earth is a "living entity", not a lump of rock. We don't have problems in software programs, we have "viruses". Stop thinking about computers as machines. Think of them as hard-skinned intelligences. If that seems too fanciful, remember this: *you* may not think of computers in this way, but the people who are designing the next generation of computers certainly do. They see computers as intelligences which mimic the human mind: intelligences to be nourished, introduced to each other, and helped to learn. They do not think of computers as machines. You will be continually surprised by the latest advance in computer communications if you do. Computers are clones of the human mind created by people working with a human, not mechanistic, paradigm. Think where the development of a young mind might go and you will be able to think more clearly about the advancement of computer technology.

Consideration of the general tendencies of computer communications— decentralization, customization, deterioration of hard linkages, universal software translation, and the development of a biological paradigm—can be used in two major ways: as a tool for thinking about how computer communications will evolve, and as a creativity generator for designing new technological applications. Try to see the tendencies at work in your organization or community.

THE DIRECT EFFECTS OF COMPUTER COMMUNICATIONS

The *direct* effects of computer communications are much more concrete and easily seen. They include:

• De-industrialization: The so-called "industrial" countries are rapidly de-industrializing. This is the result of two factors which can be attributed to computer communications. First of all, software translation of hardware goods is making it easy to produce things with fewer people and less commitment to infrastructure. Small plants with small numbers of staff can now produce as much as big plants with large numbers of staff. The result is smaller industrial sectors in the economically advanced countries.

Secondly, computer communications allows production to be co-ordinated globally, which allows companies to be headquartered in the rich countries and manage industrial production in the poorer countries. Not coincidently, these poorer countries have lower wages, less stringent safety laws, the worst forms of child labour, and weaker unions—if any. It may be that the developing countries will get what they have been asking for—industrial activity—just when it has become devalued. They may become the smoke factory towns of the Electronic Revolution—but this time not a few miles away from the rich homes of the bosses, but many thousands of miles away. Out of sight, out of mind?

• Globalization: Computer communications knows no boundaries. It is as easy to send an e-mail to a person countries away as it is to send one to the person next door. Companies can decentralize their activities and still depend on just-in-time production methods across thousands of miles. They can choose countries according to unionization rates, wage levels, safety laws, and compliant governments. If a country or workforce begins to demand better wages or safety laws, the companies can easily move production to another country.

It is no coincidence that the most successful strikes that have been held in the past few years, such as the United Parcel Service (UPS) strike in the United States in 1997 and the Australian dockworkers' strike of 1998, involved services which could not be moved. Docks have to be in one place; packages have to be physically delivered within a country.

• Virtual Companies: The most powerful companies in the world no longer have to be the biggest in terms of production facilities or workforces. Take Cisco Systems, for example. It is known as one of the world's largest manufacturers of computer network hardware, but it manufactures very little of the equipment sold under its name. It farms out most of the work to 37 factories, all linked by computer communications. Its suppliers make all the components, perform 90% of the sub-assembly work and fully 55% of the final assembly. Its suppliers regularly ship finished Cisco equipment to Cisco customers without a Cisco employee ever touching the equipment. What's more, about 80% of its sales are generated from its Web site. Cisco is a virtually non-existent company (except, of course, for the money it is earning, the power it holds over its suppliers and, most importantly, the control it has on the production methods and schedules.) Cisco has kept all the planning and co-ordinating work while farming out all the problems (such as pesky unions) to its suppliers.

• Contracting-Out: The secret to Cisco's success (which is not so secret) is that it has contracted out most of its work. It is able to do this and still maintain control over its product because it can issue orders via computer communications. More companies are looking at developing along the same lines. A study quoted by *Business Week* pointed out that in 1998 U.S. companies farmed out 15% of all manufacturing, and predicted that in 2000 they would contract out more than 40%.[1] Not only are American workers losing their jobs to contracting- out, but because of virtual companies such as Cisco, they are no longer sure who they are really working for. Additionally, the rise in contracted work is producing a pool of transitory workers who move from company to company in search of higher wages or better working conditions. The result is high turnover rates and depressed wages in the companies doing the manufacturing.

Another factor which has contributed to the increase in temporary and casual workers is the fact that employers now have computers to handle the complicated payroll systems involved in paying many outside people. Twenty or 30 years ago it would have been very difficult to track the hours of large numbers of temporary people. But now, with computers it is easier, and so employers take advantage of the capability to avoid paying the benefits due to full-time staff.

•   Different Union Structures: Unions developed during the Industrial Revolution as a response to employer actions. In many ways, they are reflections of existing management infrastructures. Today's auto unions, for example, are big partly as a reflection of big automakers. And certainly unions learned their administrative structures from the business community. So, for example, dues collection stopped being a process of meeting the members and asking for the monthly dues; it became a matter of the local union secretary-treasurers sending cheques to union accountants. Or, increasingly, computer communication is being used to send dues directly from the employer to the central union without any local union intervention.

The serious question then becomes: if employers are going to change the way they do business and morph into other sorts of structures (such as virtual companies), what will unions do? Will they reflect the employer's administrative structures? Or will they create their own? What will the unions of the 21st century (if they exist) look like? The answer may be found in a closer look at the new workplace being created as computer communication evolves.

THE IMAGINARY WORKPLACE

The electronic workplaces of the 21st century (for those who are able to participate in them) will be imaginary ones. The "Imaginary Workplace" will be one in which the human imagination (and therefore creativity) is the most important factor. For the first time in the history of humankind, men and women will work with unlimited resources—computer space and the human mind. No longer will humans be limited by the amount of coal in the ground or fish in the sea. The result could be full employment for all humans, everywhere.

That is the goal. Computer communications can help us reach it because we will no longer be limited by the natural world. But full employment policies are not necessarily supported by corporate interests. Full employment can cause sectoral labour shortages, which in turn can increase wage demands and requests for other benefits. The corporate community may feel more comfortable with a pool of unemployed or underemployed which, by its very existence, depresses wages and gives power to the managers (by allowing them to threaten employees with dismissal because others could quickly fill the jobs). If there has ever been a development in the history of humankind which could produce good jobs for all, it is the advent of computer communications. Actually producing this full employment, however, will be a question of politics and societal power relations.

Also, it has to be recognized that not all workplaces in the electronic countries will be treated as Imaginary Workplaces where workers' creativity is paramount. The people working in the warehouses of Amazon.com (the online bookseller) are not treated as people with brains; they're treated like old-time industrial workers who have to do what they are told, when they are told. The people staffing the help desks of many new computer service companies are underpaid and overworked. These workforces are perfect locales for traditional union organizing.

Still, the overwhelming trend in the electronic countries is towards the development of workplaces based on information- handling or knowledge-creation, in other words: Imaginary Workplaces. Education will play a key role in supporting the development of these workplaces.

EDUCATION IN THE IMAGINARY WORKPLACE

The Imaginary Workplace will be characterized by two major factors: speed of change and life-long learning. Assembly lines have to shut down for re-tooling every time a new product is introduced. But workplaces which are based on replicating human thought via software (which is what the Imaginary Workplace will do) can change almost at the speed of thought itself. It may take time to think up new ideas and write software to implement those ideas, but certainly not as long as re-tooling an assembly line. This means workers in the Imaginary Workplace will be expected to react constantly to re-create their jobs—every day.

The only way this can happen is if workers have access to information-on-demand, training, education and democracy in the workplace. They need access to information in order to build the software products that will provide their services or products. They need just-in-time training in order to learn a skill-set at the time it is needed. They need access to life-long education in order to keep their knowledge creatively fresh. And they need more demo-cratically operated workplaces because creativity cannot be ordered to exist. It needs to be nurtured in an environment in which people have collective con-trol over their work circumstances and feel free to express themselves. More democracy in the workplace is the key to a successful enterprise in the new electronic society. (But of course whether employers recognize this is another question.)

Life-long training and education is a prerequisite for the new workplace. Gone is the day that workers could be educated in a few years, trained in a few months, and then be expected to be employable the rest of their lives. Workers will become l'earners—people who earn a living by learning.

Computer communications, which will force the need for life-long edu-cation, will at the same time provide the tools to meet the need. Computer-based distance education could provide workers with the means to keep their skill sets relevant and ways of continuing their life-long education. But who will provide this training and education? There is no doubt that much of the educational activity will come from the private, commercial sector; that is not the problem. The problem is *how much* of this educational activity will be com-mercially-based. Primary and secondary education—for now —seems safely in the hands of the public sector (despite growing pressure to commercialize the schools). But much of post-secondary education could be privatized if public educational institutes do not move quickly to take advantage of computer com-munications for education.

A bricks-and-mortar attitude on the part of university or community college educators will result in the closing of many —half?—of the public edu-cation organizations. Workers will vote with their keyboards to stay on the job or in the home and learn at institutes which provide online courses. Those public institutes which pay attention to this phenomena will continue to exist. Those who ignore it will be shutting themselves down.

Predicting the Changes

Understanding the changes which are about to hit our workplaces involves not only understanding the general tendencies of computer communications and studying the direct effects, but also predicting what technologies will come into play in the near future. This predicting is by necessity hazy and imprecise, but it does not have to involve chicken entrails (or worse, futurists). You can learn to see what is coming in technology, at least in the short term (say, five years) by following a few rules:

- Pay attention to technologies being introduced in your sector by reading trade magazines or web sites. It always takes time for organizations to make decisions and re-write the budgets. You can think about what *currently available* technologies are likely to be introduced into your particular workplace. That is not futurism; that is paying attention to the present.
- Look at the entertainment industry, especially toy production. Most new technologies make their way into the market for entertainment or play. That is because new technologies are creative endeavours and the entertainment-toy world is geared for play. The telescope was first introduced as a toy. So was the personal computer. What are the new toys coming into the market?
- Look to corporate practice. Corporations will adopt technologies that will help them do their work. Notice this does not mean that technologies will help them make a profit. There is no evidence at all that the introduction of the microcomputer helped the bottom line. Instead, it seems to have helped companies do the old things faster, leaving room for new things to be done, or created whole new corporations such as Microsoft.
- Pay attention to democratic communities using new technologies. The Internet took off not because it enabled scientists to electronically enter far-away computers. It took off because those scientists (and later their students) used it to send personal messages. Soon millions were using it for e-mail. As another example, consider Linux, a new operating system

which could rival Windows and still be free of charge. It is being developed by programmers all over the world who are volunteering their work because they see a global community creating a new and useful product and they want to be contributing members of that community.

CREATING TECHNOLOGICAL EFFECTS

There are other thinking tools which can be used to predict what technologies will hit your workplace or the workplaces of others in the next few years. But what is important to understand here is *why* we must develop more of these tools and change our ways of confronting the future.

Why? Because of the enormous speed at which the changes are coming—and will continue to come. We will have increasingly less time to think through the consequences of our adoption of new technologies and the changes they will promote. If we do not consider how we can predict technological change, how we can react to its effects, and how to create the technological effects we want, we could end up falling into societal design driven mainly by corporate interests. That is what is happening to the design of the new global economy, which is in turn putting pressure on local societies and economies to adopt its practices.

Unlike a static society mired in traditional ways, a rapidly changing society is more easily deflected towards a new mixture of institutions and goals. Today, as in another fast- changing time—the Industrial Revolution—corporate interests are taking advantage of social flux to promote the institutions and goals they want (plus get rid of the institutions they don't want). And they are using the same arguments: less government intervention lest the wondrous technological advance be stymied; no worker organizations which could impede workplace flexibility; raw competition between workers—this time on a global basis—for lower and lower wages in the name of progress; and so on and so on. It all has such a familiar ring to it. But just because it is all so wearily familiar does not allow complacency. If we do not act now to *affect* the technological changes coming at us, we will be handing the creation of our new electronic societies to corporate leaders who may have different ideas about what constitutes a just and equitable society than do most people.

The first—and most crucial—step to understanding the technological changes coming at us, and be able to plan for them, is to build a greater appreciation of the magnitude of the changes headed our way. The simple truth is that most of the wondrous new technologies you see being applied, or hear about, are just hazy prototypes of what will appear tomorrow. The Internet may seem an awesome technological wonder. But it will soon disappear.

The Internet will disappear in two ways: First, it will be built into the material world. If you think the jerk at the next table talking into his cellphone is irritating, just wait until your fridge says: "There's a call waiting for you, and by the way, you need more butter." We are going to build the Internet into all sorts of commonplace products and consequently it will become commonplace—something to be paid less attention to as we marvel at the next technological wonder. Secondly, the Internet will cease to be a focus of societal attention in the same way radio and TV did. Both radio and TV seemed to be the ultimate in communication when they were first introduced. And both had very powerful effects on our social and political activities. But both were eventually obsolesced: radio by TV; TV by the Internet. If you think the Internet is the ultimate communication tool, then all your navigating through the next few years of technological change will head you off in wrong directions.

We are *not* building the Internet. We are building a "New Electronic Society." Computer communications (of which the Internet is merely a part) will change our industrial societies radically—so much so that to call them *industrial* societies condemns us to erroneous thinking about how they will develop. The rich parts of the world are creating *electronic* societies which will be as different from industrial societies as industrial society was to feudalism. Meanwhile, the so-called "developing" countries will be tossed the industrial dregs, and many of them will find themselves even further behind the richer countries (despite one or two golden exceptions).

The secret to understanding what the Internet is (in social, economic and political terms) is understanding that it is an *enabling, multipurpose technology*. It will promote the creation of many radically new technologies in much the same way the book did after its introduction in the 15th century, and electricity did after it was introduced in the 19th century. There are interesting times ahead.

Book production induced many radical changes. Because books became available, higher literacy levels developed. Because people could see their language in print, grammar and spelling became important. Because the Bible was translated into the vernacular and distributed widely, the Reformation was sparked. Because printed language helped define national groupings, nation states were created. Because nation states with middle classes were developed, local capital markets expanded. Because the mechanics of print (with its repeatable parts used over again to create new products) provided an industrial model, and there were capital markets, and there were books teaching people how to produce things, the Industrial Revolution was born. And out of the Industrial Revolution came unions.

The advent of electricity also provoked many societal-changing technologies, not least of which were: the telegraph, the light bulb, the phonograph, the telephone, movies, radio and television—all of which prompted many far-reaching changes.

The Internet will enable the introduction and development of many new technologies that will be just as revolutionary as the ones mentioned above. Each will have profound effects on how we organize our economies, social lives and workplaces. Talking about THE Internet in 2000 is like talking about THE Electricity in 1900. What is important to pay attention to is not the Internet, but what technologies the Internet will, and could, spawn—and develop those technologies which enhance the human condition.

(There are other very noble ideas about not being involved in *any* new technology because they are *all* tainted with the original sin of corporate capitalism and cannot be used for democratic, human-enhancing activities. This stance condemns its adherents to be continually reacting to the technological applications being promoted by the very corporate interests they decry. It closes the mental doors to understanding what radical new technologies and applications of new technologies could be developed.)

DESIGNING TECHNOLOGY

How can we be involved in the design of the new technologies headed our way? We should use our talents as people organizers to build a popular technology-organizing movement as powerful as today's environmental movement. This movement (which would include organized labour, non-governmental organizations, political parties, and other organizations) would promote new people-oriented technological designs; suggest legislative initiatives; lobby for publicly-controlled technological inquiries and regulatory bodies; encourage people in technological communities (such as workplaces) to find their group technological power; condemn technological applications which degrade the human condition; and, eventually, point to a radically different civilization based on the use of technologies which promote economic and technological activity linked directly to social well-being.

Those who would quickly scoff at this idea and dismiss it as fantasy forget that the environmental movement faced the same sort of derision when it started. But now, after only 40 years and after the development of organizations such as Greenpeace, and the rise of political parties like the Greens, environmental ideas are at the very heart of our political and economic debates. The same could happen with a technology-organizing movement and its ideas.

At the core of a technology-organizing movement must be a people-inclusive definition of technology. The engineer's definition (the one most prevalent today) is:

A technology is a tool (hardware, software or mental) which is used to solve problems.

The great difficulty with this definition is that it excludes people. It is as if technologies were not to be used by or for people. By omitting men and women, the definition excludes public debate, corporate interests, governmental action, cultural imperatives, psychological orientations, fun, love, sex, and more. It portrays technologies as entities developed as part of an unfolding of what capital 'T' Technology must be. We do not design technologies, according to this definition, as much as participate in a process of discovering the neutral laws of Technology. But this is a false extension of the scientific process to technological development. Pure science needs to be built on strict observation of life and materials in order to inoculate itself from human-produced error. A DNA molecule is a DNA molecule. But as soon as a science (such as DNA analysis) leaves the lab and becomes a technology, it enters the messiness of human activity. It becomes moulded by the prevailing power patterns, cultural activities, economic institutions, and other human-built entities and processes. Or it dies an early death (even as an idea) by not being supported once it is outside the lab.

Here is a more people-inclusive definition of technology:

A technology is a tool (hardware, software or mental) which is used *by groups of people* to solve problems.

This definition has the advantage of being closer to the truth, as well as providing an entry point for thinking about how people involved in technologies can be organized. Technologies become technologies once they come into use by people. And they are used by *groups* of people because that is how we organize ourselves (technologies are rarely designed for one person).

This way of thinking about technology opens the possibilities of seeing technological design and application almost like community organizing. Community organizers bring together people who share a common sense of community (geographical, institutional, interest, age, etc.) and facilitate the community's understanding of its power to get things done. A neighbourhood group, for example, might lobby City Hall for speed bumps on roads (a technological rather than political solution). A group of workers might organize through their union for the creation of a new workplace technology or influence the use of a technology being introduced into the workplace. In both instances, the groups come to a sense of their power by combined action. And they both face powerful, often overpowering, opponents: City Hall or the employer. But the power of their opponents does not stop them from organizing and winning what victories they can. In the end, they hope to create a society which is more responsive to the needs of its citizens, especially in whatever community they are organizing.

This sense of continuing to struggle in the face of overpowering odds is especially pertinent in thinking through a theory of technology organizing. Technology is too often seen as an all-powerful force that produces entities which appear as they do because that is the natural course of the unfolding of technology. But, in reality, technologies are the result of numerous decisions made by people working in groups (such as corporations or other institutions). They look and act the way they do because groups of people have made choices all along the path of their development.

The intriguing possibility is that, subject to other choices being made, it is possible that radically different technological forms could be developed—maybe even forms that could promote a global civilization better aimed at developing the social well-being of its people.

A small example: for years the radio was assumed to have a particular design: transistors, speakers, antennas, batteries, etc. It was what we knew to be a "radio." But a few years ago, an inventor in England made an important change to the basic design of the radio which is now helping many people in developing countries where batteries are expensive or difficult to find. He designed a radio which can be cranked up to provide an hour's worth of play time. No batteries are needed. This idea seems logical now, but for years the inventor could not interest anybody enough to get financial backing. A radio was a radio; it needed batteries, which in the rich parts of the world are cheap and easily obtainable. It was only after an entrepreneur in South Africa was intrigued by the idea that production started. And now there are villages in the developing world with a "crank-radio" that is designed for their circumstances. (Should we be thinking of crank PCs?)

As another example, the first national bilingual computer conferencing system in Canada—SoliNet—was not developed by one of the big telephone or computer companies. It was developed by a union, the Canadian Union of Public Employees (CUPE), using technology developed at the University of Guelph. CUPE was also the first organization in Canada to build a Local Area Network (a LAN) of computers, ahead of even the computer companies. SoliNet and CUPE's early use of a LAN proved that unions *can* be involved in the design of new technologies, and at the cutting edge.

These are small examples in the big scheme of technological things. But what if more attention were paid to encouraging people to be involved in the design and application of new technologies? What if more people were trained in computer system design principles or participatory software creation? What if people had access to public funds to create new technologies? What if they could sit on public boards which monitored the introduction of new technologies? What if workers were allowed to democratically participate in the creation of new, worker-oriented technologies? Might we develop different sorts of technologies which, by their very existence, could point to the great possibilities inherent in letting thousands, maybe millions, of people participate in technology design?

Andrew Feenberg, a professor at San Diego State University and one of the first online teachers, has written extensively on this subject in books such as *The Critical Theory of Technology*.[2] He argues that technologies have many "potentialities" which can lead in many different directions, according to the people making the choices. These potentialities, correctly acted upon, could lead to a radically different civilization from the one in which we currently exist: a civilization based on broader democratic participation. Labour unions, he argues, could be a part of the movement which encourages these various potentialities to be explored.

The central lesson is that within the technological world there is an array of possibilities. The existing technological world is not the result of technological imperatives which determine how a particular technology evolves or what new technologies appear. It is the result of many choices made by people working with tools to address problems and fulfill aspirations. Other choices could produce radically different technologies.

Of course, the problem is that most of the people with resources to produce new technologies are working for large corporations which have their own agendas for the world. The result is a technological world (produced by a corporate mindset) which looks "natural" and "inevitable"—something we object to only at the risk of being "unreasonable," "inefficient," or worse, "Luddite." That does not mean, however, that those outside of the corporate world should reject the practice of technology design. Rather, we should work hard to show how democratic, people-oriented technologies can be built, even with meagre resources, in order to point towards the possibility of a radically different technological civilization.

In order to do this, we need to organize communities to understand and use their group power to design and influence technology, much in the same way urban groups, organized by community organizers, influence city governments. We could train activists in the principles of democratic technology design and people-organizing skills. These activists could work in organizations, workplaces, unions and communities— anywhere people are using technologies. Generically, we could call these people "technology organizers," but they could have different titles within different communities, such as "technology stewards."

Technology organizers would not be limited to working only in the advanced electronic societies. In fact, it is possible that the most fertile work could be produced in the developing countries where technologies have to be designed to meet local circumstances. Technology organizers could work with people in developing countries to create system designs (technical descriptions) of electronic technologies which take into account factors such as undependable telephone connections, expensive Internet connections, or costly electricity. We should not assume that the way a technology appears in an advanced electronic society is its ultimate form. Like the crank radio, a technology could be designed to operate *as effectively*, while adopting a different form to meet the different circumstances of the developing world. Funding for producing the technologies could be sought after the system designs were produced. Clearly thought-out and written ideas are the necessary prerequisites for finding money.

The immediate goal of a technology-organizing movement facilitated by technology organizers would be to show that groups can influence the creation and design of technologies. The intermediate goal would be to build an international technology-organizing movement as powerful as today's environmental movement to influence governments, corporations, and other institutions in their use and creation of technology. The long-term goal would be to point towards a new global technologically-based civilization which ties economic activity to social well-being, and practices democracy in all its important activities.

TRAINING TECHNOLOGY ORGANIZERS

The key to the successful development of a technology- organizing movement would be the training of the technology organizers: the people who work within the technological communities. They would need training in the basic organizing principles of a technology organizing movement and in the goals such a movement would promote.

A basic course for a technology organizer would include:

1. An introduction to technological change, which would   include discussion of a people-inclusive definition of technology and the concept of various potentialities within technologies.
2. An overview of technologies affecting the community in which the organizer is working, with special attention paid to the technology that is most affecting the community.
3. Discussions on the basics of technological forecasting, which would include how to predict what technologies will be introduced into particular communities.
4. A module on the principles of participatory design, which is a method (originally developed in the Scandinavian countries) to effectively involve users in the development of computer programs. Participatory design principles can be learned by anybody; they do not involve extensive knowledge of computer programming.

5. An introduction to the basic strategies and tactics of organizing people within technological communities, such as:
    - Pick an initial project which is almost sure of victory to build confidence within the group;
    - Let potential solutions come out of facilitated group discussions and not the organizer;
    - Find the natural leaders within a group and train them as technology organizers;

6. A basic technology organizer course would also include a section on how to organize a computer project, including sections on:
    - Needs analysis (to determine the needs of the participants).
    - System design (a process leading to a document which describes the technical design of the software to be produced).
    - Prototyping (to provide a prototype for the participants to react to, and change, before the whole program is written).
    - Programming (the basic concepts only; technology organizers do not have to know how to program).
    - Training (how to design a training program).
    - Scheduling (how to establish a schedule for a computer project).
    - Parallel runs (operating the new and old system for a period of time in order to find errors in the new program and have time to fix them).
    - Evaluation (not only of the program produced, but of the whole process of the technology organizing involved in the project).

This last point is crucial. It is not enough to have successfully involved a community in the design of a new technology, because we know that more new technologies will appear. What we also have to do, while involved in a technology organizing project, is to pay attention to what *general lessons* could be learned about how to organize technology. Then we can apply those lessons to our technology organizing when the next new technology comes along.

In terms of technology organizing, it matters little that you learned how to work with a particular technology (like computers or the Web). What really matters are the lessons you learned in organizing the people who were involved with it. By building our stock of lessons, we can continually improve the basic principles of technology organizing and strengthen the movement's ability to confront the next wave of technological change.

Technology organizers will also need to be trained in articulating the rights the movement would fight for. A listing of rights might vary from community to community. A list of rights for a workplace community might include:

- being involved in the design of technologies in the workplace;
- privacy - no e-mail or telephone monitoring; and
- health and safety protection, especially for stress-related problems.

(For a more complete list, see the Cyberspace Bill of Rights.)

ELECTRONIC UNIONS

Each technological community will use the principles of technology organizing in their own way. They will develop novel ways of reacting to technological change. And (hopefully) they will develop new technologies. By adopting the same major goal (to uncover democratic potentialities in technologies) and sharing organizing lessons, they can learn from each other and together build a powerful, global movement.

As for the specific case of employee unions: they will need to radically reorganize themselves because their employers are in the process of radically reorganizing themselves. If they do not, they run the risk of being 19ᵗʰ century organizations facing 21st century employers. That is a risk which could very well result in the extinction of unions.

To help ensure the re-creation of industrial unions into electronic unions, we need to begin wide-ranging discussions with creative ideas. Members have to be involved in a campaign of re-thinking their institutions. Some ideas which might be introduced into these discussions include:

- Temporary local unions created for temporary projects. If employers are going to create temporary entities for their projects (possible via contracting-out and other ways), unions may have to make it easy for groups of workers to come together during the life of the project to form their own local union or branch. This may mean addressing the legislation which creates and protects unions. Maybe we should be looking at the example

CYBERSPACE BILL OF RIGHTS

As workers learn about what they need to safely and effectively navigate cyberspace they will begin to present new demands to their managers. They will ask for new rights. A Cyberspace Workers' Bill of Rights could include:

- A guarantee of the privacy of electronic mail.

- No monitoring of communications between either employees or between employees and clients.

- The ability for cyberspace workers employed by the same organization to communications amongst themselves.

- Access to outside systems such as a union computer communication system.

- No use of computer conferencing comments for job appraisals (with objective standards to be used instead).

- A policy for job advancement published on-line.

- A published and accessible policy statement outlining the organization's rules for using the computer communication system.

- Ergonomically and technically suitable equipment maintained by the employer.

- Protection for the health and safety of home-based employees.

- Compensation for home space used for work.

- Overtime for cyberspace workers to discourage the extension of the workday.

- Provision for paid sick-time.

- A guarantee of training for new software.

- Adequate technical support for software, equipment and work practices.

- Periodic face-to-face meetings of employees if at all feasible.

Originally published in *Canadian Dimension*. Dec.94-Jan.95

of actors' unions which protect members working on temporary projects (plays).

- Organize information and knowledge workers. Information workers are people such as insurance clerks who work with data that have been shaped into information. Knowledge workers are people who create new knowledge, such as university professors, scientists, computer system designers and others. Both fields of employment will expand in electronic societies. Unions have to begin organizing these people by understanding who they are, hiring some of them as organizers, and, most importantly, using the same tools they do (such as computer communications).

- Develop customized information. The key to working with people (either as clients, customers or members) in an electronic society will be to address them in customized ways. Abundant computing power allows for the tracking of minute pieces of information, such as: how many times a member sent an e-mail to the union; what are the members' interests; what family grouping do they live with; and so on. By tracking disparate bits of information on members, a profile could be built so that union organizers (or intelligent computer systems) could react to members as individuals (or individuals within particular groups). If companies are going to do this to build and maintain their customer bases, why shouldn't unions? Unions should give away customized information (such as: retirement plans, or wage analyses linked to financial plans) as an enticement for the worker to join the union in order to get more customized information.

- Organize workers' help desks. Information and knowledge workers are used to dealing electronically with computer companies for software help. They should also be able to communicate with union help desks. These union help desks could provide information on labour legislation, retirement plans, layoff provisions, etc., without charging. In order to get to a higher level of customized help, people would have to join the union.

- Lobby for truly universal pension and maternity/paternity plans. Computers allow employers to manage the payrolls of large numbers of temporary workers (in fact, this is one of the reasons for the rise in the number of casual employees). There is no reason why these very systems could not also track hourly employment periods in order to calculate pension, maternity, and other benefits. If a worker is employed by a company a total of 52 hours in a year, that employee should be able to have 52 hours counted towards a pension plan or other benefit plan. Then it would be a matter of legislation to make the plans portable between employers.

- Union education departments are usually understaffed and under-resourced. However, with the introduction of computer communications, unions could share their educational staff, or other experts among themselves. A health and safety officer based in one city could teach members of many unions who may be scattered throughout the country or international region. These activities could be co-ordinated by national and international labour bodies.

- Create databases of employers. Unions could use computers to build databases of information on employers to share with other unions (perhaps internationally), but also to track the linkage between companies (such as primary companies and suppliers). This information could help build the union's strength in bargaining, public campaigns (such as boycotts), and, if necessary, strikes.

- A union activist database could be created. This database could hold profiles of labour activists according to their interests and capabilities. For example, if a union were looking for a person with experience handling a particular health and safety problem (such as asbestosis), the database could be searched and the person contacted via e-mail.

- Hypertext contracts could be posted online. Every contract clause could have a hypertext link to an explanation of why the clause exists, why it might need improving, and what its history is. As well, clauses which do not currently exist (but the union would like to add) could be annexed with explanations. In this way, members could gain a better understanding of their contracts and be informed about possible improvements. A better-informed membership always strengthens the union's bargaining committee.

GRAND PROJECTS FOR THE LABOUR MOVEMENT

The labour movement needs some grand projects to give it focus and enthusiasm as it develops electronically. These projects might include:

- An International Labour College. The creation of an International Labour College, which uses computer conferencing to conduct online classes, would be a very important step in developing the labour movement's reactions to globalization. The college would not only train unionists in the characteristics of the global economy being created (and we desperately need more unionists informed on this topic), but also build linkages between individuals and organizations internationally.

- A Crystal Labour Encyclopaedia. If you drop a crystal into a supersaturated solution, it becomes a much larger, even more beautiful crystal. If we created a labour encyclopaedia with little articles (like little crystals) to which people around the world could attach information or comments, we could create an international encyclopaedia of enormous scope and diversity. The Crystal Labour Encyclopaedia could become a very important tool in the development of a global labour movement consciousness.

These are just a few ideas thrown into the wind for discussion. They, and others suggested by more unionists, could spark even better ideas. And it is ideas by the millions we need in order to make sure our unions make the transition to the new electronic societies that are emerging. Maybe, by adopting a program of training technology organizers and participating in an international technology-organizing movement, we can ensure the continued existence of our unions, extend our efforts to protect working people, and participate in a global movement which promotes the appropriate use of technology to celebrate the human spirit in all its manifestations.

NOTES

1   *Business Week.* (Oct. 4, 1999)

2   Feenberg, Andrew. (1991). *The Critical Theory of Technology.* Oxford University Press.

The Community Is
The Network

" W HERE DO YOU WANT TO GO TODAY?" MICROSOFT ADS PURR. "COME together...right now!" Nortel ads scream (after securing the rights from Sony to the Beatles repertoire). And IBM proclaims that they are building "solutions for a small planet."

Aside from the advertising hype surrounding the potentialities of networked communications, one of the more celebrated promises has been that of McLuhan's global village, and that of the "virtual community." But whose community are we talking about? Is it the corporate community, the local community, or the global community? In this section, several arguments are made for preserving the sense of local community using Internet tools, for purposes of social justice.

Ursula Franklin, in a speech given at the Communities Online Conference held in Ottawa in 1995, reminds us that just because a technology is available doesn't mean we must immediately run out and adopt it. We need to look carefully and critically at how we use and deploy technologies, making sure that they benefit individuals and communities alike.

Marita Moll and Leslie Shade look at the community networking movement in Canada, which has been celebrated internationally as a model for citizen-activated communication. The sustainability of community networks amid a plethora of commercial portals is a huge concern, but, as this article shows, community networks are developing innovative and unusual ways to reach and enhance the lives of communities.

Two case studies look at using networked communications for distinctly local, and often marginalized, needs. Povnet, an online commons for anti-poverty activists, is described by co-ordinator Penny Goldsmith. Garth Graham looks at the conceptualization of the Vietnam-Canada Information Technology Project, whose goals are to use information technology for development. Both cases illustrate how important it is to consult and consider the users of the technology in both design and in policy formulation.

Every Tool Shapes the Task: Communities and the Information Highway

Ursula M. Franklin[1]

INTRODUCTION

COMPUTERS AND THE APPLICATION OF COMPUTER TECHNOLOGY IS OF COURSE SOMEthing that we all have seen coming, that we have lived with. It is a very important subject—very serious, very broad. So I would like to narrow down my perspective in some way. When I speak of community groups, therefore, I will only speak about those voluntary organizations who come together to affect the lives of their community or country: people who deal with issues of environment, with issues of justice. I know them well because I have found much of my own community within these groups.

These community groups essentially are the extra-parliamentary opposition that we have had in this country for a good number of years. As communities, we took over this role when we saw the traditional parliamentary opposition more and more faded into obscurity, when we found that the moment somebody who was in opposition became government, there seemed to be a profound change in their outlook towards life.

In addition, many of the real issues seemed to get nothing but very bland responses, if any, from traditional parliamentary opposition. Of course they support human rights, of course they love nature, and so much for that. As a result, it is the extra- parliamentary opposition that provides the building blocks of democracy.

Who and What is the New Technology For?

It is these community groups that, again and again, try to cope with democracy in a technological society. Any time new technologies emerge, whether it is in the workplace, whether it relates to issues of war and peace or justice, or whether to that field that we discussing—information and structuring of discourse—it is the community that has raised the questions: what can these new technologies do in our work of furthering democracy and the process, and what do these technologies prevent us from doing?

Community groups have done that in approaches to city planning, to environmental issues, and we very much have to look at it again. What does that new technology do, what does it prevent us from doing, and what don't we do any more because that new technology is in place?

With these questions in mind, I am going to address that technology, specifically electronic networks, not so much in terms of how it has come about, but what it really signifies for me personally.

Vertical Communication

What is actually going on? I find that question very difficult. It is like a film on top of a film, on top of a film. One doesn't always really see very clearly what is going on. As community groups, we want to talk about constituency. Think of those constituencies as building blocks of democracy. Genuine democracy cannot and does not work if there are disenfranchised constituencies.

If you will, for a moment, allow me to give you a very simplistic picture. Imagine the world like a cake. Imagine that you slice it into the customary slices by vertical cuts. Each slice of that cake should signify, for us, a constituency. Each is geographically located as one segment of the larger cake. Each slice is more influenced by its immediate neighbours than by what might be in the cake quite far away.

In many ways, our communities have organized themselves by history, by necessity, around those vertical slices of cake. These are our parliamentary constituencies. That is where the member from Kicking Horse Pass resides. One knows that is where our cities, our school boards and our larger communities are.

Historically, much of the communication in those vertical slices has been vertical communication—up and down between the bottom and the top, between those who were residing in the icing and those who were the small crumbs on the bottom. We refer to the "trickle down" effects; this comes from a vertical slice model. When we deal with our members of Parliament, with our school boards, when we think of constituencies, however sophisticated we get, we work through that historical picture of a vertical cut.

THE EXPANSION OF HORIZONTAL COMMUNICATION

Of course, technology is a means to mediate the relationship between space and time. What technology has done in the world increasingly is to put horizontal cuts into that cake. You don't only talk up and down. Now you can talk across barriers, horizontally. Now we see—and this is new—to what extent the world has become horizontally sliced and how horizontal communication begins to take preference over vertical communication.

Horizontal communication, not only of thoughts but of actual real movement, takes many different forms. In the past, while slow, the horizontal movement of people was reasonably prominent. Now, if any one of you works with refugees or immigrants, you will know that the horizontal movement of people is very difficult in spite of that great horizontal slicing that has given us air traffic.

On the other hand, the horizontal movement of money is incredibly easy. The stock markets between Tokyo and New York or Toronto play on the time difference. It takes less time for money to move from New York to Tokyo than it takes the clock to move the opening time. You can speculate on currency from your desk or from your computer, always with that ease of moving money horizontally. It used to be awfully difficult to even take money from Canada to the U.K. Horizontal slicing now allows a great deal of movement, and it is very differentially specified as to who moves what.

Trade and travel is eased through horizontal slicing. You may wear a shirt or a pair of shoes that were made in China. On the other hand, you will also find that the wrapping of that pair of shoes that was made in China becomes your local garbage. Your taxes will have to pay to get rid of it.

So there is that peculiar intermixing between worlds that are both vertically and horizontally sliced. You will see, as you reflect upon it, that the legislation, the restriction, the regulation that governs the vertical movements or things that have horizontal movement consequences is very loose, even though in many ways these are the issues we face. If a nuclear reactor malfunctions somewhere in the world, the pollution is distributed horizontally. You face it in your drinking water, in your soil, and have no recourse whatsoever in terms of mitigation, responsibility or accountability, because it came to you from an unidentifiable, or occasionally even identifiable, source through an uncontrollable horizontal movement.

The Internet: Access and Advocacy

The difference between the vertical traffic and the horizontal traffic is one of the things that affects us very profoundly as we deal with community groups, with access and with advocacy. Here we have the Internet, one of those inventions that can work both vertically and horizontally. You can connect up with everybody. Wouldn't that be nice if we could gather the relevant information that we might want for our work through that horizontal slicing of our world and then use it vertically in our communities. If you are interested in clean energy, or early childhood education, you would think that there is an enormous amount of usefulness in that horizontal gathering of the best and most profound insights on the subject. Then you could, in fact, utilize it vertically to go to those who deal with implementing either clean energy or early childhood education, and say, "Look, that is the very best thing the world has to offer in terms of knowledge and insight. Let's go with it."

If I say that to you, you will say, "You must be dreaming. The world just doesn't work like that." Of course the world works very differently. There are two profound provisos to that dream of gathering knowledge or information horizontally, and applying it vertically. The one is, you aren't alone, there are the others who also run around horizontally and vertically. The second one is the place and nature of what we call information.

Knowledge vs. Action

I will go back 50 years. Right now we are celebrating the end of the Second World War. At the end of that war, the liberation of the concentration camps was a tremendous and profound shock to the world. When that became evidence in the aftermath of the war, the Germans were asked, "And what was your responsibility?" In the Germany of my childhood, the standard response was, "We didn't know." We didn't know—sometimes it was true, sometimes not, but the response meant that, had we known, we would surely have done something about it. It was the "we didn't know" that the Germans used as their explanation and their excuse for consent to tyranny.

Now, 50 years later, I don't think that there is any possibility that people could say any more with any credibility, as the Germans did, "we didn't know" about a similar profound disaster, holocaust, or negation of human rights. Assuming of course that, had they known, something would have been done about it.

The explanation or excuse of lack of knowledge may have had a part in the description in history of the Holocaust. It has no more credibility in the world because all of us know a great many things that would require from any person of conscience an immediate intervention. And, whether it is environmental disasters, whether it is Rwanda, whether it is civil rights violations in many countries, whether it is the increasing number of unemployed people in our own country, whether it is the homeless we see on our way to work—it isn't as though we don't know.

But there is that horrible realization that, while the knowledge of facts may be a necessary condition for action, and we talk about democracy in civic action, it is, unfortunately, not a sufficient one.

The mathematicians so nicely distinguish necessary and sufficient conditions. Although the knowledge of factual information is necessary for appropriate action, it isn't sufficient. What is needed for an effective mitigation and a revision of the conditions of which one has knowledge, are channels to power that are not blocked and a responsive agency of power that, in fact, can and will make the changes.

And, as you deliberate about the information highway, about your access to information, be it factual information or be it the experience of like-minded people in other parts of the world, do please remember that, while that knowledge may be a necessary condition, it may in fact be a less necessary condition than the one that makes that a sufficient condition, and that is access to power. In the end, knowledge, as one of my colleagues once wrote, has something to do with power and survival and, he added to that, we are all in the business of both.

But one cannot rest with the knowledge that one might gain in terms of information if one doesn't have a realistic grasp as to what would and could modify the conditions that one addresses. And, being chronologically challenged, I have been in this game for too long, written too many briefs, and been on too many delegations to Ottawa to address various committees to be sanguine about saying, "The poor dears need some more knowledge. If they only knew what I know, the world would be a better place to live." One begins most of these civic journeys with the idea that those in power are well-intentioned but ill-informed, and I am sorry to say that many of us ended by saying that those in power are very well informed, but ill-intentioned. They have no intention of doing what I might consider the right and appropriate thing.

WHEN TO TAKE A "DIM VIEW"

One does then have to look at another source and another need for knowledge—that knowledge of "Why do things not get done that seem to be the appropriate, useful, honourable and decent thing to do?" As we, as community groups, gather that initial information, it is only the first act of a play. The real problem for any community group is to answer the question: "What do you do after you have taken a dim view?" That is a particularly difficult question to answer in this area of access to the information highway. This is not about the gathering of knowledge, but rather about questions of structure of power and responsibility.

Now, from my own experience in this area, I should caution you about the misuse of information. I don't mean disinformation or wrong information. First of all, I would ask, "How much information do you really need before you take a dim view?"

I was once part of the small group of people in front of the then president of our university, arguing that the university should divest itself from commercial investments in white South Africa. Our president said that one had to study the issue, that he always had to see the two sides of every problem. I got very angry and said to him, "Could you please explain to me what is the other side of justice?"

That has some bearing on the pressure that is sometimes put on the community to study a question further. There may be a lot of things that have to be studied, but there is also what I call "occupational therapy for the opposition" that says, send them off to do some more push-ups on the Internet. You need to be mindful that it is possible to use information, and the need for information, as a delay for the call for action.

IRRELEVANT INFORMATION

The other area in terms of misuse of information is what I would call irrelevant information. There is an enormous amount of information that has nothing to do with anything. There is a sort of civic landfill, and you ought not to go into the business of civic landfill. If your aim is to change conditions, then there is a certain amount of information needed, but not more. After that, one needs to address the questions, "Why does nothing happen? Why do some proposals that seem to be fairly reasonable, workable, and sensible never get beyond the lip service stage?" That requires a very different sort of knowledge. That is the knowledge of the structure of power.

I have for myself come to the point where I say that people or groups or governments make the decisions that make sense to them, even if they look totally harebrained to me. My task then is to figure out the constellation of forces, the pushes and pulls, that in fact do add up to that harebrained decision-making. Then we can go into the next iteration and say, "What can we do about that balance of the push and the pull that seems to result in totally non-constructive decisions."

KNOWLEDGE AND WRONG ACTIONS

That leaves us with the experience that some of us have had and continue to have—the experience of a breed of people and politicians who do make decisions that may be morally and even nationally wrong, in the full knowledge that these decisions are wrong.

That is one of the most difficult tasks: not only to think of ways in which one could either counteract or clarify or document such decisions, but to meet up with intelligent people who, in the absolute clarity of their critical faculties, do what they know is wrong because of other narrow interests. This is one of the most disconcerting things that can happen to anyone. But don't gloss over it, don't hide it, don't excuse it. It's part of the landscape.

If you go with that sort of information into the Internet, you might very well find a lot of people who have other experiences with similar undertones in power. But you are also in a public medium, and you are flagged and visible. The Internet is not just your private multiple telephone system. It is one of the most infiltrated and infiltratable highways of this world.

It's in a way a very much more serious thing than what governments now do when they say, "We consult with community groups," and you go there and you give them all your fine thoughts and then what you find is that they are mapping the terrain in order to find a strategy to get around all those lumps and hills that have been mapped. And of course they can then say they have consulted, as they have said frequently. But the purpose was primarily to avoid trouble rather than to do the right thing.

Recently, my attention was drawn to a quote from Peter Drucker who said, "If there isn't dissent, we would not know where the problems are." I said to my husband, "Look, if there isn't dissent, we wouldn't know *whose* the problems are." I think one has to keep that in mind.

I recommend to you David Lyon's book, *The Electronic Eye*, dealing with that whole range of electronic technologies and their potential, their very great and constantly used potential for the surveillance, infiltration and containment of individual freedom.

Every Tool Shapes the Task

You can say to me, "What should we do? We live in this world. There is that Internet and obviously it has great potential. How should an organization conduct itself?"

First of all, I think one has to remember that every tool shapes the task. Whether it is a trivial tool in the kitchen, when somebody gives you a Cuisinart or one of those machines that slice and dice, suddenly you find yourself slicing and dicing and not using your old recipes any more. When you get a new tool, it affects your task.

Is there anybody here who knows what an electronic microscope does to a research group? Everything suddenly has to be observed at 2,000 magnifications because you have that expensive beast.

So, be mindful of how the tool shapes the task. And that you will only find this out when you really learn about the tool. Learn what is in this Internet. But then keep your head clear and go back to your goals. What, in fact, in the best of all worlds, do you want to do? Do any of the activities with your new electronic microscope bring you closer to that? When do you have to go back to the traditional tools of talking to people face-to-face, meeting with a group of people, having a potluck? When is it that the intangibles of the potluck far outweigh the elegance of a message on the Internet? Because, in the end, what we are all concerned about is people.

THE NOTION OF THE COMMON GOOD

The things that I most fear about the current developments is not the infiltration of the Internet. I fear the restructuring of work that the electronic media technology brings. Because we should not forget how more and more people lost meaningful work and how difficult it is for young people to get any meaningful employment. That's my first and profound fear.

My second fear is that, when the community and individuals begin to really get hooked on the Internet, using it and taking enjoyment out of the virtual communities that they can create, it gets us away from what is probably our most treasured possession, and that is the notion of the common good. If you want to grow a cactus from seed or have sightings of the Virgin Mary, you will find people who have grown cactus from seeds and who have sighted the Virgin Mary. That is nice, but that optimizing of the private creates a fragmentation that goes in parallel to the fiscal privatization that takes away from the public space.

Because, if we think that cyberspace is a public space, then let's think of the oceans. They used to be as much of a world resource as anybody could think of, but didn't belong to anybody. So everybody put their garbage into them. The potential of cyberspace as a global dump is quite substantial.

My central concern is: "What has happened to the notion of the common good?" If we, as members of a community, really think in terms of a common good, then there is a limit to the interest of particular sectors. We cannot just let labour worry about structural unemployment. Labour needs to worry about the environment and environmentalists need to worry about unemployment. We all have to worry about justice.

Does that mean we have to read every piece of miscellaneous information we can find on the Internet? Or does that mean we have to really reassess and define our common agenda? What will assure a civilized life? From there on, people can grow cactus or see the Virgin Mary as much as they wish, but it cannot be done at the expense of the time and effort that it takes to have a society that essentially promotes justice, both to people and to the environment.

Whether the information highway helps or hinders, I don't think any one of us knows at this point. But it's not a trivial issue.

NOTES

1   Keynote speech given at the "Community Access to the Information Highway" Conference, Ottawa, Ontario, Canada May 7-9, 1995. This essay was originally published by Lazara Press (Vancouver, 1996)

Community Networking in Canada: Do You Believe in Magic?

Marita Moll and Leslie Regan Shade[1]

Community-controlled computer networks attempt to reclaim electronic public space and could provide a significant challenge to corporate control of information. Freenets, or community networks . . . were set up to enrich their local communities, not return profits to investors.

—*Donald Gutstein*[2]

THE 1990s SAW THE RAPID EXPANSION OF COMMUNITY-BASED COMPUTER NETWORKS across North America. Communities, battered by the escalating rate of change that accompanied globalization, were looking for ways to maintain their primacy. They needed new educational opportunities, economic development plans, and civic participation strategies. Proponents of community-based computer networking felt that this new form of communications could serve these purposes, and they worked to make it readily available to all. In Canada, at their high point between 1995-96, there were 35 operating networks with between 250,000 and 600,000 members.[3]

Community-based computer networks are situated between commercial online services (i.e., CompuServe, Microsoft Network, America Online), Internet Service Providers (ISPs), and individual computer bulletin board services, or "BBSs." They are distinguished from commercial networks and bulletin board services in that they exhibit all three of the following characteristics:

1. Local: community networks emphasize local resources, services, culture, and people. Information, even the more seemingly mundane (local bus schedules, calendars of events, restaurant listings, etc.), and formal and informal communication forums can potentially aid in continuing education, health, well-being, and equity of citizens.

2. Access: community networks are concerned with ensuring heterogeneous access to the network at no or nominal cost to all members of the community. Schools, libraries, community information and recreational centres, and shopping malls often serve as public access points.

3. Social change/community development: the proponents and volunteers operating and championing community networks share the belief that their systems can strengthen and revitalize communities through positive and interactive communication between residents and local institutions.[4]

Community networks are variously organized, but in general they are staffed by a few paid members and a large volunteer core, who typically group themselves into several committees concerned with technology, content, volunteer recruitment, fund-raising, outreach, and training. Often they are affiliated with institutions such as universities, public libraries, or non-profit associations. Funding varies from system to system and is rarely stable. It can include a pastiche of government funding, grants, in-kind contributions, cash donations, volunteer time, donations of hardware and software from large equipment manufacturers, and sponsorship of modem lines by local businesses and individuals.

In Canada, the widespread creation of community networks became a powerful model to many for enabling citizens to support and sustain community (geographically-based and "virtual" community), participate in the public sphere, exercise democratic imperatives, and reinforce national identity.

We believe that community networking represents a grassroots effort by Canadians to create a truly citizen-based Information Highway, one which reflects what people want from this new technology: a place to think, learn, and communicate with their neighbors and an emerging knowledge-based world,

said community networking activists John Stevenson and Greg Searle in their presentation to the Canadian Radio-television and Telecommunications Commission (CRTC) convergence hearings.[5]

Electronic Catch-22

Official policy-making bodies such as the Information Highway Advisory Council (IHAC) and the CRTC also recognized the value of community-based networks by recognizing their role in supporting Canadian content, network literacy and universal access.[6] Unfortunately, the strategies which evolved to connect Canadians to new communications technologies did not capitalize on the growing experience of Canadian community networks, preferring to concentrate on the easier-to-implement but much less empowering "access to information" model represented by the Industry Canada's Community Access Program (CAP).[7] Gutstein places some of the responsibility for this development on early community networking promoters:

> Instead of challenging corporate domination, community networks and their national association, Telecommunities Canada, were largely integrated into the corporate political system, as providers of access to low-income and rural Canadians, people of little interest to the commercial ISP's that appeared on the scene a year or two after the community networks went on-line.[8]

This is a very harsh judgment. Community networking advocates were challenging corporate domination by their very presence. In the sociopolitical and policy landscape of the time, where the global dominated the local and the commercial dominated the non-commercial, just getting these networks off the ground was, in fact, a remarkable feat. It was done in the face of a singular, market-driven vision of communications championed by both government and industry. While commercial ISPs complained that publicly-supported community networks would constitute unfair competition, community networking advocates painstakingly pointed out that publicly-supported libraries were not considered to be in competition with the book publishing industry. Libraries were builders of a book-buying public. Unfortunately, even an institution as valuable as the public library might have had a poor chance of finding its way into community services, had it evolved during this period.

It is true, though, that low-cost access and community training were far more effective arguments than social change and community development in the all-important struggle to secure financial support and equipment donations to keep the fledgling networks in operation. And this is an image that has impeded the development of community networks ever since. Yes, community networks still function as low-cost access points for many users. Originally text-based systems, they still serve people whose computers would be considered historic artifacts in the current world of multimedia workstations and whose modems would choke on the Web's explosion of graphics. But it is not generally known that most community networks are now accessible through the Web from any Internet service provider, and many offer a graphical option as well as the text-only environment.

Lacking broad-based recognition as a vital public service and the funding that flows from that, community networking's financial and personnel resources are scarce and often consumed by access responsibilities. Despite this, volunteers have never seen themselves building systems to feed the information dispossessed until they could gather sufficient resources to afford a real meal at the table of the commercial providers. Community-based networks were not meant to be "soup kitchens on the Internet." Volunteers were, and continue to be, driven by the belief that their networks could strengthen and revitalize communities.

The goal of community networking is to reserve a space in this new medium that serves the interests of the community, a space not dependent on the profit motive that drives the private sector. To do this, community networks have to generate content through community interaction. Garth Graham, former volunteer Executive Director of Telecommunities Canada (TC), constantly argued that describing a community network as an Internet access provider was like describing the Canadian Broadcasting Corporation (CBC) in terms of a particular brand of radio or television set. It was the content produced through participation in online community activity, not the access medium, that was the critical component.

> Community nets are not inherently content providers. Their purpose is to defend universal participation in, and access to, electronic public space as a commons. The community itself is the network. It supplies the content as a by-product of its communications behaviours in electronic public space. [9]

Making Content Happen

Even in the electronic world, people should have a place to encounter their community haphazardly, like they do on a busy sidewalk. Otherwise it is too easy to forget that a real community is extremely diverse. Community networks offer a wonderful opportunity to provide a meeting place of the commercial sector, government, the voluntary sector, education, and the library community, says Greg Salmers, the former chair of the Saskatchewan Association of Community Networks. Bernard Hart, a director of the Chebucto Community Network in Halifax, Nova Scotia, notes that community networks help citizens explore new uses for the Internet. To provide such a meeting place where content happens, community networks have been developing enabling tools, processes and structures.

- The Chebucto community network operates a web-camera on the top of the highest building in Halifax. Originally used to feature the Tall Ships coming into the Halifax harbour, it is presently offering a view of the city's Victorian era gardens where a number of "old forest trees" are being cut to halt the spread of disease. People are able to view the park with the web-cam and also participate in a discussion forum. Chebucto also operates a project that assists people on low incomes to borrow or acquire a low-cost recycled computer for specific uses such as distance education.
- Some services developed in Saskatchewan include an e-commerce promotion in the form of an electronic community store front; a virtual reference service where librarians respond to online queries from all over Saskatchewan, Canada and beyond; and a project that cooperates with medical services to provide or facilitate remote access to specialists.
- Ottawa's National Capital Freenet (NCF) is working on a "Thin Client" project that will provide members with access to modern office automation and web-authoring software through NCF's modem pool and server infrastructure. Even those members who have relatively modest computers will have access to some of the latest Windows-based applications.

- Halinet, a community consortium of schools, libraries and social service organizations in Halton, Ontario, offers a data entry tool that allows community groups to build their own databases. Current databases include heritage collections of books, deeds, documents, photographs, memoirs, videos, maps, and other items; newspaper features about the community from the turn of the century; and a collection of documents on Great Lakes history. It also has an online volunteer centre that allows people to select volunteer opportunities according to their age, community, interests, and availability. A special search feature has been provided to enable secondary school students to find relevant opportunities to satisfy their mandatory volunteer requirements. Volunteers are able to contact the agency or agencies involved electronically through the Web interface.

The national organization, Telecommunities Canada (TC), has been developing a number of tools and services for the use of all community network members:

- open source software which enables community networks and their users to customize their opening menus. Known as a "portal," this software allows users to always have a page of their favourite destinations in front of them. Channels may be either "active" with continuously updated weather or news headlines or, "passive" with collections of links. Users can create channels and publish them for the use of the general community.
- a WebMail service that allows holders of Canadian community-based e-mail services to access their home mailboxes from any location. This service offered by TC member regional and local servers is advertising free and authenticated (i.e., not anonymous) elements of free WebMail services like HotMail that have proven problematic, especially for schools.[10] TC also offers WebMail and web page services to patrons of Canadian public access sites that do not have a local server.[11]
- streaming video services that provide an opportunity for Canadian community networks to present the activities of their citizens to the rest of the country and to the world, both live and in stored archival form. Using this service, a local Junior A hockey team was the first in Saskatchewan to broadcast games in video over the Web in real time.

- a "Network of Networks" project that will create an national community networking database. There is, as yet, no comprehensive national listing of all community networks, community access sites, and other similar network access initiatives in Canada. As a start to this initiative, a recent project with the Office of Learning Technologies has created a directory of and links to online learning opportunities offered through community networks including online courses.
- contacts with international associations, including the European Association of Community Networks. TC is participating in "Global 2000"—a series of events on community networking held around the world. Canada is seen internationally as a pioneer in this field.
- opportunities for activists to meet face to face at annual general meetings and workshops.[12]

Clearly, Canadian community networks are not dormant entities. But, even within their own communities, they are often well-kept secrets or scorned because of early ideas about their ability to scale up. Why these important services have taken such a low profile on the public radar screen has much to do with an attitude, in government and the private sector, that considers the support of public services to be an intrusion in the free market rather an investment in the health of communities. This is clearly a loss for all sectors—public and private alike—since healthy communities are essential to the existence of a flourishing market.

THE INVISIBLE NETWORKS

Community networks experience the Knowledge Society directly. How does a checklist of their concerns match up with the framework of questions addressed by the Canadian Information Highway debate? We don't know yet. We do know that the current debate carries forward assumptions about markets, communications and learning based on industrial society points-of-view . . . We also note that, well in advance of the plans of governments and business, tens of thousands of Canadians are eagerly joining community networks. *We ask – why is their experience being ignored?*

—Garth Graham[13] (emphasis added)

Without resources to promote services, community networks are in a difficult public relations bind. Not being part of the current ".com" delirium, local newspapers show little interest in them. The *Ottawa Citizen*, one of the original supporters of the National Capital Freenet, now promotes its own site, www.ottawa.com. Although the information technology industry has often been supportive by donating much of the equipment that runs the networks, they have carefully ignored these networks in public.

Meanwhile, the "co-opted" version of Canadian community networks presented by Gutstein, if correct, certainly didn't buy any favours from the country's major funder of networking initiatives. The "stove-pipe" approach to electronic networking pursued by Industry Canada's "Connecting Canadians" agenda was focused on connecting individual sectors of communities rather than the community as a whole.[14] The library community, among the original supporters of community networks, were encouraged to concentrate on creating networks of libraries through LibraryNet, schools were connected through SchoolNet, and voluntary agencies were connected through VolNet.

The Community Access Project (CAP) provided one-time grants to set up information access sites, but no assistance to help them move beyond access to enable communication and content building. Gutstein condemns Industry Canada's lack of vision. "For Industry Canada, community networks are simply another ingredient in the Connecting Canadians witches' brew, an interim stage to be tolerated until commercial interests can take them over."[15]

It didn't help that other government departments, to which community networks might have turned for support, did not see a role for themselves in this area until Industry Canada's initiatives were well under way. Severe budget cutbacks and lack of power in cabinet are two reasons advanced for the peculiar absence of departments such as Canadian Heritage and Human Resources Development Canada (HRDC) in most debates about how a Canadian perspective might be best advanced in the evolving communications environment.

Although the Industry Canada efforts have gone a long way towards establishing electronic connections in various sectors, strengthening the human connections within and among these efforts is a major weak link. This makes it an area of opportunity for community networks. It is precisely the area in which community networks excel when given the opportunity.

FROM MANIC TO MELIORISM

> Meliorism assumes that things *can* get better, but *only* if people act to ensure that outcome. Meliorism is a pragmatic viewpoint. It does not ignore problems or explain them away with platitudes or ideology.
> —Douglas Schuler[16]

Despite the difficulties, Canadian community networks are settling in for the long term. Idealism has had to give way to pragmatism as some systems that were free (or donation-driven) began charging annual fees. Others continued to rely on donations but offered enhanced services for a fee. Closer alliances with the private sector have also been part of the emerging model. A number of recent developments have helped Canadian community networks maintain their position as important community services:

- In 1996, the Victoria community network's application for charitable status, originally refused in 1993 by Revenue Canada in an application made by the National Capital Freenet, was finally successful in the Federal Court of Appeals. This was not only an important step towards financial sustainability, but also official recognition that the networks offered services that were important to the community. The decision affirmed community computer networks as a social utility and a public good.[17]
- In 1997, a "Memorandum of Understanding (MOU)" outlined a framework for cooperation between Industry Canada (IC) and Telecommunities Canada and a series of cooperative actions.[18] It defined the joint role of TC and IC in advising the government on citizen access to electronic public space and the transition to electronic public services. Although this brought no immediate changes in the policy process, it represented some formal recognition of community networks in the framework of the networked society. TC has continued to be one of the members of Industry Canada's Community Access Program (CAP) advisory board and continues to receive small project grants that have enabled it to stay alive.
- In October 1999, TC finally secured enough funding to hire an Executive Director. Much of this was due to support from the Office of Learning Technologies which encouraged and supported several projects that enabled TC to move towards a formal, rather than virtual, membership struc-

ture, imperative if the organization was to survive any longer. In contrast, the American national community networking association (The National Public Telecommunications Network [NPTN]) had ceased to exist in 1997. Ironically, October 1999 also saw the closing of the historic and visionary Cleveland Freenet, which, since 1985, had provided a model for other community networks to follow.

- Some community networks have found ways to fit into the "Connecting Canadians" agenda. Community networks in Ottawa, Vancouver, and Halifax have a role in delivering the VolNet program in their region. Ottawa's National Capital Freenet has a big piece of Ottawa's winning bid for a "Smart Communities" project.[19] Various networks have also participated in the rural and urban CAP projects. Each one of these projects represents revenue and, perhaps more importantly, new members for the networks. In an in-depth report on the sustainability of the National Capital Freenet, Executive Director Chris Cope says: "So long as the National Capital Freenet relies on donations from its members to support the cost of day-to-day operations, it must set membership as its highest priority. The very nature of NCF is often to provide an introduction to the Internet and the natural attendant outflow of members must be offset by an equal or greater inflow. Methods of attracting new members is therefore of paramount importance."[20] The report suggests that new members would most probably be found among the estimated 30% of Ottawa residents who are not connected to the Internet, either because they lack the know-how or sophisticated equipment.

There is still enough of the original magic that brought community networking activists together under the local, access, and community development/social change umbrella to keep scores of volunteers busy implementing new programs. But the challenges to community networking in the next few years will surely test their resolve once again. Clearly, funding must be stabilized and much of this depends on a clearer definition of their role in the networked world and official recognition of their importance in filling that role. The MOU with Industry Canada serves as a basis for such recognition, but the structures and processes that would make the agreement a basis for action are still far from reality. Similar MOU's with other departments might also be useful.

Beyond this lies what might be an even greater challenge. Even with sustainable funding, community networks must develop ways to maintain a sense of "neighbourhood" in the non-jurisdictional Web-based online world. The NCF report points out that the participation in the governance of NCF has fallen off sharply. In 1995, 13% of members voted in the annual elections for board members. In 2000, participation was down to 2.6% "[Though they] value the service we provide and are willing to support it through their donations, just as they might support public television, the majority feels no particular connection to NCF as a particular community but rather is a user of our service and a participant in other communities of his/her choosing."[21]

Ian Allen, community networking activist and former technical director for the National Capital Freenet, points out that the new environment of PPP/Web access cuts away the structures that give context to community networks, causing the sense of neighbourhood to fade. There are no more sidewalks where you might bump into people not going your way. Says Allen:

We can try to find out "how to do "community" in the non-text, non-captive-audience, full-Shockwave/ICQ/MP3 Internet domain. Nobody has figured out how to capture or create community in that realm yet, not even the big and rich guys. Remember: to attempt this is to have your site try to compete for attention with every other online site on the planet. Good luck!

The conclusion of the NCF report is pragmatic. "NCF's best opportunity to remain sustainable is to continue to help the people of our community to access technology which otherwise might be unavailable to them, and to continue to provide a service that remains relevant and useful." Community networks must still focus their resources on access. But the landscape of physical access to the communications network may look completely different within five years.

FIBRE TO THE PEOPLE

In the information technology community, customer-owned dark fibre networks, dedicated to a single customer where the customer is responsible for attaching the telecommunications equipment and lasers to "light" the fibre, is being promoted as the access route of the future. According to Bill St. Arnaud, Senior Director of CANARIE[22] Advanced Network Projects:

> Customer-owned dark fibre is a basic infrastructure like roads and bridges. It is not a telecommunications service. But governments are starting to recognize that customer-owned dark fibre is a powerful economic enabler of new commercial services and will be as fundamental to the economic and social well-being of the community as publicly-owned roads and bridges have been in the past. [23]

Several such projects are already underway:

- In the first national dark fibre project, Sweden has established a funding pool of over $20 billion (U.S.) "that will be used to connect the main localities of neighbouring communities—forming a grid across the country."[24]
- A recent article in *Wired* magazine describes a project in La Grange, Georgia, which offers all residents free internet access via cable modems and low-cost broadband access to residents and local businesses through its municipally-owned fibre and broadband hybrid fibre-coax networks.[25]
- The London edition of the Financial Times reports that the U.K. government is looking at ways to guarantee universal access to high-speed, broadband communications networks by 2005. The government is considering making universal broadband access a part of the next election platform.[26]

In Canada, some current projects include:

- a consortium of school boards in Quebec connecting schools with dark fibre;
- a dark fibre project initiated by universities in the Halifax area that might support access to the community network; and
- a consortium of businesses, school boards, hospitals, universities and government departments who have signed an agreement to create a locally owned and managed municipal fibre network for Ottawa.[27]

Describing the communications infrastructure as a public service, like sewage and water services, is a dramatic change of direction for the official rhetoric around new communications technologies. Communications corporations will not be happy. This will remove the infrastructure from their growing world of integrated products and services. But it could provide a major boost to community networks and their users, both in terms of legitimizing the concept of a community-owned communications channel and in terms of physical access to that channel.

If the road into the neighbourhood is paved by the municipality, communities can finally focus their resources on services and activities, rather than access. Community networks have already shown that they are representatives of community online and should be considered natural participants in these projects. This may be a renaissance opportunity for community networks.

CLARIFYING ROLES FOR COMMUNITY NETWORKS

Physical access, of course, is only one out of the seven levels of access that make up the "access rainbow."[28]

7 GOVERNANCE
6 LITERACY/SOCIAL FACILITATION
5 SERVICE/ACCESS PROVISION
4 CONTENT/SERVICES
3 SOFTWARE TOOLS
2 DEVICES
1 CARRIAGE FACILITIES

Access "Rainbow"

Community networks play an important role, as indicated in the NCF report, in providing training and assistance. Even if universal access becomes a reality, "I expect that there will be a substantial segment of our population who will not embrace Internet use, either because they don't know how or perhaps because they don't understand why they might need it and have no idea how it will enrich their lives. These people will need the traditional community network approach to outreach, training, and just plain hand-holding," says Chris Cope.

Agreeing with the NCF report, Ian Allen suggests that one way to maintain relevance is to "give up the 'mass market' for community networking and appeal to real, existing groups that need to be online. Programs like VolNet may be the natural place where community networks find the real, physical communities of people who want to use computer-assisted interaction. These groups will find that going online dilutes their community with all the distractions of the Internet, and that, rather than enhancing local community and communication, it causes local community to fade." A community network can at least help stem the flow.

These suggestions reflect the realities of operating community networks in the year 2000. But many argue that the health of a nation depends on the strength and vitality of its cultural industries, and, although community networking has not secured the same credibility as the broadcasting, publishing, and film industries, it has proved to be a very responsive and viable "local culture" and can play an important role in the development, organization and dissemination of content that matters to the community. Paul Neilson, a Canadian Internet activist, raises some red flags on the promise of high bandwidth:

> The cry should go out across the land: Give me: Content! Content! Content! Give me the critical thinking skills to evaluate it and know when substantive content is missing. Most concerned people are stuck on bandwidth. I am not prepared to go with the flow. If you are buried in advertising, propaganda and schlock on your bandwidth, it won't be a technical problem!

The final word goes to Chris Cope, who says, on the subject of recovering online neighborhood in a Web-centric world:

It behooves us to see if we can find ways to re-create some of the tools and benefits we have offered in past [text-based world]. While we may have to pace technology as things change and become increasingly web-centric, we need to re-create some of the things that served to introduce our members to each other. Whether this means the operation of a dating service, or maintaining buy-sell forums, or finding ways for members to meet and help each other with technical and topical concerns, or whatever. We'll have a continuing role with access. We'll need to be providers for quite a while yet, and as the need for access provision diminishes, the need to help people find good ways to meet people and do useful things will increase . . .

In other words, we are not defining the space, but helping people understand what it is. Our position may be that of facilitator, teacher, mediator, champion, and maybe a bit of Cupid.

Cupid? Now, there's a bit of magic . . . .

Notes

1   And a host of Canadian community networking activists who contributed to this article via informal online discussions.

2   Gutstein, Donald. (1999) *E.con: How the Internet Undermines Democracy.* Toronto: Stoddart. p.260.

3   Graham, Garth and Leslie Regan Shade. (1996, June 27). *Rhetoric and reality in Canadian community networking.* Paper presented to the INET 96 Conference, Montreal.

4   Beamish, A. (1995, February). *Communities on-line: Community-based computer networks.* Unpublished master's thesis, Massachusetts Institute of Technology. URL: http://alberti.mit.edu./arch/4.207/anneb/thesis/toc.html quoted in Shade, Leslie Regan. (1999) "Roughing it in the electronic bush: community networking in Canada." *Canadian Journal of Communication.* 24: 181-182.

5   Stevenson, J. and G. Searle. (1995, February 13). *New voices, new visions: Community media and the information highway.* Submission by the Internet Public Interest Research Group in response to Public Notice CRTC 1994-130: Call for Comments Concerning Order-in-Council P.C. 1994-1689.

6   Graham. (1996).

7   According to the website "Connecting Canadians is the federal government's vision and plan to make Canada the most connected country in the world. In an increasingly competitive and knowledge-based global economy, Canada can benefit by becoming a world leader in the development and use of advanced information and communications technologies." For more information see: http://www.connect.gc.ca/

8   Gutstein. (1999). p. 261.

9   Graham. (1996). p.2.

10   Chilibeck, John. (1998, Dec. 7) "Government bans free E-mail in N.B. high schools." St. John, N.B.: Times Globe.

11   Telecommunities Canada (1999, Sept. 2) "A Canadian alternative to 'HotMail'" Press Release Ottawa: Telecommunities Canada. Available at: http://www.tc.ca/

12   All of the community networks and the services mentioned in this section can be accessed through the Telecommunities Canada home page http:// www. tc.ca

13   Graham, Garth. (1995) "A domain where thought is free to roam: the social purpose of community networks." A background paper supporting Telecommunities Canada's appearance, March 29 1995, at the CRTC public hearings on information highway convergence. Available at: http://www.tc.ca/crtc.brief.html

14   For example: In the February 1998 budget, the federal government announced the creation of the Voluntary Sector Network Support Program (VolNet) to "expand the technological capacity of the voluntary sector" and to "enhance the capacity of voluntary organizations." It established a target of offering connectivity to 10,000 voluntary organizations by March 31, 2001. This target was to be reached by providing organizations with access to computer equipment and Internet connections, support and Internet skills development.

15   Gutstein (1999). p.269.

16   Schuler, Douglas. (1996) *New community networks: Wired for change.* New York: ACM Press. p. x

17   Shade, Leslie Regan. (1999) "Roughing it in the electronic bush: community networking in Canada." *Canadian Journal of Communication.* 24: 183.

18   Telecommunities Canada and Industry Canada. (1997) "Framework for Co-Operation between Telecommunities Canada (TC) and Industry Canada to enhance the ability of Canadian communities to utilize electronic public space." Available at http://www.tc.ca/framework.html

19   for more information see: http://smartcommunities.ic.gc.ca/

20   Cope, Chris. (2000, July 16) "The National Capital Freenet; Opportunities, challenges and a sustainable future." Report to the NCF Board. Available at: http://www.ncf.ca/execdir/ncf2000/

21   ibid

22   i.e. Canadian Network for the Advancement of Research, Industry and Education

23   St. Arnaud, Bill. (Version: July 6th, 2000-07-06) "Frequently Asked Questions about Customer Owned Dark Fiber" For the most recent version please go to the CA*net 3 web site at www.canet3.net

24   CA*net 3 news. (2000). "Government's role in developing broadband infrastructure." June 19. http://www.canet3.net/frames/canet3newsarchive.html

25   Delio, Michelle. (2000, Aug. 22) "A city with a broadband future." *Wired* Available at http://www.wired.com/news/culture/0,1284,38346,00.html

26   From the London edition of the Financial Times. http://news.ft.com/ft/gx.cgi/ftc?pagename=Viewc=Article&cid=FT36MP9KGCC&liv

27   Ottawa Centre for Research and Innovation (2000, May 3) "Ottawa's Optical Fibre Initiative - Historic Agreement Signed." News release. Available at: http://www.ocri.ca/about/hitech_news/news/ocri_053000.html

28   Developed by Leslie Regan Shade and Andrew Clement.

POVNET: An Online Commons for Anti-Poverty Activists

Penny Goldsmith

INTRODUCTION

A FEW YEARS AGO I HAD A MEETING WITH A WOMEN'S CENTRE IN THE DOWNTOWN eastside of Vancouver. I was waxing on eloquently about why they should have a public access site via the local community network so that women could go online in a place where they felt comfortable. The staff person I was talking to looked at me somewhat blankly, and then pointed out that, if they had the resources for an extra phone line, it would be used instead to enable women to telephone friends, make doctors' appointments, and phone potential employers for job interviews.

Dr. Ursula Franklin, an eminent scientist in experimental physics and a longtime feminist and community organizer, has written and spoken extensively on the impact of technology on issues of peace and justice. According to her, "Any time new technologies emerge ... it is the community that has raised the questions: what can these new technologies do in our work of furthering democracy and the process, and what do these technologies prevent us from doing." [1]

WHO'S LEFT OUT OF THE NEW TECHNOLOGY?

The issue of a growing gap between people who have access to electronic information and the technology that creates it, and those who do not, is one that has been surfacing more and more as resources, job postings, and information about living in our local communities become increasingly available only electronically. People who can't afford computers at home (a 1998 Angus Reid survey reported that 62% of Internet[2] users access the internet from home in British Columbia[3]) and who don't have access to public access sites are rapidly becoming part of an information "have-not" ghetto.

Women are one group that is left out of the technology loop. According to Monica Townson, 57% of single-parent families headed by women are in poverty.[4] Shelagh Day and Gwen Brodsky point out that "Aboriginal women, immigrant women, visible minority women, and women with disabilities are more vulnerable to poverty than other women. In 1990, 33% of Aboriginal women, 28% of visible minority women, and 21% of immigrant women were living below the low-income cut-off, compared to 16% of other women."[5] Certainly, poor women are not obvious candidates for access to new technology. PovNet is firmly rooted in the needs of such groups.

POVNET's History

PovNet as a project had its beginnings in the anti-poverty community in British Columbia in the summer of 1997 as anti-poverty advocates began recognizing the need to communicate with one another more cheaply and efficiently. It is now run by a provincial steering committee of anti-poverty groups, including groups representing women, people with disabilities, tenants, poor people, libraries, refugees and immigrants, legal aid advocates and public bodies like Community Legal Assistance of B.C. and the B.C. Public Interest Advocacy Centre, who take test cases to court on behalf of these organizations.

That first summer, a community meeting was held in Vancouver, with advocates from around the province in attendance. It was a meeting of people—not a computer in sight—and it started PovNet off on a foot that continues to this day: computers are a resource, but the technology does not drive PovNet. At that meeting, a list of ideas surfaced about how PovNet could help facilitate an online communication network using confidential discussion groups and a public web page. The lists of needs were long; advocates wanted to talk to each other about all sorts of areas of poverty law.

Now, three years later, I recently spent a couple of months talking to anti-poverty advocates and groups across Canada about the need for PovNet in other parts of the country. The overwhelming response from anti-poverty workers everywhere was that they wanted a way to talk to one another about what they were doing: information and ideas still needed an online communication voice. Consequently, we are applying for money from the federal government to expand PovNet. Initially, we will hold a national meeting. There will be no computers.

POVNET as a Political Force

> The central problem with using the Internet for strategies of social change is still mostly on our (the social organization's) side. Whatever the forms in which it will evolve: we still have to learn how to use it productively and efficiently to "deliver our messages" and cause structural impact.
> —Carlos A. Afonso on the "Corporate Watch" web site.[6]

Canada is a country with a social safety net. And right now, Canadians are fighting to keep it. As well as specific education, training, communication and other resources, PovNet provides a place where advocates can exchange information about what's happening in different parts of the province, and the country. Law reform is one way to keep the social safety net from sprouting even larger holes. Advocates need to know what other advocates are up to.

For example, the B.C. government introduced a form which people on welfare had to sign before they could get assistance. On this form, those who were applying for welfare were asked to sign away their rights to privacy. This allowed the government to go to landlords, the tax department, anywhere, for information about a person seeking assistance. It took a bit of time for advocates to become aware of the form; meanwhile, people were signing it because they were told they had to in order to get their cheques for food and rent. Advocates across the province were outraged. A court case was launched arguing that the form violated the Canadian Charter of Rights and Freedoms. A provincial coalition, 'federated anti-poverty groups of BC,' produced a revocation form for people on welfare to sign if they felt they had been coerced into signing the government form. The provincial government did eventually modify the form somewhat. In the meantime, the PovNet discussion group became a quick route for advocates to know what was going on in different parts of the province.

Two organizations, End Legislated Poverty and the Downtown Eastside Women's Centre, are currently involved in a national campaign to prevent the deduction of National Child Benefit Supplements from families' welfare payments. This is a postcard campaign with real postcards. But people will be able to send the postcards electronically, too, via links from the PovNet web page.

Member organizations of PovNet are also taking test cases to court to challenge anti-panhandling laws in municipalities throughout Canada and to defend "squeegie kids"—young people who are getting arrested as they wash car windows at red lights to make money. PovNet provides the links for advocates to keep up to date with these cases.

COMMUNICATION

PovNet currently facilitates five e-mail lists on the topics of workers compensation, unemployment insurance, welfare, housing, and mental health issues. Specific lists about women and poverty, First Nations and aboriginal issues, and lists in languages other than English are pending. Advocates using the e-mail lists represent women, Aboriginal and First Nations communities, homeless people, injured and unemployed workers, poor people, people with disabilities, and others. Several of the groups are co-facilitated by community advocates. The PovNet office provides a central place and a person for people to call to find out why their message didn't get posted, why they can't get online, and why the filtering system we set up on the phone together the day before suddenly doesn't work.

EDUCATION AND TRAINING

I use the word "education" more these days when I talk about learning, because someone pointed out to me recently that people with money get educated, but poor people get trained. Education and training is a big part of PovNet. British Columbia is a large and diverse province. In the north, communities are small and spread out; in some, there are still no phone lines, and in others, getting on the Internet involves long-distance charges.

As well as doing a great deal of educating and training over the telephone, I spent a lot of the first three years of the project travelling around the province and visiting advocates where their computers were. Sometimes this was in a community centre; sometimes in someone's home. Invariably, there was not a dedicated line to the Internet; groups were using fax lines or phone lines, so sessions had to be scheduled at the beginning or end of the day.

I discovered lots of practical details early on. For example, there's not much point doing a training session at a high-tech computer lab, and then finding out that a group is dealing with a 386 and a 14.4 modem. But, more importantly, there always needs to be a human face attached to the technology. That way, when I get back to Vancouver (where the PovNet office is housed), people know they can call. And they know that, when problems arise, there are no stupid questions and that it is *always* the computer's fault, never theirs.

THE WEB PAGE

The PovNet web page is the public presence of the project. All of the information on the page is designed from the point of view of the needs of the advocate. The page contains local up-to-date information about B.C. government policies and community initiatives, as well as international events that involve Canadian advocates (for example, the United Nations Human Rights Committee meeting in Geneva, links to information about the World March of Women, books and other materials about poverty in Canada and internationally). At this point, the web page is directed by local information sent to the PovNet office. This will expand as PovNet moves across the country.

And when I'm travelling, I invariably give a workshop at the local library about online poverty resources. Part of PovNet's role is to create an online home for people whose starting reference point is not e-Bay.

FUTURE PLANS

We are talking to advocates across Canada and to the federal government where funding is available for "community learning networks." We are hoping to be a resource for advocates who want to set up PovNets in other parts of the country.

Future plans also include:

1. creating online resource kits with precedent forms and sample letters;
2. developing training courses for advocates;
3. providing web forums for homeless people via public access sites; and
4. creating an events calendar and discussions about law reform.

Attached to all these things, of course, are real people, showing each other how the technology works and how to make it work for them.

Conclusion

> The reality is that the 'big' issues and distinctive features of our lives are still very much those that occupied our non-networked ancestors. Charles I, on reading a declaration of his treasons, squirted down the line from Oliver Cromwell's headquarters somewhere in England during 1649, still gets to hear that he is going to lose his head. The 'defining moment' had nothing to do with the technology that brought him the message.
> —Trevor Haywood, "Global Networks and the Myth of Equality"[7]

We are not going to patch up Canada's social safety net or create a just and equal global society with e-mail lists and web pages. But we are working with activists who function in real time, not in the asynchronistic floating world of cyberspace. When an advocate at a women's centre is helping someone get a welfare cheque, she knows that the woman needs it today. When someone has been turned down for welfare in a small rural community in northern B.C., that person knows that the local advocate, often working out of his home, will help right away. And the advocate knows that he can connect with others who are doing the same work in different parts of the province to get advice and suggestions.

PovNet works because community anti-poverty advocates have no illusions about technology. But we can use online space to communicate with one another as long as we have access to it and know how to use it.

To get to the PovNet web page, see *http://www.povnet.web.ca.* To e-mail PovNet, contact povnet@web.ca.

NOTES

1   Franklin, Ursula. (1996). *Every Tool Shapes the Task: Communities and the Information Highway.* Vancouver: Lazara Press.
2   I tend to use lower case for internet deliberately to make a point that it is not actually a place or a person.
3   Angus Reid. (1998, January) *Internet Survey for Information, Science and Technology Agency.* Government of British Columbia.
4   Townson, Monica. (2000, April) *A Report Card on Women and Poverty.* Ottawa: CCPA.
5   Day, Shelagh and Gwen Brodsky. (1999). *Women and the Equality Deficit: The Impact of Restructuring Canada's Social Programs.* Ottawa: Status of Women Canada.
6   http://corpwatch.org
7   Haywood, Trevor. (1998) "Global Networks and the Myth of Equality" in *Cyberspace Divide: Equality, Agency and Policy in the Information Society.* N.Y., London: Routledge.

Networking Community, Not Technology: Informing Development Choices In New Ways

Garth Graham

I believe it is the responsibility of any civilized society to ensure human dignity to all members and to offer each individual the best opportunity to reveal his or her creativity. Let us remember that poverty is not created by the poor but by the institutions and policies that we, the better off, have established. We can solve the problem not by means of the old concepts but by adopting radical new ones.[1]

—*Muhammad Yunus, The Grameen Bank*

INTRODUCTION

DURING MY FORMER WORK WITH THE NATIONAL GRASSROOTS ELECTRONIC COMMUNITY networking association, Telecommunities Canada, I came to realize that, when we globalize, we also localize. When the middle disappears, communities stay. Governments, as we know them now, change. I am now in Vietnam, but regardless of what county we are in, we need to design this awareness as part of the default settings.

This essay grew out of a presentation made to a workshop on changing planning methods in Vietnam.[2] The workshop was an initial step toward drafting a national information technology strategy for 2001-2005. Although it is therefore a product of the Vietnam-Canada Information Technology Project, it is very much a personal expression. It should not be considered to reflect the official views of the Project, Government of Vietnam, or CIDA. My Vietnamese colleagues have referred to it as "philosophy" and I accept that classification with thanks. Policy as an expression of peace, order and good government is much more a matter of values than of economics.

WHEN WE GET TO 2005, WHAT CAPACITY WILL WE NEED TO DO INFORMATION TECHNOLOGY POLICY?"

The Vietnam–Canada Information Technology Project (VCIT) supports Vietnam's capacity to use information technology policies for its development. That is to say, we do not view IT policy as an end in itself. We seek to understand how IT policy serves strategic national purposes. The outcomes of the project have more to do with the results of the policies to shape the environment in which technologies are applied and less to do with the technologies themselves. At the moment, VCIT is supporting a group that is drafting the new national 5-year strategic plan for the use of information technology, 2001 to 2005. But just what does the capacity to create and apply information technology policy actually require?

When expecting visits of Canadian policy experts to Hanoi, I am often advised, "They must just tell us their experience and we'll adapt it to Vietnam. The experience comes from outside. The initiative comes from inside." That consistent advice reveals a Vietnamese intention to contain an alarming Canadian propensity to rush toward dialogue, just as if open dialogue was a normal first step in establishing personal relations. But their concern restates an essential principle of sustainable capacity building. Appropriate external intervention should facilitate local action, not initiate it.

Today, I hope, in keeping with that principle, I'm going to share both my experience of doing information technology policy, and my sense of how the capacities required to do that are changing in both Canada and Vietnam. Since that requires a deeper understanding than I actually have of the Vietnamese context in which social, economic and political change occurs, I hope I don't succeed in demonstrating merely the opposite—that "participant observation" is an oxymoron.

My "online" experience is that everything conventionally assumed to be true about information technology policy can and should be very carefully questioned. My sense of the factors driving changes in the capacity to do information technology policy is that the role of leadership awareness is greatly exaggerated. When we look back from 2005, we will see that the significant changes in our understanding will have been driven by our experience of changing patterns in daily life.

One lesson learned from the VCIT Project is that the capacity to think about the uses of information technology for development is an essential part of a national development strategy. VCIT supports Vietnam's uses of information technology policy formulation to act as levers that influence other beneficial development results. This requires a group of people with the ability to synthesize the high-level lessons learned from exercising that influence and to feed back messages that then dynamically change the policy formulation system. Often, we get so involved in the details of policy formulation and implementation that we forget to do the feedback.

The location of responsibility in the Government of Vietnam for national information technology policy formulation has recently moved from the former independent Steering Committee for the National Program on Information Technology to a new Information Technology Management Agency in the Ministry of Science, Technology and the Environment. Because of plans for government restructuring, we don't know if this "transition" of responsibility will have moved again by the year 2005. But we do know that a transition is necessary. In every country, many things affecting information technology policy responsibility are changing rapidly. Because of its former isolation, this is particularly true in Vietnam.

Today, I'm going to talk about four factors that affect policy formulation capacity:

1. *Asking good questions:* different ways of thinking about the questions that information technology policy must address.
2. *An alternative model of change*: new ways of thinking about the consequences of living in a political economy of ideas (or, if you must describe it that way, the "knowledge based economy," although I've never been comfortable with that concept).
3. *Anticipating the future of policy:* measuring the content of current issues in information technology policy in Vietnam against the picture I intend to draw of doing information technology policy in an online society. Are current policy pre-occupations a useful guide for anticipating the problems that information technology policy makers will face in the future?
4. *Survival rules*: concluding with a summary of rules of thumb for surviving daily life online, some "life lessons" based on my experience.

ASKING GOOD QUESTIONS

Where you look for answers depends on the questions you ask. I am going to begin by outlining some concepts that should challenge policy makers to think about the role of IT policy in different ways. These include:

> A. THE SOCIAL, ECONOMIC AND POLITICAL IMPACTS OF GLOBAL NETWORKING;
>
> B. A FRAMEWORK FOR UNDERSTANDING THE THINKING OF VARIOUS TYPES OF IT POLICY PEOPLE; AND
>
> C. A "MAP" OF ONLINE SOCIETY.

A. Global Networking Impacts

The transition from agricultural to industrial economies caused fundamental political realignments. The transition from an industrial economy to a digital economy is also causing fundamental realignments.[3] Global networks:

- reduce the power of nation states
- destabilize élites
- transform work and daily life
- change how people identify themselves
- form ruthless entrepreneurial environments that disrupt the power of big corporations
- cause spontaneous communities of interest, not geography, to bloom.

So far, because it is not yet online,[4] the society inside Vietnam remains isolated from these impacts. But its external relations are shifting rapidly to take these changes into account. For example, the integration of Vietnam into the telecommunications infrastructure of its neighbors in South East Asia necessitated active participation by Vietnam in regional efforts to address Y2K telecommunications network problems.

B. Finding a Middle Way in the Attitudes of IT Policy Makers

Richard Heeks,[5] University of Manchester, developed the framework below:

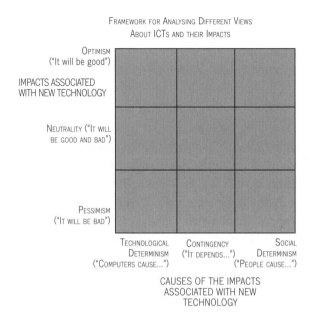

FRAMEWORK FOR ANALYSING DIFFERENT VIEWS
ABOUT ICTS AND THEIR IMPACTS

OPTIMISM
("It will be good")

IMPACTS ASSOCIATED
WITH NEW TECHNOLOGY

NEUTRALITY ("IT WILL
BE GOOD AND BAD")

PESSIMISM
("IT WILL BE BAD")

TECHNOLOGICAL   CONTINGENCY   SOCIAL
DETERMINISM   ("IT DEPENDS...")   DETERMINISM
("COMPUTERS CAUSE...")   ("PEOPLE CAUSE...")

CAUSES OF THE IMPACTS
ASSOCIATED WITH NEW
TECHNOLOGY

The framework provides a way of analyzing the claims made by IT policy-makers and people involved in technology transfer projects. When we can classify their point of view, we can better assess the value of the advice they give. Both Heeks and I fear optimistic technological determinism. Policy development is inherently political, not technical. The fact that the content of policy debate is concerned with appropriate trade-offs in the use of technology does not change this. Keeping Heeks' framework in mind, we can assess biases that may colour the views of those who profess to decide things for us.

For example, how many of us believe that technology in itself is the key to reducing inequality in the global economy? U.S. President Bill Clinton does. He says, "How can we continue to grow the economy? You can bring investment into places that are left behind. I think we should shoot for a goal with the developing countries of having Internet access as complete as telephone access within a fixed number of years. It will do as much as anything else to reduce income inequality."[6] In terms of the Heeks framework, President Clinton is clearly an optimistic believer in technological determinism. If he is commenting on your national IT policy, you might like to take his viewpoint into account even if you agree with it.

Here's a second example. This is David Crane, economics editor for the *Toronto Star*, commenting on changes in the education policies of the Conservative government of the Province of Ontario. "Education and knowledge are the primary sources of economic growth. The knowledge-based economy is about people . . . Investment and growth will go only to where the educated and skilled people are found."[7] In Heeks' terms, David Crane can be seen as an optimist, but also as a social determinist. He sees people's actions, not technology, as the primary cause of change.

Heeks notes that "ICT fetishists have so far been unable to demonstrate how ICT-based information represents a more important resource than water, food, land, shelter, production technology, money, skills or power in the development process."[8] He also notes that the indigenous knowledge systems of poor communities are being systematically ignored and overridden. He makes good points. A balanced approach to formulating IT policy must accept that: there are both good and bad impacts; and that the causes, the factors influencing those impacts, are complex. But, even if I did get labelled an "ICT fetishist" by Heeks, I am going to insist that becoming informed, not "ICT-based information," is, in fact, a basic need. When you hold that view, you cannot ignore the fact that every social network has an "indigenous" knowledge system.

The goal of IT policy-makers must be to centre themselves in the middle zone of that framework, the box where neutrality and contingency converge.

C. Seeing the structure of online society

The majority of people in Vietnam have no experience of making daily use of the Internet. Many of them desire to do so as soon as possible, in spite of a concern that it will have a negative effect on social and cultural values. Many have heard that it is an information system, a communications system, and that it is "interactive." But those concepts don't help them imagine how it feels to inhabit the Internet as a "place." Only by being "hands-on" can you experience the liquidity of the many new online communities and the positive opportunities to structure social and economic interactions that the Internet's vastness creates.

Here is a map[9] that portrays, in a graphic way, the sense of how social networks structure relationships in an online society. If you think of this as an organization chart, it does not resemble the organization charts used to describe Vietnamese institutions. Although the World Wide Web has hundreds of millions of pages, this map shows the links between merely hundreds of pages.

The map was drawn by software called "Clever" that analyzes how particular kinds of web pages, authorities and hubs are linked together. Authorities are sites that other web pages frequently link to on a particular topic. Hubs

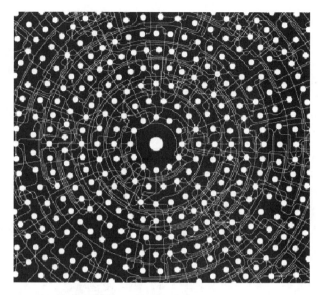

are sites that happen to cite many authorities. This underlying pattern emerges because individuals make millions of decisions to create pages with links and thousands of decisions to link authorities and hubs. Zones in the overall pattern define "communities of interest." These communities grow themselves. That is to say, they are self-organizing. They are not planned.

Another example of a self-organizing community that forms a new social zone within the Internet is the worldwide group of programmers who voluntarily participate in the dynamic evolution of the open operating system called Linux.

You might think that all graphic maps of the current structure of social organizations and communities in Vietnam would always look different from the one that emerges from tracking links on the World Wide Web. But, in fact, there are analogies to self-organizing systems within Vietnamese society; the flow pattern of bicycle and motorcycle traffic on city streets, the shape of rice paddy terraces around mountain farms, the commercial distribution systems for food from rural areas to urban neighborhoods. Such analogies may be useful in assisting IT policy-makers to begin thinking about future social and economic changes in a different way.

An Alternative Model of Change

If we are to assist IT policy-makers to think about future social and economic changes in a different way, we must get them to ask: is there a model of change that fits with that map of online society? If a model was not based on

technological or social determinism, what would it look like? We need a model
that is:

- contingent on the complex self-organized links and experiences of transactions in an online society;
- based on an understanding of how individuals and communities actually
  learn within that society; and
- dynamic and organic, rather than "engineered."

Here are three principles, based on the experience of Telecommunities
Canada, the national voluntary organization of the online community networking movement in Canada,[10] that begin to structure such a model.

A. TECHNOLOGY IS THE WAY WE DO THINGS
B. THE COMMUNITY IS THE NETWORK, NOT THE TECHNOLOGY
C. NOW WE MAKE OUR NETWORKS AND OUR NETWORKS MAKE US

A. Technology is the way we do things

Underlying the first principle of the Telecommunities Canada change
model is the idea that you should carefully examine your assumptions about
the concept "technology." Canadian senior scientist Dr. Ursula Franklin, in a
speech about the impact of the Internet on society, defined technology as "the
way that things are done around here."[11] She defined technology as practice
rather than focusing on the tools themselves as objects. Such a process definition lets you see that the tools in a culture and the way those tools are used tell
you something about the nature of that culture. A set of "technologies" is, in
and of itself, a kind of information system.

When we can imagine a different "way of doing," whole new ranges of
tools will begin to express that difference. The emergence of new technologies
tells a story about the way the culture that produced them is changing. That is
to say, they are a symptom of the change, not a primary cause of it. This is a
point that technological determinists resist accepting. As a communications
technology, the Internet is a symptom of a changed way of seeing, not the cause
of it. Looking at what people do with new ways of connecting to each other,

and how that alters their relationships provides a view of the new culture of society online.

Accepting that definition of technology and its consequences, then what are its implications for national IT policy? It has to be more about understanding social and economic change than it is about causing it. This shifts an appropriate response to the expression "just share your experience and then we'll adapt it" into an entirely different context. Seeing technology transfer as the communication of practices and behaviors that are embedded in cultural perspectives ensures that we will not be underestimating the difficulty of obtaining the necessary "skills" that successful use requires. It should also ensure, but rarely does, that we begin to design the new systems with a careful exploration of intentions in order to discover common values.

B. The community is the network, not the technology

To avoid IT policy formulation based simply on technological determinism, it is essential to remember that networks are inherently social. We are connecting or linking people to people, not machines to machines. If pessimists exclaim that our communications systems isolate people, we might then ask ourselves: are they right? Are we merely designing systems that connect people to the machines rather than through the machines to each other?

That map illustrates a significant difference in community online. The online context specifically enhances self-organizing processes in social networks. But, at the same time, it gives hugely enhanced access for its participants to the rules that structure it. Everybody "on" a system now knows what that system knows. Because of this inherent characteristic of dynamic self-organizing systems, people own the communities they inhabit in a powerful new way. This has one interesting impact. What would formerly have been seen by the business that supplied it as merely its "market" is now being revealed as a community of interest that is owned by the consumers that demand it.

Many online communities come alive fast, and die young, but in their brief span those communities behave more coherently in relation to their social ecologies than traditional communities of place. Each member's actions are transparently linked to the pattern of collective behaviour, so the accountability for responsibility is explicit and revealed. The community as self-organizing dynamic system can shift its rules and remain coherent. The equilibrium of open and dynamic systems is not an absolute or a stable state. Every community is always continuously emerging out of a wider context of social networks, and it sustains itself in interaction with that wider context.

In North America, grassroots community networking associations synthesize and share the experience of creating and sustaining community online. They are advocates and practitioners of community development online. The basis of their practices is the way in which electronic networks assist and sustain the emergence of communities as self-organizing systems.

C. Now we make our networks and our networks make us

But I would be guilty of the alternative sin of social determinism if I simply told you that "the community is the network," and left it at that. The tools, the way of doing, and the social networks within which the doing gets done, intertwine. When people make and use new tools, they change the world, and that changes them. When you connect to networks in new ways, you can only do so by changing your "way of doing things." In anthropology, this process is called acculturation. We cannot give you our experience as if it were an object or a tool. We have to understand your context —your way of doing— before we have anything of value to share. We know, if we share, we'll be changed in the process. That's called learning.

ASSUMPTIONS ABOUT THE NATURE OF INFORMATION

Now I want to explore the idea of information as property. If the first look at a different change model begins with carefully examining our assumptions about technology, the second look begins with carefully examining our assumptions about information. The key product of a knowledge-based economy is ideas, not information as a commodity.

Governments cannot tax ideas. Global corporations can't really control ideas. This makes both of them very nervous. So they both insist on the enforcement of copyright laws. Copyright is based on an abstract notion that ideas can be considered as private property. But, historically, that notion was only half of the concept of copyright. The other half had nothing to do with the current emphasis on private gain. The laws were enacted for the public good of rewarding people for sharing knowledge about their way of doing things, rather than keeping it secret. It was philosophically sloppy, but pragmatically useful.

When you begin to focus on changing practices, on the way we do things, your thinking shifts to learning, informing, and knowing as verbs, rather than on information or knowledge as things, as nouns or as property that can be owned. Changing the way we do things or the way we see things—that is to say, the way we become informed—is not the same thing as managing a scarce resource. Our new political economy of ideas has some very strange new rules, and one of them is that use of information does not consume it. Attempting to control access to information as if it were property or a scarce resource stops innovation, profiting some at the expense of the many.

A recent Microsoft ad illustrates the consequences of the global corporate belief that information is property. It re-states a classic proverb about the nature of development.

> *"Give a man a fish, he eats for a day.*
> *Teach a man to fish, he eats for a lifetime.*
> *Enlighten him further, he owns a chain of seafood restaurants.*
> *....Where do you want to go today?"*

Where indeed! For Bill Gates, the end result of enlightenment is that practice knowledge gets turned into a commodity. If the proverb is re-written to make clear the dynamic systems view of how the connecting processes of social networks inform relationships in communities of interest, it might read like this:

> *"Give a man a fish, he eats for a day.*
> *Teach a man to fish, he eats until the fish stocks collapse.*
> *Enlighten his understanding of the system in which he,*
> *his neighbors, and the fish stocks interact,*
> *and the eating of all three will be sustained forever."*

RURAL FARMERS AS DECISION-MAKERS:[12] APPLYING THE CHANGE MODEL IN VIETNAM

Influencing the choices that people can make is a powerful means of breaking free from cycles of poverty. Remembering that information is a verb, not a noun, provides a way to link IT policy and the design of projects for poverty alleviation in a new and direct way.

VCIT supports a project involving the Interministerial Centre for Spatial Applications (CAIS) of the Ministry of Agriculture and Rural Development and Radarsat International (RSI) to produce a Rice Crop Monitoring System as a pilot Geographic Information System database. The model of rice crop production combines Radarsat images of the Mekong Delta and crop production modeling software called "Agroma." In the first workshop on project results, September 1999, Dr Cu of CIAS was using the slide below to discuss the future uses of the model in decision making.

The inset photo on the left is a satellite image of the Mekong test area and the inset photo on the right shows combined field crops of flowers and rice. Since I had been with Dr Cu when he took the crop photo, I knew that the farmer had said, "I can make more money growing flowers than rice." When I noted this, the workshop decided that his slide should include what I've added here, "Rural producers are decision-makers, too."

Looking at development from the point of view of those who are being "developed," their key problem is knowing what to do next when the cost of making a wrong choice is extremely high. Becoming informed about the choices they can make can improve their daily living. Taking that view during development project design and implementation would turn the focus away from the information technology itself and toward information use and the processes that inform.

The geographic information system data analyzed by AGROMA is not really a model of rice crops. It is a model of human behavior in land use. To create the model in the first place, the project staff had to "ground-truth" the satellite images by referencing them against site visits to sample by direct observation what the image actually displays.

But, if you must ground truth to produce the image, you must also ground truth later to prove the utility of its use. If you share the results of the model with the people whose behaviour it models, they will do two things. They will provide you with new information that then changes the model. If it's a good model, one that fully realizes a new view of their circumstances, they will change their behaviour. The better the interaction of the model and its use to inform decision-making, the more the system of behavior that is being modelled will change. That is to say, if the model is effective, it will alter the interaction of people and the land they inhabit.

Thinking about future uses of the Rice Crop Monitoring System has led us to conclude that classic methods of community-based or participatory rural development should be incorporated into any follow-up project. The concept would be to share information about choices and about the results of changes, not to focus on GIS hardware or analysis software or particular information technologies. In this manner, we may discover what happens when we inform people's choices in a different way.

The design of such an agricultural information network for farmers would need to begin with an essential first step, an "information system" analysis stage. In participatory rural development, it is necessary to understand the system that exists before external intervention begins. That we are considering "information" systems as interventions, in fact, intensifies this need. There is going to be an existing "indigenous" knowledge system that informs rural producers in their rice growing and marketing behaviours, and we will not understand very much about our potential impact unless we go and look at it.

There is one more way that the concept represents a new potential. If you think about systems that inform decision- making as "top-down" or "bottom-up," you are modelling behaviour in a linear way. But the patterns of people's behaviour that emerge in social network interactions are dynamic. In the same manner as the web communities' map, dynamic systems organize themselves. Their patterns of organization reveal "rules" that are internal, not externally imposed. They are "self-organizing."

Improving their ability to self-organize is easy. Just increase the feedback loops. Then the people in the system become more aware of the consequences of their mutual interactions and they modify their behavior accordingly.[13] In effect, what we propose to do next is an analogy to the individual decisions to establish "links" on the World Wide Web. We propose to ground-truth the model in the dynamic way that human behaviour actually operates.

To sound a final note of caution, such a model is not intended to predict what they will do. That is impossible. We are merely trying to inform what they do differently. We can connect together the parts of rural development communications systems in different ways. So then those systems themselves begin to "think" or behave in different ways. Then people can know about their development choices in different ways, hopefully better ways, resulting in better choices. But, whether the choices are good or bad, the responsibility for the consequences of those choices remains, as it should be, theirs.

ANTICIPATING THE FUTURE OF POLICY

Four scenarios

Is the current information technology policy environment in Vietnam a useful way of anticipating the problems that information technology policy-makers will face in the future? As Mr. Heeks said, "It depends." In this case, I'm going to suggest that it depends on how the interaction of two key factors governs the attitudes of those people who will shape the policies. So far, in describing what influences the doing of information technology policy in an online society, I have stated that:
• Global networks will cause fundamental political re-alignments.
• Policy-makers must balance a range of factors in their understanding of

the cause and impacts of changing uses of information technologies.

- The shape of online society is best seen as an organic structure of self-organizing communities of interest.
- Technology is not tools, but practice: the way we do things.
- Information is not a noun, it's a verb, and therefore the real goal for the use of information technology in development should be informing choices, not creating information systems.

In the chart below, I've summarized these ideas along two dimensions:

- In the vertical dimension, the question is: will policy- makers be governed in their thinking by seeing the parts or the whole of the development dilemma? Will they split development projects into specific sectors or functional programs, or will they be more broadly focused on the lumps of results and outcomes that occur in attempting any new actions for social change? In effect, to what degree will they consider the context of a problem and the value of addressing it rather than just the problem itself? The question is important because, in society online, anything can link to anything and often does. The complexity of factors attempting to ignore or reconfigure sector boundaries will overwhelm those that try to maintain them.
- In the horizontal design dimension, the question is: do they see themselves as constructing machines or as realizing dynamic relationships? The question is important because, in society online, the "rationalist" must find a way of abandoning mechanistic predictability as a goal. An online society organically learns and re-learns its way into unpredictable configurations. It does not "build" them.

FOUR SCENARIOS:
FUTURES AFFECTING IT POLICY PLANNING

SPLIT or LUMP:
Sector or program driven

NEED FOR CONTROL RESULTS IN FOCUS ON IT APLICATIONS IN SECTORS	THE VCIT-SC/NPIT ZONE TRANSITIONAL CONFLICT ENROUTE TO LEARNING SYSTEMS

DESIGN: ENGINEER   GROW DYANMIC
MECHANISTIC CLOSED SYSTEMS ———————————————————— OPEN SYSTEMS

HIGH TECH SOLUTIONS TRANSITIONAL CONFLICT TO KEEP THINGS CLOSED	NEED TO INTEGRATE CAUSES POLICIES SUPPORTING ADAPTATION AND LEARNING

BROAD FOCUS ON
SOCIO-ECONOMIC IMPACTS

Control!:

Vietnam in 2005 could have a policy environment governed by program splitters who view the technology as a solution rather than a means to an end. That would be a future of strong technocrats whose needs for efficiency, for control, and for predictability of outcomes cause them to narrowly focus on information technology applications within carefully defined sectors. In this scenario, the risk of picking the wrong applications is extreme.

High tech solutions:

In this scenario, Vietnam "leapfrogs" backward into industrial society rather than going "fast-forward" into an online society. Vietnam in 2005 could have a policy environment governed by technocrats whose commitment to an optimistic technological determinism is weaker than in the control scenario. Their actions would be tempered by some concern to understand the social, economic and political consequences. It would be easier to effect change in this scenario than in the control scenario, but the tension between the demands to adapt to an online society and the demands to achieve an out-of-step industrial society would increase the level of conflict produced by the changes.

The essential purpose for having a national capacity to do IT policy is to discover and communicate fundamental processes of social, economic and political change that result from the interaction of technology and society. The design of the systems that apply what is ordinarily called "high technology"[14] must have simplicity as a goal. If not, they risk being "half-way technology" instead of high technology. Simple solutions cost less, but require profound understanding to achieve. Profound understanding comes from a mix of both insight and innovation, from the continuous process of better, faster, cheaper. It comes from a conscious intention to change "the way things are done around here." Half-way solutions, because of waste in their creation and inefficiency in their use, are incredibly expensive, far more expensive than a developing country can afford.

Transitional conflict:

Vietnam in 2005 could have a policy environment governed by program splitters with some understanding of the necessity of moving toward the growth of dynamic open systems. That would be a future of social determinists with a perception of the need to modernize Vietnam as a learning society. But it would tend to view Vietnam as on the road to an industrial society with an information technology sector that supports the introduction to a market economy. This is, in effect, a "more of the same" scenario, growing out of the experience of the Steering Committee for the National Program on Information Technology. There would still be differing agendas for change. But the conflict would tend to be about options to open outwards rather than, as in the high yech solutions scenario, to keep things closed.

Integrate:

Vietnam in 2005 could have a policy environment governed by a holistic necessity to adapt to an online society. These policy-makers would balance neutrality of beliefs on good and bad information technology impacts, with contingent views about their causes. They would be comfortable with the idea that online communities of interest self-organize, and that informing systems of poverty differently enables the individuals trapped within them to make choices in a different way. The need to integrate with new structures internally and externally would result in an accelerated adaptation of Vietnam's traditional reactive isolation into a new mode of interactive participation.

FITTING IT STRATEGY TO NATIONAL DEVELOPMENT STRATEGIES

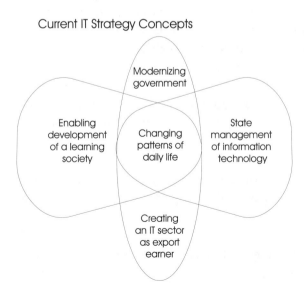

Current IT Strategy Concepts

Modernizing government

Enabling development of a learning society

Changing patterns of daily life

State management of information technology

Creating an IT sector as export earner

Here are some of the concepts that seem to be driving discussions of the strategic role of information technology policy in Vietnam's official strategies for development.

New technologies are the carrier wave of a signal about new ideas and about changes in the way that things get done. In Vietnam, the code word that allows for indirect discussion of changes in the way things are done is "renovation." In development, the code word that allows for indirect discussion of changes in the way politics are done is "governance." The wide-scale acceptance of new information technologies, as evidenced by their use, sends a signal about massive realignments in the structural connections of society, economics and politics. If you can read that signal, you have a different way of understanding both reform and processes of change in governance.

Near the beginning, I stated that where we look for answers depends on the questions we ask. If we explore these current strategy concepts by asking questions based on them, are they good questions? Some of them are, and some of them are not. Again, it depends. In addressing the four questions below, I am of course setting up my own targets. But I do so in order to find a way to examine what I suspect are some underlying assumptions.

1. Can the state actually *manage* the strategic use of IT for development?

    Accepting my description of the dynamic factors structuring society online, obviously my personal answer to the question as asked is: no, it cannot. While you can apply management principles to the operation of an information or communications system, you cannot predict the impact of its use on the environment it serves. While there can be "management" of the large-scale application of systems within specific services, the impact of those systems on reconfiguring the delivery of public services overall will be learned, not managed. Also, I suspect that such a question assumes that information technology policy is merely a subset of technology policy.

    2. Who sustains capacity to *think* about the use of IT for development of Vietnam as a learning society; what do they need; and how would they apply what they learned?

    This question assumes that information technology policy is inherently socioeconomic policy and, while neutral on impacts, is driven by social determinism.

3. How does Vietnam develop a set of strategies for the use of the Internet to *enhance* the quality of daily life?

This does sound like a question that seeks for contingent causes. But I suspect that such a question begs a second question. Does the questioner assume that information technology policy plays a minor or major role in effective development policy? If I am correct that changes in technology reflect and are a consequence of underlying changes in society, then a development process that cannot read that message is operating blindly. As the interconnections that affect daily living become increasingly complex, having the means to remain informed about the consequences of emerging networking phenomenon should be viewed as a basic function of the capacity to design development strategies.

4. Are there technologies that *inform* our abilities to make personal and community choices in different and more effective ways?

Remembering that technology is really a symptom of culture change processes, of changes in the way we do things around here, this is closer to a real contingent question. Good policy formulation questions take us out of our comfort zone and into the unknown. Can we see our dilemma and its challenges differently? Can we change the way we do things? If our networks and our choices become different, can we—or how can we—accept the degree to which we become different? Does the risk of error remain so great that we prefer to stay trapped in a cycle of poverty? Does a shadow still fall on the gap between becoming informed and acting on what we now know?

SURVIVING DAILY LIFE ONLINE

I hope that you are all still with me, at least to the degree that this very personal view of the consequences of living in a political economy of ideas gives you pause for thought. I'm going to conclude with a few ideas about how acting within this different way of doing might feel.

A Vietnamese friend, in describing Vietnam's behavior in the face of change, once told me the story of the small farmer who, seeing the gathering storm, brought everything inside and tightly locked the windows and doors. And, in the dark and thunder, he and his family waited patiently for the storm to pass, and he congratulated himself on his intelligence. Here is a better way of anticipating the storm.

I do not want my house to be walled in on all sides
and my windows to be stuffed.
I want the cultures of all the lands
to be blown about my house as freely as possible.
But I refuse to be blown off my feet by any.

Mahatma Gandhi

If Gandhi was confident that he could, with advantage, let the "cultures of all the lands" blow freely about his house without being blown off his feet, why should we accept any less? We have to understand each other's context—our ways of doing—before we have anything of value to share. We know, if we share, we'll be changed in the process. But we may without fear call that process "learning" when we have a sense that the choice of receiving the cultural winds full strength was our own.

It is impossible to use planning to make the future predictable. But, if you must, you can use planning as a means of deciding which of thousands of possible outcomes is the most useful to attempt. Anticipating the future is not about predicting the future. It is about deciding what you want to do and why. Ultimately, the heart of that task is not about society, or economy or politics. It's about values. What do I need? What do I want? What do I care about? Whether the possibilities are broad or narrow, what commitments or responsibilities will flow from my choices?

Based on my experience, here follows some very personal rules of thumb for crossing the digital divide into the online world of 2005. Vietnamese culture places great emphasis on the values that shape a person of good character. These rules of thumb describe the behavior of a person of good character in a digital world. Adaptation to them will challenge a Vietnamese sense of integrity in very complex ways.

Seven rules of thumb for surviving daily life online:

1. Systems that inform choice increase equity and social justice. In designing them, avoid the nouns information and knowledge. Prefer the verbs to inform and to know.
2. Real learning is discovery. Tell your own story. Act on your own knowledge. Let no one control or commodify the expression of your identity.

3. In resource economies, reality and ideology will always be in conflict. In an economy of ideas, reality is optional. Imagine that!
4. Local is the other side of global. When the middle disappears, think local.
5. Communities do not create content. They are the content.
6. Ignore technocracy and ideology. Understand conventional wisdom so that you can do the opposite. Make choices based on understanding changes in daily life as if you were learning to live in a new culture.
7. A knowledge-based society is closed. A learning society is open because it increases autonomy and cooperation at the same time. Do not isolate. Always connect.

When facing external interventions, Vietnam has centuries of experience in practising a particular kind of cultural adaptation. It adds layers of complexity, Buddhism, Taoism and Confucianism, for example, to an unaltered substratum of the animism of village life. Vietnam expects to do the same with the fundamental materialism of Western thought. And in fact, in the yin and yang of communism and capitalism, it already has years of experience of accommodating one-half of that thought. However, I believe it is risky to assume that information technology is merely another manifestation of Western materialism.

The shift to a market-based economy is not the most significant change in Vietnam's future. Both the developing and developed economies are all at the same stage of adapting to a profound cultural shift. They are all becoming digital. Digital is liquid. Don't plan. Float.

A true capacity to formulate information technology policy would sustain an evolving means of understanding the economic, political and social impacts of the changing uses of information technologies. Most countries do not attempt to have such a comprehensive national capacity. Instead, they narrowly define information technology policy as part of policy for science, or for technology in general, or for economic development. In the Socialist Republic of Vietnam, it would be unusual if the present attempt to develop such a comprehensive capacity was not sustained.

The culture shift that information technology symptomatically foretells is the one that is superseding Western materialism. The "ism" in question doesn't really have a name yet. But, whatever its name, its philosophy faces directly the consequences of understanding the "meaning" inherent in knowing that Western materialism ignores. It is an expression of a way of doing things and a relational way of seeing things that departs significantly from the automatic atomism of the previous 2000 years of Western methods and practices. It allows indigenous knowledge systems to flow together and apart at will.

As Vietnam contemplates how best to accommodate yet another layer of cultural complexity, while still protecting its essential being, it might usefully assist its planning to consider that it is facing not one but two new cultural traditions. And, for the one that's about becoming digital, any nation's guess is as good as another's.

The emerging social structure of a political economy of ideas is not the same as that of an industrial economy. The experience of online communities of interest is in advance of what businesses and governments understand to be occurring. Businesses and governments believe that the present society goes online as is. They see the citizens of industrial economies as passive "consumers" of services, not as active extensions of the self into a dynamic and alterable set of communications systems. But seeing daily life online clearly is not just a question of understanding a problem of "access to services." It is a question of understanding alterations to daily life as it is lived.

In the mass markets of the industrial economy, socialization to social norms is thought of as a process that is external to the individual. But integration into online communities is a matter both of individual choice and of responsibility. The individuals create their networks and, in turn, their networks create them. But they do have much more choice because their choice has become de-institutionalized. For the poor, becoming better informed about the choices they can make increases the possibilities they have for improving their daily living on their own. Taking that view in the design of development projects that use IT turns the focus away from the information technology itself and toward information use and the processes that inform. The real goal for the use of information technology in development should be, not creating information systems, but informing choices.

NOTES

1   Muhammad Yunus. (1999). "The Grameen Bank." *Scientific American*, November. p. 119.

2   Seminar on Current Planning Methodologies, Vietnam-Canada Information Technology Project, Vietnamese Executing Agency, MOSTE, Hanoi, December 10, 1999.

3   "Liberty.com: politics and Silicon Valley." *The Economist*, October 30, 1999, 23-24, 28.

4   Citizen access to the Internet in Vietnam began in 1997. Currently, out of 76 million people, there are only approximately 45,000 registered Internet accounts. The impact of the Internet on daily living in Vietnam is a secondary consequence of global integration, not a primary factor in the personal experience of ordinary citizens. All forecasts of Internet growth in Vietnam conservatively anticipate a slow growth. I do not believe this is what will happen. Because of the convergence of descending bandwidth costs with a certain threshold of use, there will be a takeoff point beyond which growth will explode.

5   Richard Heeks. (1999). *Information and Communication Technologies, Poverty and Development.* Paper No. 5, Development Informatics Working Paper Series. Institute for Development Policy and Management, University of Manchester, June. p. 14. http://www.man.ac.uk/idpm/idpm_dp.htm#devinf_wp

6   President Bill Clinton speaking at the Third Way Summit, Florence, November 21, 1999. *Toronto Globe and Mail*, November 22, 1999, A13.

7   David Crane. (1999). "Harris must learn to support education." *Toronto Star*, November 21, A17.

8   Heeks. (1999) p.16.

9   The Clever Project, IBM Almaden Research Center. (1999) "Hypersearching the web." *Scientific American*, June. p. 55. http://www.sciam.com/1999/0699issue/0699raghavanbox1.html

10 www.tc.ca

11 Ursula Franklin. "Beyond the hype: thinking about the information highway." Address, Breakfast on the Hill Seminars, Social Science Federation of Canada.
"It is important to me to define technology and to say that technology, in my definition, is practice. Technology is, essentially, the way we do things. It is quite clear that many of the human tasks of providing shelter, food, guidance and order have not changed throughout history, however, how we provide food, shelter, health and housing has changed profoundly. The way we do things – which today involves, of course, machines, but also considerable knowledge and organization,

planning and management. That is what I call technology, i.e. the way that things are done around here."

12   The "Agroma Concept" graphic is borrowed and modified with permission from: Pham Van Cu and Kevin Jones, Introduction to Agroma, a powerpoint presentation made to the Workshop; RADARSAT data application on rice monitoring, Ho Chi Minh City, 21-24 September 1999. PCI Geomatics 1999.

13   "The standard scenario for economic development in a poor country calls for industrialization via investment. In this 'top-down' view, creating opportunities for employment is the only way to end poverty. But for much of the developing world, increased employment exacerbates migration from the countryside to the cities and creates low-paying jobs in miserable conditions. I firmly believe that, instead, the eradication of poverty starts with people being able to control their own fates. It is not by creating jobs that we will save the poor but rather by providing them with the opportunity to realize their own potential. Time and time again I have seen that the poor are poor not because they are lazy or untrained or illiterate but because they cannot keep the genuine returns of their labor... Self-employment may be the only solution for such people, whom our economies refuse to hire and our tax payers will not support." Muhammad Yunus. (1999). "The Grameen Bank". *Scientific American*, November, p. 119.

14   Halfway technology tries to cure existing conditions; high technology aims to prevent those conditions from ever existing. It is prophylactic rather than therapeutic. ... The point is that the aim of high technology should be to simplify, not to complicate. The true high-tech device is not the gadget with the most complicated mechanism, the most incomprehensible bells and whistles, and the most arcane operating manual. On the contrary, mature technology works on the simplest imaginable principles, which are, often as not, copied from nature, but which could only be unraveled by scientific resrearch." Hans Christian Von Baeyer. (2000) "The Lotus Effect." *The Sciences*, January-February.   p.15.

Postscript

I N THIS FINAL ARTICLE, HEATHER MENZIES OFFERS A MORE DYSTOPIAN VISION OF THE future of digital public spaces. This isn't a piece of sci-fi, although some of her (really true!) examples are chilling in their insular extremes. The erosion of public spaces and the increasing customization of our everyday lives, propelled by digitization, is reason enough for us all to heed the call of:

LOG OFF AND TURN ON!

* * * *

On Digital Public Space and the Real Tragedy of the Commons

Heather Menzies

"No one can predict the future; the future is always in motion."
(Yoda in *The Empire Strikes Back.*)

"It ain't over til it's over."
(Yogi Berra, baseball player.)

INVITED TO CHECK OUT THE FUTURE, I CAN GO FOR THE BIRD'S-EYE VIEW, PREDICTING THE lifelines of cyberspace. Or I can take the plunge, submerging myself probelike in the churn of the social backdrop. Emulating Dylan Thomas, I plunge my hand into the close, dark bag of lived particulars, groping, and grabbing on.

First, it's the squeegee kids in Toronto, New York and other major cities being criminalized for having become so marginalized in their society that they live on the street eking out an existence panhandling and washing car windshields. Next, it's "Operation True Blue": the Toronto police union's telemarketing fund-raising drive in which, depending on the donation, you got a gold, silver or bronze decal to put on your windshield, a small badge of identification with the boys in blue—and their identification with you.

Both are significant for what they suggest about the growing inequalities in our society. While upscale incomes rose through the 1990s in Canada, average household incomes dropped by 10%, and the proportion of low-income young families increased by 15%.[1] In the United States, the numbers are starker still. Between the late 1970s and the late '90s, the poorest fifth of U.S. families lost 6.5% of income, while the richest fifth posted a 33.3% gain, according to the Economic Policy Institute in Washington.[2]

More significant still, these inequalities are not being viewed as a collective public concern flagged as such in the mainstream media. Rather, they are being labelled for easy identification, and individual treatment, either in passover rituals or for criminal prosecution. For the time being, therefore, I expect that the inequalities in our society will deepen. They could even intensify into a class-like polarization, and this could become the backdrop for much of everything else, including the unfolding hopes for digitally networked democracy and social justice.

Moreover, the political left, savaged by a hostile media and internal divisions, is down for the count these days, and the mainstream media so merged with the corporate mainstream that the social divide has virtually vanished from the screen of public attention. Until the grassroots social and media activism in evidence around the World Trade Organization (WTO) protests in Seattle can achieve a level of sustained organization sufficient to change public policy, I expect that the future will feature a lot of individualized solutions to the intensifying social problems of intensified inequalities. Individualized solutions largely for the rich, that is, where, in the U.S. at least, according to the Economic Policy Institute, wealth is so concentrated that the richest 1% spends as much as the poorest one million.

So invest in customization and miniaturization, folks, if you're into cynicism and defeatism. Just as prison management companies were touted as "theme" stocks for the '90s, this could be the wave of the Millennium.

Miniaturized medical diagnostic and treatment devices are an obvious example, with IBM cultivating quite a niche for itself there. Meanwhile, Bill Gates is staking out the home, and somewhere in or near Dallas, a computer systems manager called Mitch Maddox is doing his bit to help him. He's locked himself into his home for a year, alone (or so he says) with merely his modem, his computer, and his Internet connections. He's determined to prove that, as he puts it, "we need never walk into a store, grocery, library, school, government office, movie house, arcade, or repair shop again." He's even changed his name to DotComGuy to bond more completely with his dot.com web I.D.[3]

Who knows where Bill Gates will take similar DotCom guys and gals with his dream of smartening up the home? There's talk of downloading recipes into ovens, of wiring thermostats into "personal digital assistants," with these modelled as upscale cell-phones, or even digital watches for remote control of things back home, and elsewhere. What's significant is that Gates has teamed up with General Electric in this digital I.Q. effort. Not only is G.E. the world's second most valuable corporation, but it also has extensive information industry holdings, including in multimedia (It owns NBC, the third largest network in the U.S.), and it controls a strategic distribution infrastructure and right of way.[4]

Finally, General Electric has a valuable history lesson in its founding principles of massive vertical integration and scale. As Thomas Hughes argues, founder Thomas Edison didn't so much invent the electric light bulb as he invented the electrical system.[5] He engineered a total systems environment that made electricity (rather than natural gas) North America's taken-for-granted power source from the outset, creating an integrated infrastructure of large-scale power production, distribution and appliance uses that made "living better electrically" irresistably accessible, ubiquitous, convenient and cheap. So, wherever this research is going, it promises to be a mass.com ride. The model home for this is already up and running. It's the Gates's own $75 million "estate" home, filled with "intelligent" gadgets and digitally latched doors reminding guests, outfitted with swipe cards, that some private spaces are more private than others.

PUBLIC SPACES

Meanwhile, what's happening to public spaces as we know them—spaces that social and cultural activists are trying to extend through digital networking? There are two parts to this: 1) the built environment of welfare state public institutions like libraries, schools and liberal arts and science universities; and 2) what's left of the traditional "commons" of common ground where the public is free to come and go. Both are taking a beating these days, reminding us that, as ecofeminist Maria Mies points out, development tends to be a polarizing dynamic, with underdevelopment often accompanying new development.[6]

In this case, digital and cyberspace development is occurring simultaneously with cutbacks in public and social spending, and public space is diminishing. Budget cuts have forced many libraries to close branches and reduce hours, and to levy user fees for some new services. In post-secondary education, cutbacks and government-controlled re-engineering are lowering the window on public interest and civic studies in the humanities and liberal arts, most noticeably in Ontario. What's good for General Motors has eclipsed what's good for society, not just taken to mean the same thing.

It seems that there's a new enclosure movement afoot as well. Bits of public space and public institutions are being retooled and redirected toward narrower, more private interests and concerns. In fact, the words "public" and "public interest" are heard less and less these days; instead, it's the public as "clients" and "customers." And even there, "matching grants" and targeted and applied research are taking their toll, with this client base increasingly meaning business and industry. Similarly, stores and public buildings where the general public traditionally assumed a right to wander at will are quietly acquiring magnetic-card readers on their doors and by the elevator. It suggests that "public access" (including even to malls and hotel lobbies) could soon mean card-carrying "members" only.

In turn, this leaves more of the non-card-carrying public out on the street, or taking refuge (rolled up in sleeping bags, bits of plastic and tarpaulin), in city park remnants of the traditional commons. In the historically open public space of streets, sidewalks and parks, bylaws not only now ban squeegee makework projects and panhandling. They also require permits to sell things, to congregate or to hold a march. It's hardly conducive to an inclusive public culture. Especially if the people zooming by in cars are buckled into upscale armoured vehicles which, in addition to global positioning systems, feature bulletproof glass and frame, remote starting system, siren, intercom and cellphone, halogen front and rear blinding lights, and dual ram bumpers (a standin for, or supplement to, gold-plated decals marking them for special protection). Clients for these worked-up sedans and sport vehicles include doctors, lawyers and business executives, all sharing "a fear of being assaulted in their vehicles."[7] Why? In part, because social polarization breeds mutual isolation, and that breeds fear and hostility.

When a plurality of people share a common public space, they rub up against each other's differences on a regular basis. In small and large ways— or, as Michel Foucault would say, in the microcapillaries of power that is daily life—they learn to negotiate these differences, contending with their fear of the strange. They learn to cope with difference and to accommodate one another— social habits that are vital to social cohesion and democracy.

As inequalities intensify, as more and more people opt for "extreme nesting," as e.home shopping is called, this withdrawal from public space on the ground could become a serious social and cultural issue. The individualized e.commerce solutions to the inequalities of time which leave the rich too harried to go shopping the traditional hands-on, face-to-face way then do double duty. They promise to "solve" the social polarization problem, as well. More and more people isolate themselves inside their homes, keeping their security systems on by day as well as by night. As they do this, they implicitly act out a perception of the environment beyond their windows and doors as hostile and threatening. People are spending less time attending functions in civic society these days, more time in solitary activities.[8]

The home could become not only a silicon work and sleeping cell, however artfully decorated; not only a cyber version of the astronaut's individualized life-support system, but with a garrison mentality toward a presumed-to-be hostile world outside its perimeter. Such a mindset could corrode the public domain of cyberspace as it corrodes the trust necessary to build and sustain it. Furthermore, as the rich and powerful buy into "public interest" surveillance and control of the Internet, an assumption of mistrust toward whatever is outside the supervision of mainstream Internet service providers could readily spread. Evidence of this trend is spotty, yet suggestive.

In the U.S., wide media coverage of Internet "terrorism" and a high-profile White House meeting paved the way for a massive upgrade of FBI cybercrime investigators after a 15 year-old Canadian prankster (dubbed "Mafia boy" by the media) had disabled some of the biggest commercial players on the net last February. In March, the British government introduced legislation to expand traditional wiretapping and extend it to the Internet. It included clauses that could require Internet service providers to install surveillance software capable of turning over information, detailed to the level of e-mail addresses and correspondence, at government request.

In a possibly related development, a British court supported a libel suit brought against Britain's largest Internet service provider (Demon) by a physicist claiming he'd been defamed by two anonymous postings on its net sites. Since then, there have been isolated reports of non-profit groups being dropped by local Internet service providers on the excuse that they don't fit the profile of a public interest group, or because of complaints about the content. As well, college and university students have had their computer privileges revoked after their involvement in online acts of civil disobedience. Nor, it seems, is there a public third party to which such cases could be appealed. Similarly, workers have no recourse as employers install sophisticated keystroke-cop software under brand names like Silent Watch and Investigator. User companies include Ernst & Young, Delta Airlines and Lockheed Martin.

These developments—quite apart from the commercial ones such as the MP3 court case affirming corporate music producers' intellectual property rights over user groups' freedom of communication and expression—evoke a sobering backdrop for speculating about the future of public interest networking in the digital New World Order. It suggests that the assumption of freedom and private autonomy that prevailed through the '80s and much of the '90s must now be tempered with caution as the Internet becomes a hotly contested terrain of political and cultural activity.

Furthermore, the overreaching strengths of the commercial conglomerates and their government supporters suggests that community nets and their variations in the excellent Canadian Women's Health Network, Povnet, community nets, etc., will not succeed in creating a viable public digital space by expanding on the goodwill and commitment of their activist founders and members alone. Expanding and enriching that public space (and continuing the late-modern thrust of it toward user-controlled rather than state- or corporate-controlled structures), and at a level that can be called mainstream will become increasingly difficult, if not impossible, without a public policy commitment at the level of enforceable public legislation and enabling public finance.

Meanwhile, the commercial players are moving to consolidate a sponsored and supervised broadcast and "value-added service" model for the Internet, and to discredit and dismantle what's left of the public system. If they succeed, there is a real possibility that the public-commons community networking initiatives that flourished through the '90s could be channelled into a path similar to the truncated development of community-access cable. They could end up as enclosed miniparks of participative public space, paternalistically kept and supervised by commercial broadcast service providers. This would betray the dream of plurality, inclusivity and social justice that have propelled so many committed public-space practitioners over the past ten to 15 years. The struggle, of course, is far from over, nor the outcome predictable.

THE SPONSORED PRODUCTION MODEL VS. THE PARTICIPATIVE CREATOR / END-USER MODEL

In the early months of the new Millennium, the broadcast model gained some important strategic victories. The first of these was the merger of Time / Warner / Turner and the music conglomerate EMI with America Online. The second was the move by Bell Canada to take over the CTV broadcasting network and, later, to merge with Thomson Corp. involved in print and web-based news. The latter move is particularly significant in that it will merge carrier and content on a scale that will vault this model to dominance in the new political economy of communications. It also compromises the largest existing common-carrier infrastructure on which a mass-scale space for participative, user-controlled democratic communication could be built.

These mergers won't necessarily shut down the telephony model of user-controlled content and participation. Nevertheless, they tip the scale of development that much more decisively toward a production model as they position most of the key players in new communications technology clearly to the camp of traditional industrial production—however post-modernized through customization and virtualization. This won't make it impossible for non-profit groups to leverage ad hoc deals for participatory content with would-be service suppliers.[9] But it suggests that corporations might be less receptive to these proposals over, for instance, broadcast-like content proposals as the emergent pattern seems to favour good old mass (if customized) production, distribution and consumption. Furthermore, such proposals might come from some of the more traditional players in business and industry who have developed vast expertise and resources in digital information networks in financial and business management, including IBM, Microsoft, and the major banks.

There is much reason for optimism, given the record of what popular movements have accomplished in appropriating the Internet from the military / research establishment since the mid-1980s. They range from women using the net to organize the UN Women's Conference in Beijing despite efforts by the world's largest dictatorship to thwart them[10] to the Zapatista uprising in the Mexican state of Chiapas[11] and, in Canada, community networking through freenets, Community Access Programs and Community Learning Networks.[12]

Nick Dyer Witheford not only argues that the move toward globalized digital capitalism was big business's counterrevolutionary response to the success of postwar social movements around the world. He also offers a persuasive array of examples to support his hopeful thesis of a new countercorporatization dialectic, with social justice and democracy groups appropriating the very tools big business has deployed to defeat them through Peacenet, Usenet, anti-free trade networks, plus those in the Chiapas and Indonesia.[13] Still, it would be naive to ignore the systemic biases built into the now commercial infrastructures on which all these initiatives depend.

It would also be instructive to note the absence of Sub-Comandante Marcos from the celebrations marking the fifth anniversary of the Zapatista uprising, explaining in a taped message sent from the mountains instead that "we have turned inward to organize the resistance among our people." Marcos's decision to at least hedge his bets on global digital "hacktivism" would suggest the importance of having a mix of older and simpler media to fall back on (face-to-face meetings, community radio, radio-telephone, Gestetner machines, etc.) even as they continue the struggle to preserve the Internet as a viable medium for broader collaboration, networking and solidarity building.

WHAT'S NEEDED

In his excellent book, *Reconvergence*,[14] Dwayne Winseck set out a number of critical public policy issues that will strongly influence whether there will be a viable scope and space for public interest communication in the global digital networks linking Canada into a globally networked world. These include 1) the importance of retaining a separation between carrier and content; and 2) the importance of building the Internet on a telephone model of ubiquitous, transparent, cheaply accessible user control and participation, rather than letting it move toward a broadcast model where participation for most is limited to multiple-choice consumption.

Related to this, he stressed the importance of open-network architecture and open-source software, much on the model that is being actualized by the Linux operating system developed by Finnish university student Linus Torvald. Even in a mediascape dominated by the broadcast model, a network of micro-networks grounded in both social activist participation and public interest culture and communication could continue to grow and flourish if a commitment to open access participation was entrenched in communication regulation internationally. The World Intellectual Property Organization (WIPO) treaties on copyright (1996) endorse a new right of communication to the public. This needs to be interpreted as including the right to communicate among a diverse public of its own definition and choice.

Similarly, public understanding of communication rights as fundamental human rights has to inform a concerted campaign to hold public regulatory agencies like the CRTC accountable to the public interest. Such rights should inform a redefinition of "basic" or "core" communication services to include, as Andrew Clement and Leslie Shade suggest, Internet service, which in turn should be guaranteed to include transparent easy access to all sites broadly defined as in the domain of public culture and communication, possibly with accessible public Internet service providers across the country as part of a multimedia digital infrastructure dedicated to public culture and democratic communication. [15]

The struggle, it seems, must be engaged at two levels equally. Not only at the ad hoc level of on-the-ground activism, online coalition building, and pragmatic deal-making (including with commercial Internet and telecommunication service providers), but also and equally at the public policy level, with a critical eye for seeing how the micro-moves on the ground can be coordinated to advance the larger policy vision.

A key question for me is whether there is enough political vision and sustained inter-organizational networking and coordination to advance the larger agenda.

THE REAL TRAGEDY OF THE COMMONS

The question reminds me of what I consider to be the real tragedy behind what is popularly understood as the "tragedy of the commons" of two centuries ago. The tragedy I refer to operates at two levels. First, as a text, the original essay was a piece of propaganda; yet its author and distributor had such clout that the rhetoric of inevitable, unavoidable "tragedy" became a self-fulfilling prophecy. In other words, the rhetoric of an inevitable outcome helped to make the "foretold" outcome (the tragedy of the loss of the commons) inevitable.

Most people are familiar with this story as republished by Garrett Hardin, and take it at face value: the tragedy is that self-interested individuals grazing sheep on common pasture lands will inevitably destroy its reproductive base by overgrazing their sheep because an unavoidable human tendency to maximize personal gain would prompt each one to pasture that one more sheep which would push the carrying capacity of the commons beyond the threshold of sustainability. Some 140 years after the original tragedy was foretold, in the form of a lecture delivered by William Forster Lloyd published by the prestigious Oxford University Press in 1833, Garrett Hardin recycled it as truth: Everyone is locked into a (modern, liberal, utilitarian) system that compels them to maximize their personal individual gain. "Freedom in a commons brings ruin to all," Hardin wrote.[16]

But there's no evidence to support this. Lloyd's 1830s assertion merely assumed that everyone is locked into the modern utilitarian production-model mindset, and supplied no evidence from the commoners to support it. Yet evidence of commons-sharing practices from Canada's First Peoples clearly refutes this simplistic duality between monad-individualism and self-abnegating collectivism. Intricate customs governed the sharing of firewood, waterfowl eggs, and other materials, and traditional borders marked one family's use-domain from another's. However, the refusal to acknowledge and respect this (certainly on the Canadian Prairies)[17] and the moves to undercut its integrity and to replace it with the individualized private property and the Enclosure movement combined to make the "tragedy" a self-fulfilling prophecy.

Something similar could happen here and now. If we cannot retain the customary practices and courtesies of our existing public spaces, both on the ground and in cyberspace, it will be that much harder to resist the many ways in which our public and civic spaces are currently being enclosed and commoditized. Eventually, what had been a groundswell of digitally networked social and cultural activists might dwindle into a handful of hackers and geeks, merely another consumer group to be targeted for product and raided for cutting-edge fashion ideas.

It's important to remember this hidden underside to the tragedy of the commons story, because much the same double loss could, in fact, be happening now. Not only as the powerful in media and government circles proclaim the desertification of our public spaces, undercutting the possibility of trust and cooperation in the digital commons with White House meetings and cover-story portraits of self-serving terrorists and criminals both on the net and on the streets; but also and equally, the commons could be threatened as the social habits of trust and cooperation for sharing diverse public space are allowed to atrophy by isolation, social fragmentation, and polarization.

All of which is to say that the task ahead is about solidarity building to mitigate and reverse the inequalities of globalization in the name of social justice and democracy. Using (globalization's) digital networks is important in this work, tooling them into a universal service model with access and participation on users' terms. But the technology is, as usual, only part of the picture.

Equally important is the trust and cooperation essential to motivate and sustain this solidarity and to both assert and reassert democratic and human rights across social divisions. And to do this locally as well as globally. That requires time. More time than it takes to log on and process e-mail. It requires the slowed-down time of empathetic conversation, breaking bread together, and other shared experience. It requires the commons of common, shared time and the social habits of a pace essential to community.

NOTES

1   Sauve, Roger. (1999). *The Current State of Canadian Family Finances*. Ottawa: Vanier Institute of the Family

2   Monkerud, Don. (2000) "The American Left has Left us." *San Francisco Chronicle*, Feb. 13

3   See HYPERLINK "http://www.dotcomguy.com" www.dotcomguy.com

4   Tuck, Simon. (2000) "His New Job? Controlling your Home" *Globe and Mail* Jan. 14: A-1

5   Hughes, Thomas. (1985)."Edison and Electric Light" in *The Social Shaping of Technology*, Donald MacKenzie & Judy Wajcman (eds.) Milton Keynes: Open University Press.

6   Mies, Maria, "Liberating the Consumer," in *Ecofeminism*, Maria Mies and Vandana Shiva. Halifax: Fernwood Books, pp. 251-264.

7   See the Armet Armored Vehicles site at HYPERLINK "http://www.aavi.com" www.aavi.com\

8   Putnam, Robert. (2000). *Bowling Alone: The Collapse and Revival of American Community*. NY: Simon & Schuster.

9   Reddick, Andrew. (1997). *LMCS in Canada: Opportunities and Implications for Consumers*. Ottawa: PIAC. p.21.

10   Davis, Dineh M. (1998). "Women on the net: implications of informal international networking surrounding the Fourth World Conference on Women," in Cynthia J. Alexander and Leslie A. Pal. (ed.). *Digital Democracy: Policy and Politics in the Wired World*. Toronto: Oxford University Press. pp. 87104; Shade, Leslie Regan. (1997). "PostBeijing and beyond." in Rachel Lander and Alison Adam (ed). *Women and Computing*. Intellect Books. pp. 181-189.

11 Dyer Witheford, Nick. (1999). *CyberMarx: Cycles and Circuits of HighTechnology Capitalism*. Champaign, Il: University of Illinois Press. p.343.

12 Reddick, Andrew. (1998). *Community Networking and Access Initiatives in Canada*. Ottawa: PIAC.

13 Dyer Witheford, Nick. (1999). p. 317380.

14 Winseck, Dwayne. (1998). *Reconvergence: A Political Economy of Telecommunications in Canada*. Hampton Press.

15 Clement, Andrew and Leslie Regan Shade. (2000). "The access rainbow: conceptualizing universal access to the information/communication infrastructure." in Michael Gurstein (ed). *Community Informatics: Enabling Communities with Information and Communication Technologies*. Hershey, PA: Idea Group Publishing. pp. 32-51

16 Hardin, Garrett. (1968). "The tragedy of the commons." *Science* 162(1968):1243-1248.

17 Spry, Irene M. (1983). "The Tragedy of the Loss of the Commons in Western Canada," in *As Long as the Sun Shines and the Water Flows*, Ian Getty &Antoine Sussier (eds.), Vancouver: U.B.C. Press.